KT-498-576

A Long Lunch

My Stories and I'm Sticking to Them

SIMON HOGGART

JOHN MURRAY

First published in Great Britain in 2010 by John Murray (Publishers)
An Hachette UK Company

First published in paperback in 2011

7

© Simon Hoggart 2010

The right of Simon Hoggart to be identified as the Author of the Work has been asserted by him in accordance with the Copyright, Designs and Patents Act 1988.

All rights reserved. Apart from any use permitted under UK copyright law no part of this publication may be reproduced, stored in a retrieval system, or transmitted, in any form or by any means without the prior written permission of the publisher, nor be otherwise circulated in any form of binding or cover other than that in which it is published and without a similar condition being imposed on the subsequent purchaser.

A CIP catalogue record for this title is available from the British Library

ISBN 978-1-84854-398-0

Typeset in Bembo by Hewer Text UK Ltd, Edinburgh
Printed and bound by Clays Ltd, St Ives plc

John Murray policy is to use papers that are natural, renewable and recyclable products and made from wood grown in sustainable forests. The logging and manufacturing processes are expected to conform to the environmental regulations of the country of origin.

John Murray (Publishers)
338 Euston Road
London NW1 3BH

www.johnmurray.co.uk

To Alyson, Amy and Richard, who have been supportive beyond any call of duty

Contents

Introduction

Even I would find a book about my life pretty dull. Unless you have become Prime Minister, mounted the first single-handed ascent of Everest without oxygen, or been the greatest pianist of your generation, there usually isn't a lot to say that rises above the average or the quotidian. It's one of those popular myths that everyone's life is, in its own way, fascinating. Some people lead lives of dullness, even in many cases lacking Thoreau's quiet desperation. The ranks of self-published books, now growing at speed since computers made them much cheaper, are full of titles such as *An Eventful Life*, or *Here, There and Everywhere*, *Life As It Is Lived*, *Along the Way*, or *It Seemed to Me*. The very titles depress the soul and I have made these titles up. Sometimes people who have led lives crowded with incident manage to make it all sound like an extended version of a trip to work on the 7.29 from Weybridge. I recently ploughed through a self-published autobiography of an elderly Tory MP who had been in the House for the resignation of Margaret Thatcher, and who had noticed nothing, felt nothing, and recounted nothing except his own doughty refusal to tell his local party how he had voted.

To be fair, many do contain elements of interest: the businessman who suddenly found himself flying bombers over Hamburg, the professional soldier who worked for Montgomery or Churchill, the bond trader who rebuilt a castle in Slovenia and turned it into a home for orphans. Some are written with flair, wit and observation. When I am retired, I may – if I have the time and the energy – acquire a hundred or so of these books, cut out the pious tributes to family and colleagues, the dreary details of deals done or lost, and create a collection of first-hand observations and adventures.

So this is in no way a life of me. On the other hand, I have encountered some interesting people who have said and done intriguing or amusing things. Like almost all journalists, I have been on the fringe looking in, sometimes a welcome, occasionally an unwelcome guest in the lives of people who have been someone or achieved something: Princess Diana, Bill Haley, Enoch Powell, Ian Smith, Joyce Grenfell, W.H. Auden. Journalists are forgotten more or less on the day they retire, unless, like Keith Waterhouse, they have produced other work of lasting value. I am pretty sure that even George Orwell would be a footnote if he hadn't written *Animal Farm* and *1984*. William Russell of *The Times* is remembered for his despatches from the Crimea, not for what he wrote, but for the fact that he wrote it. G.K. Chesterton is generally described as a journalist, but I wonder when anyone last read one of his articles, as opposed to the Father Brown stories or *The Man Who Was Thursday*.

Some journalists cannot bear to be only looking on and get involved in other activities, occasionally, though not often, with vast success, like Robert Harris, who was a colleague of mine on the *Observer* before he understood that there was more satisfaction and far more money in novels. Derek Taylor worked for the *Guardian*, part-time at least, then hooked up with a group called the Beatles who had realized they needed a press officer. Quite a number go into government departments, and others become MPs themselves, with mixed success. Ruth Kelly, who worked in the *Guardian*'s City office, rose to the Cabinet, while Julie Kirkbride, once of the *Daily Telegraph*, was forced out of Parliament because of her part in the great expenses scandal.

So this book is really a string of anecdotes, observations and stories. I play a minor role, a walk-on part as an observer in some of the tales, but that is all. However, I should give you a framework of what I was doing at the time. I was born in 1946, lived in North Yorkshire till the age of three, then in Hull until 1956, when my family spent a year in Rochester, New York. I have a younger sister, who is a retired teacher, and a younger brother, who was a teacher and is now a journalist himself. In 1959 we moved to Leicester where I went to Wyggeston Grammar School, whose most famous alumni are the Attenborough brothers, the naturalist David and the film director Richard, though I acted with Tim Piggott-Smith, who sat next to me in class and, showing early promise, naturally got the best roles in the school play. These plays were directed by our history teacher, Edgar Rayner, whose best friend was Colin Dexter, who wrote the *Morse* books. Dexter moved to Corby, where he taught classics to a close friend and neighbour of ours. This is a very small country.

At the beginning of 1965 I went to do voluntary service, teaching in western Uganda, where I was a failure, and learned far more than I contrived to teach my pupils. Later that year I started at King's College, Cambridge, where I worked on the student paper, and participated in a somewhat limp fashion in student revolution. While the students were rioting in Paris, we were gathered round gas fires, drinking tea, eating crumpets, listening to the Beatles and fooling ourselves that we were on the cutting edge of a new world.

The *Guardian* began to recruit graduates again in 1968, and I got one of the places, which was a great relief as everyone else had turned me down. I reported on Northern Ireland occasionally, then full-time for two and a half years until 1973, when I went to work in London as a political correspondent. I left in 1981 to write features, largely political, for the *Observer*. In 1983 I married my wife, Alyson Corner. The *Observer* sent me to Washington as US correspondent in 1985, and both our children were born there. We returned to Britain in 1989 and in 1993 the *Guardian* bought the *Observer*. I was transferred back to the *Guardian* and have written the parliamentary sketch since then.

I chaired *The News Quiz* on Radio 4 for two periods, totalling a dozen years. This is the eighteenth book with my name on the cover, though only one, *The Cat That Could Open the Fridge*, about round-robin letters, was even a medium seller.

That is enough about me. If I had to sum up my life, I'd say that I moved from being a promising newcomer to clapped-out old has-been, with no intervening period.

A small proportion of the material in here has appeared elsewhere but I have never been afraid of repeating myself.

AT HOME

I
At Home
Auden & Lady Chatterley

Having left the army – I was born nine months after he was demobbed – my father got work as an adult education teacher in the North and East Riding of Yorkshire. I had been born in Ashton, Lancashire, in the hospital nearest to Stalybridge, Cheshire, where my mother had been raised. However they lived at the time in Marsk, then moved to Redcar, the seaside resort that served the people of Middlesbrough.

I went back to Redcar for the first and only time forty-nine years later, for the 1997 general election, since Mo Mowlam was the local MP, seeking re-election. The town looked poor, tatty, in need of a lick of paint. And on the promenade someone had thought that a plaster statue of a penguin would enliven the atmosphere. They were mistaken. Ms Mowlam, who was still claiming that the brain tumour that later killed her was benign, sashayed down the main street, receiving greetings and plaudits from the people, and returning the compliment with enveloping hugs and kisses for friends and strangers. Her progress resembled a cross between a Roman emperor returning after a successful campaign against a distant tribe, and Thora Hird.

Apart from Boots and other chains, all the shops seemed to be selling cheap goods of one kind or another, mostly made from raw materials not found in nature. Even Marks & Spencer, where

I popped in for a bottle of wine to cheer up my evening, sold no men's clothes and only two types of wine, red and white. But there was money around all the same: at the till the tanned woman in front of me was saying that she and her family were just back from a holiday at Disneyland in Florida.

~

(Mo always made any man – especially any journalist – feel for the moment that he was the most important person in the world. She would take you by the arm and lead you off to coffee, as if your arrival could not have been more perfectly timed, since she urgently needed to consult you on a matter of vital importance. Meeting a third person – once it was Lord Attenborough, outside the Tate Gallery – she would introduce them to you as if it was you who were the famous person she was showing off.

One of her devices was to grab your face with a meaty hand and smooch you ferociously, even – especially – if you were on the phone. Then she would stroll away, pausing to throw back, 'I've got flu!' She did this to a lot of men.)

~

We moved to Hull in 1950. Dad published his first book, on Auden, the following year, and in 1956 we went to the United States, to spend a year at the University of Rochester, New York. In the years leading up to this Dad wrote his most famous book, *The Uses of Literacy*. He was putting the final touches to it in the months before we went to America, when the publishers, Chatto & Windus, sent the manuscript to a libel lawyer. One of the central sections of the book was an attack on tabloid newspapers and pulp fiction, illustrated by extracts from real books, magazines and papers. It seems almost inconceivable now, but the lawyer warned that if the writers quoted were to sue, they might win up to a million pounds – a substantial sum today, an almost unimaginable amount then. The idea that someone might have gone to court to defend the quality of writing along the lines of: 'I watched her brains splatter on the wall. I figured I owed myself a drink . . .' seems grotesque, but at the time Chatto unsurprisingly decided not to take the risk.

There was only one thing for it. Dad had to invent examples of the kind of thing he was criticizing, which he did with speed, relish and inventiveness. The lawyer was satisfied, and Dad could sail to New York knowing the book was going ahead smoothly.

The incident had a curious afterlife. Dad greatly enjoyed creating these fictional fictions and one of the crime novels he invented was called *Death Cab for Cutie*. Someone in the Bonzo Dog Doo Dah Band, the comedy rock group, must have read the book, been attracted by it, and wrote a deliberately awful song with the same title. The chorus, sung in a morose mumble, was 'Death-cab for Cutie / Death-cab for Cutie / Someone's gonna make you pay your fare.' You can see the band perform it in a strip club during the Beatles' television show *Magical Mystery Tour*, an undistinguished film now largely remembered for John Lennon's 'I Am the Walrus'. Then a west coast American band that was looking for a name seized on it, and they became a cult success, touring the UK as well as the States. They were for a spell the favourite group of our son, also called Richard Hoggart. In such ways do jokes trickle down the generations.

~

We came back from America in the summer of 1957 to discover that the book had not only been published without attracting a writ for libel, but had received considerable acclaim. In a small way, Dad had become famous – or at any rate was asked occasionally to appear on television which in those days amounted to the same thing. It's hard to remember now when there are scores of channels available, most of them broadcasting twenty-four hours, that appearing on TV was an astounding brush with fame. There were only two channels – ITV had started two years before, and there was no daytime television at all, only the test card.

He appeared on a high-minded BBC (there was no BBC 2) religious programme one Sunday evening, talking to schoolchildren. The whole neighbourhood came into our living room to watch, not because they didn't have televisions themselves, but because the very fact that someone they knew was on TV was a great communal event, a sort of indoor street party.

~

The book (it was originally called *The Abuses of Literacy*, but Dad thought that sounded off-putting) went on selling and selling. It became an A-level set text which helped the family finances, though probably made it disliked by a whole generation of young persons. But even now my brother and sister and I meet readers for whom the book bulked hugely in their lives, often highly intelligent people from working-class backgrounds: 'It was my story'; 'I didn't realize there were others like me'; 'It was a perfect description of the world I came from.' Tony Warren, who invented *Coronation Street* at the age of twenty-three, told Dad that he inspired him to believe that the lives of ordinary working-class people could be as rich and fascinating as anyone else's. The first episode was transmitted in late 1960.

~

That was the year the *Lady Chatterley's Lover* trial was held. *The Uses of Literacy* had been out for three years, and had caught the attention of Sir Allen Lane, the founder of Penguin Books, who published it in paperback. Lane thought that Dad would be a good addition to the *galère* of witnesses – academics, politicians, and various *bien pensants* – who were to give evidence in the book's favour. I am sometimes doubtful whether the trial, and Penguin's acquittal on a charge of publishing an obscene article, really was a turning point in British society as Philip Larkin implied in his poem 'Annus Mirabilis': 'Sexual intercourse began / In nineteen sixty-three / (which was rather late for me) / Between the end of the Chatterley ban / and the Beatles' first LP.' Still, it certainly symbolized a change, and the BBC in particular returns to the topic over and over again.

I was fourteen at the time of the trial, and had not even read the book, though I made up for that omission very quickly, and long before I read another word by D.H. Lawrence. Naturally the family followed the reports in the papers very closely. We could not know that the trial had, in effect, ended almost as soon as it had begun. The prosecuting counsel, Mervyn Griffith-Jones, had been deeply shocked by the book and genuinely appalled at the idea of it being generally available. In his opening speech to the jury he spoke at length about its iniquity, then suddenly and catastrophically added, 'Is this a book you would wish your wife or servants to read?' Even then the idea that a man should determine his wife's choice of reading seemed hopelessly dated, and as for the idea that the jury might have servants . . . The prosecution case never recovered.

Forty-odd years later I met Griffith-Jones's son, an extremely amiable Church of England minister, who told me that his father always wrote his opening and closing speeches with immense care, and read them out to juries verbatim. On this occasion he thought the speech was going so well that he could risk an ad lib, with, for him, terrible consequences. If he had not said those words, would the jury have convicted? And would the permissive society have simply failed to occur? I am pretty sure the answer to both questions is no, but it's an intriguing thought.

~

Dad had paid close attention to the evidence of the other defence witnesses (it cannot have helped the prosecution case that they called nobody at all, possibly because they couldn't find anyone, or perhaps because they felt that the book was so disgusting that no jury could rule in its favour and that therefore they needn't bother). He had noticed the way Griffith-Jones tended to bully the witnesses, who were largely academics and used to the kind of 'on the one hand, on the other' arguments you get at universities. (Roy Jenkins, then a backbench Labour MP, gave some of the briefest and most effective evidence. It was his private member's bill that had become the Obscene Publications Act, under whose provisions Penguin Books were being prosecuted. He was asked if he was indeed the private member behind the bill, and replied, 'Yes, and if I had thought for one minute that—' He was quickly interrupted, since in a British court it is only the wording of the act, not the presumed intentions of the legislators, that is deemed relevant. But the point had been made: the man behind the act did not dream that it could have covered *Lady Chatterley's Lover*.)

Dad decided that, come what may, he would not back down from anything he said. Hence his claim that *Lady Chatterley's Lover* was 'puritanical', in the sense that Lawrence demanded complete respect for one's conscience. This caused Mr Griffith-Jones to come close to an explosion, and one can see why. One doubts that, for example, the Pilgrim Fathers would have approved of Constance and Mellors's behaviour, even if a certain amount went on anyway. Of the innumerable headlines about the trial, the one that stuck in my mind was 'Lady C "puritanical" says the potty prof'. I had mixed feelings about this kind of thing. Nobody wants to see their much loved father described as 'potty' in the public prints. But it briefly won me more prestige at my grammar school in Leicester than any number of tries for the First XV might have brought.

~

At one point, Dad talked about the 'reverence' shown by Lawrence. Once again, Mr Griffith-Jones came close to spontaneous combustion. 'Reverence! Reverence?' he demanded. 'Reverence for the weight of a man's balls?' As for the word 'fuck', which Mellors uses tenderly, and purely to mean 'make love', Dad pointed out that he had heard the word used in a different sense several times as he passed a building site on his way to the trial. Whether the court liked it or not, it was certainly in common usage.

After the victory, Penguin and the defence team heaved a sigh of relief: Griffith-Jones had not noticed one passage which at least implies that the couple are having anal intercourse. That might have been harder to explain. (Though of course these days magazines offer young women careful and sympathetic instruction in anal sex. I would love to have seen Mervyn Griffith-Jones leafing through a contemporary edition of *Cosmopolitan* and contemplating 'Twelve ways to drive him wild in bed!'.)

~

The after-effects of the trial continued. Dad was asked to write the introduction to the first legal edition of *Lady Chatterley's Lover*, for which he was paid a flat fee of £50. When the book went on to sell three million copies, he became slightly aggrieved, or at least rueful, that the sum had been so small. His children had to point out to him that of the three million purchasers, not one had bought it for the introduction.

~

Now and again the BBC revives the trial. In one of these films, in 1980, Dad was depicted wearing a sort of mud-coloured sleeveless pullover, which caused him some annoyance. That was, he thought, the type of dreary, cheap garment BBC producers imagined that provincial lecturers wore in the early 1960s. Things looked up in 2006. The corporation got Andrew Davies, a screenplay writer who could work sex into the Morris Marina owner's handbook, to create a drama around the trial. Presumably they felt that there was not enough sex in it already. Davies imagined an affair between two members of the jury, who faintly echoed the characters in the book: an upper-class woman, and a young, recently married and very timid clerk, played by Rafe Spall. The idea was that there would be lots of flesh, plenty of bonking, and revealing discussions of the trial in bed.

Dad was played by David Tennant, who was fairly well known already, but had yet to reach the level of fame that meant that it was possibly illegal for any BBC drama not to include him in the cast. (The *Daily Mail* worked out that in the three weeks over Christmas 2009, and including repeats, he had appeared in seventy-five BBC radio and TV programmes.) My wife and I were invited to watch him spend a day filming Dad's evidence, at the old Kingston Crown Court, a building that often serves as the Old Bailey. He had done his homework immaculately. He had a picture of Dad on his mobile phone. He had studied every picture he could find from the time – including one that clearly showed Dad in a mud-coloured sleeveless pullover. He had somehow found old TV interviews, so he could get the accent and speech inflections right. He was charming, and very anxious for us to approve his performance. I said he had got pretty well everything right, except that Dad had never worn long sideburns.

'Ah,' he said ruefully, in his normal Scottish accent, which you only occasionally hear on air these days, 'I had to get special permission to leave the set of *Doctor Who* for a day, and if I had shaved them off they wouldn't have grown back in time.'

I thought that was an extraordinarily modern form of fame – to be played by an actor who has gone to immense trouble to get everything right, but topped off with Doctor Who's face furniture.

~

Very occasionally, famous people would visit. Between 1960 and 1962 Dad was a member of the Pilkington Committee on Broadcasting. Other members included Joyce Grenfell, who became a lifelong friend, and Billy Wright, the footballer, who had played for England 105 times, and had captained the team 90 times. Now and again the committee would visit members' homes for their discussions, and in due course our turn came. The neighbourhood, or at least the young males, were in a state of fevered excitement. The great man had agreed, very willingly, to play football with us in the garden. We crammed in as many friends as we could. But he got it wrong. One of us would tackle him, always successfully, and he would say, 'Got me that time! You're too good for me!' He was being kind; he thought we wanted to be able to boast that we had beaten Billy Wright. But we knew he was faking it. What we really wanted was a demonstration of his skills.

~

Joyce Grenfell was one of the kindest people I have ever met. Her eyes seemed to dance with warmth and enthusiasm. As Clive James records in his rightly adoring memoir of her, once she was your friend she was your friend for life. She was one of those people constantly on the lookout for treats and favours she could bring to people. For example, Leicester City, the team both I and my brother supported, reached the Cup Final for one of their rare, and always doomed, attempts to win the Cup, at a time when this was much more important than the First Division Championship. Joyce had been coming to stay with us, and on the way she got into a minor accident with a man who turned out to be a trainer at West Bromwich Albion. He didn't want to lose his no-claims bonus, but would Joyce like two tickets for the Cup Final? Naturally she agreed, and handed them straight over to us.

She and her husband Reggie came to a party we threw for both our parents at their house in Farnham, Surrey. It was summer and we had planned on holding it in the garden, but it rained, so everyone was crammed indoors. I can still see Joyce sitting on the arm of a sofa, doing her act, the guests all in a trance of delight.

~

The visit of W.H. Auden was anticipated with nerves, excitement and planning that was, perhaps, not quite careful enough. Dad was a huge admirer of the poet, which was why his first book – Auden had written at length to say he liked it – had been about him. Dad nominated him for an honorary degree at Birmingham University, where he then worked. Auden had been partly raised in Birmingham and said he would be delighted to come. Could he stay for a few days? It was customary for the nominator to put up the honorary graduand, and though most would stay for just one night, my parents were very pleased to host a longer visit. It was the end of the academic year, and the weather was sunny and warm. We had expected that he would want to spend much of his time revisiting places he knew in and around the city, but he preferred to sit in a deckchair in the garden, reading and chain-smoking Lucky Strikes.

~

On the first evening my parents had invited a smallish group of friends and colleagues round to meet the great man. I was put in charge of drinks. Just before they arrived, he bustled into the kitchen and asked if I knew how to make a dry martini. I said I thought I did. 'Probably not the way I like them,' he said, and showed me how he did like them. He rummaged round the cupboards and found a three-pint jug. Into this he poured an entire bottle of gin. He added a whole lemon, sliced, then a tray of ice. (Already in America people kept vast quantities of ice in their freezers; that tray was all we had.) He then finished off the drink with a single capful of dry vermouth, took it into the sitting room, arranged a small table in front of the comfiest chair, placed the jug on it and held court. He finished the martini when the last guests left.

~

Then it was time for dinner. In those days people drank a lot less, mainly because they had less money. There was a residual fear of drink, too. These days we fret about young people drinking too much, but in earlier decades the terror was of the breadwinner spending the family's money on booze. My parents were far from tight-fisted, but would have thought a bottle of wine quite adequate for three people at dinner, and a bottle of wine is what they served. It was probably the only bottle in the house. (We did have beer delivered. The Davenport's man came every Friday with a dozen one-pint bottles for Dad, and a stone flagon of ginger beer for the children.) Auden kept himself well topped up, then when the bottle was empty, simply reached across the table and took Dad's glass. When he had finished that, he announced that he was going to bed, and took Mum's glass with him. He must have slept pretty well on a bottle of gin, four glasses of wine, and a capful of vermouth.

~

I had been worried that he might demand to know what I thought of his poetry, which, since I hadn't read any, would have been quite a facer. Luckily he had no wish to discuss his work at all. Instead he wanted to talk about food mixers, the Kenwood Chef in particular. According to him this was a wonderful machine, and he couldn't imagine how my mother got by in the kitchen without one. She should buy a Kenwood Chef immediately – it would transform her life. I recall the family being slightly baffled, even disappointed, by this encomium. It was like one of those imaginary 'who would come to your dream dinner party?' columns that appear in the newspaper, and all Shakespeare had wanted to talk about was house prices and why they were perpetually digging up the M40.

Later Auden talked about drugs. He and his partner, Chester, had read a great deal about LSD and had decided they ought, in a spirit of enquiry, to try it. So they had invited a doctor friend round to their apartment in New York one morning. He was to inject them with the drug, and stay to observe what happened. After some time, nothing had happened, so the doctor left, and the two men went to the local diner for lunch. There Auden suddenly saw the spectacle of his mailman doing a dance in the street, a wild, uncoordinated fandango, quite unlike any he had seen. Clearly the drug had taken effect, so they hurried home.

Next day the mailman knocked on their door. 'What's with you, Mr Auden?' he had asked. 'I had a package for you yesterday. I saw you in the diner and I jumped around in the street so you'd see me, but you looked right through me . . .'

~

The last day of his stay was a Sunday. I was first up from our family, and came downstairs to find Auden on the sitting-room sofa, with a piece of greaseproof baking paper that he had clipped to the *Observer* Everyman crossword. He was tracing out the grid so that he could do the puzzle without spoiling it for anyone else. It was a touching gesture. He finished it, and left soon afterwards.

~

A year or so later J.B. Priestley came to stay, for the same reason, but for a shorter time. The local Birmingham BBC station sent a reporter round, a young woman who was in training. Priestley had established himself in a vast armchair, and was vast himself, so it was not easy to see where the armchair ended and the writer began. He gave an interesting interview at some length and, deeply grateful, the reporter disappeared. Then half an hour later she phoned in tears to say that she had failed to make the machine work. Could he . . . 'Of course,' he said, 'you come here again.' And he gave the same interview. It would be silly to say that the world is divided into nice people and self-important people – most of us hover between the two – but it was good to see that he was firmly on the nice side. Though it would have been a touch hypocritical for him to refuse: *An Inspector Calls* is entirely about a young woman whose life is destroyed by the viciousness of people more powerful than her.

~

In 1970 Mum and Dad went to Paris, where Dad had accepted a job as an assistant director-general for UNESCO, the United Nations cultural organization, which devoted some of its time to preserving world culture, for example Venice, Angkor Wat, and recordings of folk music from around the globe, and most of its time to bureaucratic in-fighting. Dad would come back with elaborate tales of how such and such a factotum had arranged things so as to frustrate another factotum, or how one country was digging in its heels because of a quite trivial slight imposed on it by another country. Now and again, nations would pull out, generally resentful communist nations, so the delegate would be sent to protest and announce his withdrawal. The Chinese, for example, became tremendously upset when an LP of Tibetan music included sleeve notes describing Tibet as a 'country'. It was not a country, it was a province of China. Sometimes officials withdrawn from Paris to return to their own cheerless and impoverished capital would break down in tears.

~

I was already working for the *Guardian* but would visit my parents in Paris whenever this was possible. Dad had a generous salary, beefed up for everyone to make it possible to attract Americans. He and Mum decided that they would pay for their children to visit at any time. So we did. I learned a certain amount about France in that time. For example, there was a restaurant a short walk from their apartment. It was called Le Lloyd's, because a nearby building had been the Paris office occupied by Lloyd's of London. It looked beguiling inside, all warm oak panelling, and souvenirs that the owner had brought home from years of foreign travel. But every time my parents looked in and asked for a table they would be turned away, courteously but firmly. '*Désolé*,' they would say, '*nous sommes tout à fait complets.*' But they weren't. There would be perhaps two tables occupied.

Dad explained the problem to his secretary at work. She was appalled. The solution was simple. She phoned the restaurant and in a voice radiating the grandeur that only someone who works for a magnifico can produce, declared that she was calling on behalf of an assistant director-general of UNESCO, who *commanded* a table for that evening. Miraculously a table was free, and from that moment on there was much bowing and scraping when they visited. It is not only the British who adore their class system.

~

The director-general of UNESCO was M. René Maheu, an *énarque* who, though just as unknown in France as he was in the rest of the world, carried with him all the style, grandeur and selfish self-assurance of those mightier figures who have ruled the French state for so much of the past hundred years. This meant having several women, including his wife, with whom he did not live, but to whom he returned for care and attention whenever he was ill, his mistress, who was his official companion at formal ceremonies and on trips abroad, and various girlfriends. These were generally selected from the ranks of secretaries and assistants. Dad used to get particularly annoyed if someone in his department was sequestered to accompany the DG on a visit abroad. Once, for example, he had arrived in Dad's office and admired a young American woman who was working for him. Colour TV had only just come to France, so he essayed a topical pick-up line. Gazing down her dress he remarked, 'Ah! *Deux chaînes. Et en couleur!*' (Two channels. And in colour!) Around this time, Dad put his foot down and refused to allow the woman to accompany Maheu to Venice, an event that led to considerable friction, as the French grandee faced off against the more puritanical Brit.

I was working in Northern Ireland at that point, and I had written a jokey sketch about Ted Heath's surprise visit to the province. It was not entirely complimentary to our then Prime Minister, but Dad enjoyed it, and during a long meeting, pushed the clipping over to Maheu – who had perfect English, never used in public. He read the piece without any flicker of amusement, then handed it back, saying, 'In France, your son would not be allowed to write such a thing.' Which was true.

In 1975 my parents returned from Paris. Dad, now fifty-seven, took a job as Warden of Goldsmiths' College, London, where the main building is now named after him. (Years later I mentioned this to a student at Goldsmiths, who expressed puzzlement until it clicked into place. 'Oh, the RHB,' she said, 'I had no idea . . .' Even fame in the form of a brass plaque is fleeting.) They lived in

Farnham, Surrey, for the next quarter-century. Dad was constantly working, on a book, or a talk, or an article, or marking students' essays. I have never known a man to work so hard. (None the less he always had his study door open, and we were always welcome to go in, to ask for money, or help with a problem, or just a chat. I followed this practice in my own home, even after our son, then aged twenty months, crawled into my room, gave me a big toothy smile, and switched off my computer at the mains. I was unfamiliar with the way computers, unlike typewriters, need constant attention, and so lost a whole chapter.)

Even on Christmas Day, when he liked to be surrounded by children and grandchildren, he would bring out the battered old board he had saved from army days, and scribble notes while the shrieks, giggles and tears of children and, later, grandchildren filled the room. The board would be put away for Christmas dinner and for the *Morecambe and Wise Show*.

~

I got a place at King's College, Cambridge, where my stay was clearly undistinguished. When my daughter applied to the same college we carefully prepped her on her reply to the inevitable question, 'Why did you choose King's?' One of her reasons was to be, 'Because my father came here, and he said he had a wonderful education.' One of the dons said, as if dredging up a distant memory, 'Oh yes, your father. Is he still a teacher?'

In every first-year undergraduate's room there was a copy of the *Varsity* guide, *Varsity* being the student newspaper. It contained a huge and bewildering list of the various clubs and societies you could join, and asked if you'd like to be a journalist. I can still remember sitting on the bed, my anxious parents having just departed, and thinking, Yes, that'll do, for a career as well.

~

All journalists need butterfly minds. If you don't have one, you're ill-equipped for the job. A mind that can fix on a topic to the exclusion of pretty well everything else is useful for an academic. A journalist isn't generally interested in a subject; the question they ask is: 'How can I make this information seem interesting to anyone?' Easy when you're describing an air crash, or the resignation of a Prime Minister, but much harder when you're dealing with quotidian news, which is often much the same from one day to another.

At Cambridge there was plenty to write about. The Pill had just arrived, though it remained, with all colleges single-sex, quite difficult to find a young woman who was prepared to make use of that wonderful liberation we had all read about. There were lots of drugs around. I tried marijuana, but it gave me horrible, paranoid dreams, and I only ever tried it again, by accident, when a friend, trying to convert me, had baked it into cookies. On *Varsity*, the watchword was near total irresponsibility. For example, there was an American graduate student who always seemed to be annoyingly busy with some good works. He ran the Student Representation Council, which had a certain reach-me-down left-wing feel to it. (We in the Labour Club, renamed the Socialist Society, thought we were frightfully left-wing, and even handed out leaflets at factory gates, where as undergraduates we were received with ill-disguised glowering.) Once, just to annoy the American, we ran a stop press item: 'ERNIE BRAUCH ARRESTED. Ernie Brauch said yesterday, "I have been arrested by the wonderful response to my SRC guide." ' He threatened to sue. Some years later he was genuinely arrested, on fraud charges.

In my last year I ran for editor of *Varsity* but received only one vote. It was just as well; even now I would be hard put to edit the back of a cornflake packet. In the same way, competent footballers often make terrible managers.

~

The sixties began late, round about 1967, and brushed us only in a marginal fashion – we wore multicoloured shirts, torn jeans and absurd neckwear. There were demonstrations to mark the visits of politicians – one of the liveliest was against Denis Healey, who was then defence secretary. But few people graduated and went on to change the world, or even devoted as long as a year to trying. We went into jobs in the media, or the law, or accountancy. Mervyn King was at my college, a year below me, so I never met him. I did encounter him in the middle of the economic crisis of 2009, and remarked that you knew you were getting old when the Governor of the Bank of England looked young. He sighed. 'Yes,' he said, 'but I looked an awful lot younger six months ago.' On the whole, I'd say that if you can remember the sixties you weren't there – or you were at Cambridge. They may have clearer recollections in Oxford, as Oxford has always been the more romantic of the two universities. Cambridge people tend to think of Oxford as a cross between a finishing school and a late-night party. Meanwhile, in the cold, damp Fens they get on with discovering gravity, or evolution, or DNA.

~

People from one's student years fade in and out of one's life, like characters occasionally resurrected when the plot of a soap opera demands it. The novelist Salman Rushdie (q.v.) I haven't seen for years, and neither of us would be pleased to meet the other. I bump into the playwright David Hare at election times, when he is usually employed by one of the more serious papers to give a writerly view of events. Jonathan King, the pop singer and record producer, was inescapable, driving round Cambridge in his E-type Jaguar. I have always liked Britain's best-loved celebrity paedophile, and have some sympathy with his claims of innocence. However, he is not a father himself, and presumably has little idea of the skin-crawling horror every parent feels at the thought of their teenage son falling into the hands of an older, predatory man. I see him now, perhaps once a year, and feel awed by his ability to shuck off the recent past, to keep a personality that might have been preserved in amber.

~

Now, at the time of writing, our parents are both living in a home in north London, near to my brother's house. They are well cared for, fed, cleaned, dressed, put to bed and got up, under frequent care from trained medics, and are visited by a member of their family almost every day. But week by week they are losing their memories and, I fear, their minds. They have a great-grandson, with another baby on the way, but are only dimly aware of him. Mum once said in one of her more lucid moments, 'I know we had a really interesting life, but now I've forgotten it, it might as well not have happened.'

Now and again, we bring Dad some pleasing news: *The Uses of Literacy* is back in print, Radio 4 has run a programme devoted to his work, an appreciative article has appeared somewhere. People, usually strangers, write fan letters, or ask for help for a thesis they are writing about him. He takes little of it in. People often say, 'At least they are together,' which is true, and a comfort, I suppose, but dementia is a form of separation from the whole world, including those who have been closest to you for seventy years. Seeing them both fade before our eyes has been the most miserable experience for their family and their friends.

AFRICA

2

Africa

Ian Smith & Boys in Kilts

I first went to Africa in 1965 as part of what was not yet called a gap year. I flew to Entebbe, Uganda, the day after Winston Churchill died. My posting was in Nyakasura, a Scots Presbyterian school near a town called Fort Portal, in the foothills of the Rwenzoris, the fabled Mountains of the Moon. Because it was Scottish, the pupils – many of whom were older than me – wore khaki kilts, and sporrans made from goatskin. On chilly days, and there were many, they also wore scarlet pullovers. In a group they looked rather good, as if members of some long forgotten native regiment raised by the British to fight a rebellious tribe.

I learned two important things while I was there. First, I was a terrible teacher. If I couldn't hold the attention of pupils who desperately wanted qualifications so they could get a decent, well-paid job, a car and a brick house to live in, what chance would I have at home? My strategy in the end was simply to read to them. More than anything else they loved hearing stories about young people from other countries, so I could read *Oliver Twist*, *Emil and the Detectives*, and the big hit, *Things Fall Apart* by Chinua Achebe. There was no television to distract them, so they were happy and pleasingly silent as the books carried them to worlds that must have seemed infinitely strange – Victorian

England, pre-war Berlin, or Nigeria, which in its own way must have been every bit as foreign. In spite of this literary laudanum, I was rated 'very poor' by a schools inspector, an Englishman who sat at the back of one of my classes and scowled. Any faint chance I might have had of going into the profession vanished for ever. Since virtually all my family were or had been teachers of one kind or another, I was in the position of someone coming from a military family who realizes, somewhat to his alarm, that he is a pacifist.

~

The second important lesson resembled a discovery that C. Northcote Parkinson (of Parkinson's law) might have made, and probably did: in any committee, time will be spent in inverse proportion to the importance of the topic in hand. Thus at one staff meeting we had to decide whether to spend thousands of shillings (the currency system was the same as it was in the pre-decimal UK, but without pounds) on a new chapel which I, being irreligious, thought unnecessary. As a temporary volunteer teacher my view, rightly, counted for nothing and the chapel went through on the nod. The next discussion was on whether boys who broke their garter elastic (they had scarlet woollen socks, similar to British schoolboys, or, come to that, to kilt-wearing Scottish clansmen) should be given new garter elastic on the grounds that it was of poor quality and likely to tear anyway, or charged sixpence for a new garter because they had probably used the old one to make a catapult. This matter occupied the remainder of the meeting and caused lasting ill-will between liberals and disciplinarians, the soft-hearted and the sceptics. All but four of the staff were British, many of them idealists who wanted to do their best for a newly independent nation, Labour supporters who felt we owed it to the people; others were perhaps more attracted by a life that involved sunshine, servants and far less pressure than anyone would face in a school at home, even in those better disciplined days. With some, I suspect, it was a mixture of both. For months afterwards people would occasionally snarl at each other: 'We all know how you voted on garter elastic!' as if that invalidated the view they might have on any other topic.

~

The Rwenzoris were covered by rainforest. On one occasion the teachers held their own expedition into the mountains. We saw giant frogs, and earthworms two or three feet long. But the mist came down, and while most of us got home safely, two of our number, disoriented, went down the wrong side of the mountain and arrived in the Congo. They sought help in a village where they were the first white people the inhabitants had seen. At this time there was, as was fairly common, a civil war in the Congo and it was feared that it might spill over into Uganda. To reach Fort Portal, however, troops or refugees would have had to pass over the Rwenzoris and through the rainforest. So we were perfectly safe, though enjoyed terrifying each other with images of crazed soldiers sweeping through the school, forcing the boys to join their army and raping the girls. The teachers finally returned.

~

Social life centred, as it did throughout the old empire, on the club. (The British Council library was good for books and magazines, chiefly old half-forgotten periodicals like *Plays and Players*, the bookshelves well stocked with Agatha Christie and Ngaio Marsh. They felt old-fashioned even then – but the Council has modernized its ideas a lot lately. One of my fantasies was that John Major, who spent some of his youth in Nigeria, actually was Nigerian, and had learned his English in the British Council library. Hence his curiously old-fashioned turn of phrase. 'Fine words butter no parsnips,' he would say, a line rarely used since, I suspect, the 1950s.) We played hockey – what North Americans call 'field hockey' – against the local Indian community, who invariably thrashed us. The manager of National & Grindlays Bank, one of two banks in the town, organized Scottish country dancing nights. I was recruited because they were short of numbers, but I have always been a hopeless dancer and inevitably got it badly wrong. As when one car spins out of control during a Formula One race, the knock-on effect could destroy the whole dance. This drove the manager to a gibbering fury. Scottish country dancing is entirely prescriptivist and obliges every participant to be in precisely the right place at precisely the right time, over and over until the wretched thing comes to an end and you can plead that you need the lavatory, or a drink. This form of dancing was perfect for Jane Austen's day when it reflected society's obsessive concern with place and timing. It also worked well in Scotland. In Africa, in the sixties, it was wholly inappropriate. Or so I claimed.

~

The younger teachers spent Saturday nights at a sleazy bar in town, where we were usually the only white people drinking. It seemed daring and exciting. I was a virgin, but one particularly beautiful young local woman seemed attracted to me and soon, as we sat at the bar, had entwined her legs with mine. For an inexperienced eighteen-year-old this was almost impossibly exciting. Years of fantasizing were about to end with a sudden burst of dreamlike reality. I discovered she was a prostitute at more or less the exact time as I fell into a drunken stupor. Waking up the next day – a kind colleague had driven me home – I felt sorry for her. She must have assumed that I would have given her quite a useful sum (I was paid pocket money by the school, around £8 a week) and she had wasted almost an entire evening on me.

Some of the pupils at the school were influenced by a certain innocent desperation. Any qualification would make an enormous difference to their lives. One boy, whose work had been consistently lazy and second-rate, appeared at the back door of the house where I was lodging. He was with a girl, whom he introduced as his sister. If I gave him better marks, I could have sex with her. I very much doubt that she was his sister; she was almost certainly a prostitute from the town, but that would, he assumed, sound less beguiling. Also, I might be impressed by the notion that his family were so supportive they would do anything to help him reach his goals. The desperation was obvious, but there was an element of innocence too: clearly he believed that there was no problem that could not be solved by the application of sex, money or both.

~

At that time it was literally impossible to starve in Uganda. The staple diet was plantains – *matoke* – and these grew on trees, everywhere. Under the relatively – for Africa – benign rule of Dr Milton Obote, it was also peaceful. The horrors of Idi Amin and the Lord's Resistance Army were decades away. The other volunteer, Chris Mallows, and I set out to hitch-hike to the Kenyan coast. On our first night we set up our tent in the grounds of the Queen Elizabeth National Park. All meals cost 10 shillings a head, which was more than we could afford, so we ate cold baked beans from the can washed down with condensed milk. It is customary at this point to say that the food could not have tasted better if it had been a five-course meal prepared by a Parisian chef, but that would be nonsense. It tasted like cold beans and sweet milk. It was, however, aromatic enough to attract a herd of elephants, who stomped around outside the tent, like nervous guests afraid to walk into a party. Finally trunks started appearing inside the tent and waving around. Elephants are herbivores, but even a herbivore can step on you, and we spent an anxious night.

I was reminded of the old joke about the householder who is asked if the family has any pets.

'An elephant,' he replies.

'Where does it sleep?' asks his astonished questioner.

'He sleeps where he bloody well likes, of course,' is the reply.

I felt, instinctively, that elephants know this. (Apart from mosquitoes, and of course other people, the animal responsible for killing most humans in Africa is the lovable old hippo. They are ferociously protective of their territory and their young, and can shift their massive bulk at startling speed. Buffalo and elephants come behind, with more obvious killers, such as snakes, crocodiles and lions, hopelessly back in the pack.)

Next day a young black couple, a civil servant and his girlfriend, gave us a lift all the way into Nairobi where they owned one of the brick houses that were so large in the imagination and ambitions of our pupils. They put us up, then the following morning we stood waiting for a bus to take us into the city centre. A white woman was so astounded by the sight of white youths waiting at a bus stop that she not only gave us a lift, but insisted that we stayed at her beach house near Mombasa. Here we met other volunteers, and sang folk songs to Chris's guitar. It was, as I say, a very innocent time, at least for me.

~

I now realize that this was – if not the end of empire – at least the end of a transition stage. Uganda was moderately well governed. There was almost no hunger. For a European, life could be delightful, without any sense that your enjoyable existence was at the expense of the local population, though of course it must have been to some extent. On Saturdays we would go to Bimji's store in downtown Fort Portal where you could buy almost anything, including bound editions of the *Daily Mirror*, which arrived some weeks after they had been published in London. It didn't matter; in those days news could be just as entertaining after a month as it might have been the day after it happened. There was a market where perfectly good meat and vegetables could be bought and back at one's bungalow in the school grounds there were servants to cook it all. You could listen to the BBC World Service, and it was on their Wednesday lunchtime rundown of the 'hit parade' that I heard the Rolling Stones' 'It's All Over Now' and 'Satisfaction'.

Now and again, at entirely erratic intervals, a flimsy blue aerogram would come from home. Sometimes two or three weeks' supply would arrive at once, though I knew that my mother had written them on successive Sundays. Nowadays such a form of communication seems only slightly more up to date than a messenger with a cleft stick. When our daughter went on her gap year to Sri Lanka in 2005, we expected an email from the local internet café almost every day. If she missed two days, we would feel the first slight stirrings of panic. My parents must have gone several weeks without hearing from me, and seemed to cope perfectly well.

~

I cleared off home a month early, little regretted by the school, where I had been such a hopeless teacher. I had, however, made friends there, and former teachers back in the UK still hold reunions.

~

Fifteen years later, in 1980, shortly after the Lancaster House Agreement brought an end to Ian Smith's unilateral declaration of independence in what was still called Rhodesia, I flew into Salisbury on the first British Airways flight since the lifting of sanctions. As a student I had had lunch with the late Nicholas Tomalin, a journalist, who had recently returned from Rhodesia, not long after Smith had declared UDI. The white people there, he told me, were the worst kind of British petit bourgeois, being narrow-minded, parochial, mercenary and insufferably self-satisfied as a result of their sense of superiority to the native population. He was right about many of them, though others were brave and determined, while generous and liberal in their attitudes.

At their worst, they were strikingly unpleasant. I hired a car from the local branch of Avis. 'You'll have to wait a few minutes, the Munts haven't got it ready yet,' said the woman in the Avis office, a young and attractive blonde. I assumed the Munts were a husband and wife team who worked on the cars. I soon realized that 'munt' was the nastiest term of abuse for the native people, meant to be as offensive as, say, 'niggers' or 'yids'. The casual rudeness some white people employed all the time was breathtaking. The sense of being constantly humiliated in your own country and among your own people must be dreadful. The violence of Robert Mugabe's goons, the starvation, the miserable poverty, the lack of any healthcare – all these are loathsome beyond measure, yet I suspect many Zimbabweans feel that it is to some degree bearable because it is not being inflicted on them by an arrogant and alien race. In my limited experience, when people are going to hell, they usually prefer it to be in their own handcart.

~

These thoughts came to mind when I visited a white farming family in the north of the country. Tomalin's strictures about such people struck me as having a degree of truth, and yet were deeply unfair about some of them. My host and hostess were justifiably proud of the school they had built for their employees' children and the medical centre. It was inconceivable, they said, that under black majority rule these people would be any better provided for. Indeed, they implied darkly, they would probably be a great deal worse off. All horribly true, but missing the point. Even paradise would be intolerable if you could never have any realistic hope of leaving.

They were nice people, anxious to do the right thing by their own lights, which had nothing to do with what we members of the chattering classes in Britain regarded as the most obvious wisdom. But they lived miles and miles from anywhere, and in their way were as cut off from the modern world as the women walking alongside the dusty roads with water pots balanced on their heads. It was impossible to get hold of hard currency to spend abroad, and so their son, on a trip to London (easy to reach; you just changed planes in Johannesburg), had taken an elephant-hide briefcase in the hope of selling it. It was, they insisted, immensely valuable, and even if he raised only half what it was worth it would pay for all his board and accommodation. Their description of this lad standing in the City of London, stopping passers-by and asking them to fork out a vast sum for a mottled grey briefcase, hovered between the tragic and the pathetic. In the end he had brought the thing back. They showed it to me, perhaps hoping I would buy it. But it was deeply unpleasant to look at. A leather case doesn't bring to mind a cow, but this looked far too much like the animal that had died to provide it.

~

A couple of colleagues and I had dinner in Meikles, the main hotel in Salisbury. At a time of swift change in the UK, sanctions had frozen time in Rhodesia. Brand names that had long ago vanished from our shelves were still found there, such as Lyons

Maid ice cream. Meikles had an excellent wine cellar, and sold it at pre-inflation, pre-sanctions prices. In the restaurant a half-bottle of excellent Châteauneuf-du-Pape cost the equivalent of £2. They still had all five types of Pimm's: gin, rum, Scotch, rye whiskey and brandy. I hadn't seen any except the gin in Britain for years. (Sanctions had made the Rhodesians very resourceful, and alcoholic refreshment was important. They had whisky made from fermented cane sugar flavoured with barley, gin from fermented cane sugar flavoured with something or other, and pastis made from fermented cane sugar flavoured with aniseed. All tasted dreadful, but they induced oblivion with gratifying speed.)

There were tennis clubs and horse races. It was a little like being in the Home Counties between the wars. I half expected William Brown and his family from Richmal Crompton's novels to turn up for Pimm's on the lawn; Violet Elizabeth Bott would have looked and felt entirely at home. The main difference was that the great majority of the population were servants or menials.

We were joined – she invited herself – by a good-looking if slightly tarty blonde woman in a scarlet silk dress who was clearly drunk. After a slow start she tore into us. She was a schoolteacher, she said. She taught black kids English. There were never sanctions against educational material, and Rhodesian children, black and white, still took British exams with British textbooks which could be freely exported to the rebel state. She was furious because the set Shakespeare play that year was *Othello*, a choice that she thought had been deliberately made to infuriate her and other white teachers. 'It's about a black guy who fucks a white woman, and I have to teach this to a big buck nigger sitting in the front of my class!' she exclaimed, the alcohol intensifying her anger. I wondered at the time whether her rage might not be bound up with her own unacknowledged sexual attraction to the pupil in the front row, but there was no way of knowing, and it seemed an ill-advised point to pursue.

~

I had been having some R&R in the north of the country with a colleague, and on our way home we stopped to pick up a young 'troopie', one of the white soldiers who had been fighting the guerrilla insurgency that had finally brought Ian Smith's Rhodesian Front to negotiate in London. Being a soldier was something of a part-time job, and like many young soldiers he loved it: the danger, the camaraderie, the admiration of grateful civilians.

What he wanted to talk about was a recent trip to South Africa. For a Rhodesian, South Africa was as startling and wonderful as Texas might be for a Mexican peasant, being similar in many ways yet bewilderingly different in others. 'In Sith Efrica,' he said, 'they have these things called [he pronounced it] div-eye-did highways! It's like two roads nixt to each other, and all the treffic going in one direction is on one road, and all the treffic going in the other direction is on the other road! Do you hev dividid highways in Britain?'

We assured him that we did and he seemed a little disappointed.

'End the television is in colour, not like the bleck and white television in Rhodesia!' he said. Did we have colour TV in Britain? He was rueful when he learned that we did. 'They have this fentestic American TV show, it's called *Dellas*! It's really great! I watched all of Series 3 when I was there!'

I was beginning to feel sorry for him. 'Who do you think shot JR?' I asked affably, since that was then the only talking point among *Dallas*'s millions of fans.

There was a silence from the back of the car, until he said with surprise and distress, 'Somebody has *shot* JR?'

I realized that in the past we measured how advanced a civilization was by the point at which they had invented the wheel, or discovered fire. Now we could make that same judgement by what stage they had reached in American TV soaps.

~

The young man described some of the larks they got up to at weekends. (It was, on the whole, a surprisingly low-intensity uprising, and weekend leave was usually available.) They liked to get drunk on lethal cocktails. One was the Gorilla. You put an inch of undiluted orange squash in the bottom of a pint glass, filled it to within an inch of the top with beer, then stood with your back to the bar and flung a coin behind you. The remaining space had to be filled from whatever bottle the coin had struck. (I later learned that this derived from a game played in some British pubs. A correspondent in the *Guardian* mentioned that it had come to an end in his pub when the coin had hit a bottle of winkles in vinegar.)

Another drink popular with the troopies was kudu piss. This was Rhodesian pastis, mixed with American-style green cream soda. It sounded repulsive. It was. My colleague and I decided to throw a party the night before we left for London and invite all the people who had helped us. As a joke, we made a great bowl of kudu piss, and as the African night descended, it actually began to fluoresce. You could have read a large-print book by the light it emitted. Everyone there tried it, but only once, with the exception of a local journalist, who decided it was delicious and drank the lot.

~

The governor for the transition period between the end of UDI and the elections that brought Robert Mugabe to power was Sir Christopher Soames. He was the son-in-law of Winston Churchill, all of which stirred a deep and atavistic longing in the breasts of white Rhodesians. They yearned to be invited to

Government House, if not for dinner, then for drinks alone, and they queued up to sign the visitors' book if only to leave their mark there, like dogs peeing on a lamppost. Soames knew how to act the panjandrum, and did it very well. For example, when a military plane flew over the territory, it was obliged to engage in 'contour flying' which meant keeping the plane at an extraordinarily low level, making it virtually impossible for anyone with a ground-to-air missile to take aim in time. This technique, I learned at first hand, since the military love little better than demonstrating their kit and their training to the media, required immense skill on the part of the pilot and iron stomachs for his passengers, since if a mountain, or a hillock, or even an elephant appeared ahead the plane had to climb suddenly and at great speed. This would clearly not do for the governor, so when he travelled his plane circled around a secure area, then climbed until it had reached a height deemed to be safe from rocket attack. Thus Sir Christopher and his staff were able to enjoy tea served on bone china, scones and sandwiches, without the risk of the whole lot being hurtled to the floor when the pilot spotted a tree.

~

French wine was imported in substantial quantities for the dinners at Government House. But since it was so expensive, others had to rely on more local wines. On one occasion I was at a dinner attended by Dmiso Dbengwa, who was a senior aide to Joshua Nkomo. Our host, the *Guardian* correspondent James McManus, had recently returned from Pretoria, and had brought with him a case of South African wine. This was at a time when a liberally minded person in Britain would no more have bought South African wine than served his guests strychnine. Anyone who bought it – and some wine merchants kept a small selection – was, in the view of most people one knew, little better than a Nazi. Mr Dbengwa did not share that view. 'Ah,' he said, with immense satisfaction, as he glugged the delicious knock-off claret. 'This South African wine is so much better than the rubbish here in Zimbabwe!'

I was, in my innocent and naïve way, quite shocked at the time, though explained to myself that since Britain did not groan under the South African hegemony, we had no excuse but to maintain our boycott, even if African guerrillas were indifferent.

~

Once, visiting Matabeleland, the tribal region to the west of the country, I had an appalling Chinese meal in Bulawayo washed down by an even more appalling wine grown nearby. I felt sorry for the winemaker, trying to create something drinkable on soil that grapes detest and in a climate far too hot. Most red wines, even bad ones, improve on being exposed to the air, but this was the opposite. The first glass was almost tolerable; the second tasted of sulphur mixed with the flavour that hit your tongue when, as a child, you licked an old penny. There wasn't a third.

~

I tried to get into South Africa, but this was notoriously difficult for anyone with the word 'journalist' in their passport. My paper wanted me to write about the steam train that still went from Bulawayo to Johannesburg. I presented myself at the office of the South African consulate in Salisbury, where a functionary implied he did not believe a word I was saying. 'Don't you have trains in England?' he kept asking. I explained that we did, but they were not romantic steam trains, ploughing through the soupy African night past native kraals, kudus and lions, sparks briefly illuminating the velvety blackness.

'I will forward your request to Pretoria,' he said, 'but I have little hope that it will be granted.'

He was right: it wasn't. I had learned another useful lesson. I am almost certain that if I had said, 'My paper wants me to write an exposé of the evil apartheid system that destroys families, demeans humanity and kills all hope,' he would have said, 'Ach, why didn't you say so?' and stamped a visa straight into my passport.

~

At this time of transition the various guerrilla armies that had been fighting the white government had allowed themselves to be herded into encampments. They kept their arms, but the notion was that, isolated in distant terrain, they would no longer be an overarching presence in the shift to full democracy. Max Hastings, who had come out on the same plane as me, decided to drive to one of these encampments to meet the guerrillas and the British soldiers in charge of keeping them there. It was a perilous journey. We went in the Avis car that had been prepared by the 'Munts' and someone had – deliberately? – put all the equipment required in the event of a flat tyre in the boot with the exception of a jack to raise the car. So when, bowling down an appalling dirt road, I felt the car slither underneath me, the discovery of the missing tool was bad news. I was, frankly, terrified, since other journalists travelling down the same road the previous day had been shot at by men with Kalashnikov rifles. By incredible good fortune we were near a police station. There the police chief, who had a Boer name, and who looked as if he would be perfectly content if we were stranded there for days, at the mercy of irregular soldiers or savage beasts, was persuaded against his better judgement to lend us a jack.

~

We set off again, with Max driving. Now and again he would take his hands off the wheel out of sheer exultation, and cry,

'And to think they pay us to do this!' He said then that he only felt truly alive when in danger. The happiest moment of his life had been when, during some unpleasantness in Angola, he had ridden into the danger zone at night, sitting on the coal tender of a train.

I had first encountered Max in Belfast, where he showed more courage than the rest of the press pack put together. When the real trouble started, in August 1989, the B Special constabulary, founded to keep the uppity Fenians in order, were mobilized and toured the Catholic streets in armoured cars with Browning machine guns mounted on the roofs. The rest of us had fled to the safety of the hotel, piecing together what was happening by listening to the police radio, the local BBC and bits and bobs we picked up from people fleeing the flying lead. Max, however, was out there cruising the streets. At one point he learned that a Browning had fired into the first floor of a terrace house, the bullet going straight through the wall and into a small boy. Max hurled himself up the stairs of the house, grabbed the child, and while waiting for the ambulance to arrive stood in the street cradling him and dangling a white handkerchief. The B Specials continued to fire, and various impromptu mobs hurled bricks and petrol bombs at them. To us, Max's behaviour was unimaginably foolhardy; to Max it was living.

~

I don't know anyone who blends such bravery (though he told me some time after the Falklands War that he felt he was losing his bottle, and no longer had an appetite for putting himself in harm's way) with occasional silliness. Once he came through the door of the Europa Hotel carrying four dead pheasants. I asked where he had been. 'Shooting with Lord Larne!' I asked if those were the birds he had shot. He gave me a pitying glance and said, no, when you went shooting all the birds belonged to the owner of the shoot. However, Lord Larne had kindly made him a gift of these two brace.

Next morning I found him in the bar. 'You know those pheasants I brought back last night? I have had a word with the restaurant here. They're going to roast them for me, and I'm going to organize a dinner party, for a few interesting, sophisticated and knowledgeable people. But you can come if you want.'

With anyone else you might take umbrage. But Max wasn't trying to be rude or sarcastic, and I wasn't going to miss such an event for a non-existent slight. Sadly, Max couldn't find any interesting, sophisticated or knowledgeable people to share the feast, so the guest list turned out to be me, plus the camera crew from *Panorama* for whom he then worked.

One of them said, 'Here, Max, this pheasant, what does it taste like?'

I said, 'It tastes like chicken that's just beginning to go off.'

'I couldn't have put it better myself!' said Max.

'In that case, do you mind if I have a steak?' asked the cameraman.

'Me too,' said the assistant cameraman.

'Yeah, steak for me,' said the sound man. In the end Max and I chomped through as much pheasant as we could, and very good it was too.

~

So we were back on the road, heading for the guerrilla encampment. Several thousand of them were gathered in fields at the bottom of a mountain. To one side there were maybe two dozen British soldiers who could do little more than keep an eye on them, since they were outnumbered by several hundred to one. They made us very welcome; doubtless bored with each other's company after some weeks unable to move or do anything interesting or talk to a woman, they would have fallen happily on anyone. They described how they had planned what to do in case the negotiations in Salisbury went wrong, and their nominal charges decided to slaughter them before moving elsewhere. They'd identified a cave thirty metres or so up in the mountain. This would be their redoubt, where they could have defended themselves until help arrived, if ever it did. It struck me that a couple of grenades would have made short work of the cave and anyone inside it, so that the event would have resembled *Zulu* without the happy ending. But that wasn't the point; I have often noticed about British soldiers – no doubt the same is true of other armies – that they positively enjoy danger, that it is constantly and not unpleasurably in their minds. It's the equivalent of that gorgeous new secretary at work, something to keep in mind whenever work is a little dull.

After lunch, we set off back, arrived without incident, and guzzled great quantities of Pimm's, in various flavours.

Before I left what had become Zimbabwe I wanted to meet Ian Smith, the Prime Minister who had declared UDI. He was – this was a given among nearly all the people I knew – the evil racist who had taken this extraordinary step in order to keep the majority population of his country in virtual slavery. Thinking of Smith as a sort of British Hitler was as much taken for granted as the necessity of not buying anything from South Africa. (The late Paul Foot used to tell a story about buying some oranges, then noticing they were Outspan brand. 'I'm not buying them,' he said, 'they're South African.'

'Quite right,' said the greengrocer, 'all those nasty black hands touching them.')

Smith had a secretary, a young, attractive and highly intelligent woman who liked to hang out with the visiting press corps. I asked her, more in hope than expectation, if she might arrange an interview for me. She said she would try, but the *Guardian* was not exactly his favourite paper. On the other hand, he did read *Punch*, for which I had started writing. She had just returned from a trip to the UK, and he had come into Salisbury from his farm. She was chatting enthusiastically to a female colleague about a Jean Muir dress she had bought in London. 'It's really great, and it shows off my tits!' she said. At this point Smith walked in. It is hard to realize now, when such a remark would be the subject of casual laughter by anyone who heard it outside a fundamentalist mosque, how old-fashioned he was, and how deeply embarrassed he was at overhearing this remark. She later told me, 'I said as quickly as I could, "There's this British journalist who wants to interview you, and he writes for *Punch*," and he was so desperate to get out of the room that he said, "Yes," and I put you in the diary!'

It was sweet of her to go to this trouble and to take the risk. The interview was fascinating rather than interesting, if such a distinction exists. Smith believed that both Rhodesia and South Africa were victims of a communist plot organized by the Soviet Union, and that the Western powers were blind to this obvious truth. He repeated this view several times. As for the black people of Rhodesia, he said, they would quickly realize that they had been much better off under white rule. He was clearly wrong about the Soviet puppet masters, though his second point may seem more moot these days.

~

I returned two years later. It was the beginning of the nation's descent into horror, although no white farmers had yet been forced off their property at gunpoint, and nobody was starving. But the political signs were there. I saw Mugabe address a rally, and noticed how the biggest cheers were for his attacks on the British, white people, and imperialism in general. And there was a sense that time for the whites was limited. The farmers were to bear the full horrors of Mugabe's rule, though even they suffered less than the local African population. In the city, there wasn't a lot to do. Europeans would join each other to sit around someone's pool for lunch, waited on by servants. Much of the conversation was devoted to whose pool they would be sitting around for dinner that night, and so on, a continuous loop lasting for days. I broke away as often as I could, for trips to Victoria Falls – if you are lucky enough to go, make it the dry season, as for much of the year the mist created by the flow obscures everything – and the Great Zimbabwe, the monument after which the country is named. I am a connoisseur of those little cardboard signs you sometimes see in hotel rooms warning, in a chirpy, reassuring way, of the perils you face. In the West Indies, 'In the unlikely event of a hurricane . . .' and here, 'In the unlikely event of a rocket attack on the hotel . . .'

~

Years later I returned with my family to Africa – to Kenya this time, to visit my sister-in-law and her family. We went to the Masai Mara game reserve, camping in tents with beds, to which servants would bring coffee at 6 a.m. We would then bowl out on to the plains to spot animals and to eat a hot breakfast as the sun rose. We were lucky. Most of the visitors stay in giant lodges, from which vans with windows emerge one after the other to pursue the wildlife. The drivers are wise in the ways of the plains, and almost instinctively know the signs that tell them a BBC camera crew is lurking somewhere. They contact each other, and soon the BBC team has been cornered, as scores of tourists gaze in awe at the wonderful sight. At one point we spent a couple of hours looking at a pride of lions under a bush, the cubs playing, the father cuffing them to keep discipline. Later, back at home, we watched the entire thing again as part of the BBC's

Big Cat Diary series. You would have imagined that the lions were alone in this great, hot wilderness; what you couldn't see was the whole BBC outfit, plus us in a Toyota Land Cruiser plus jeep, plus eight vans from various lodges, all clustered round in the hopes that at least some of their customers might get a view.

Do the lions have even an inkling of what is going on? It's said that they would never try to hunt humans in a vehicle, regarding us as Captain Scott might have contemplated a can of bully beef without a tin opener. Do they accept all this attention as an inevitable part of their existence in the wild, like vultures and occasional storms? Perhaps it is part of nature's great cycle: wildlife programmes create an interest in wildlife so that people come to Africa to see it. But once they get there, the only way they can find the wildlife is to track down the people who are filming it for the wildlife programmes that attracted them in the first place.

MANCHESTER

3

Manchester

George Best & Mia Farrow

It was largely luck that I went to the *Guardian*, after graduating, in 1968. I was given the job – technically as a trainee – by Harry Whewell, the then northern news editor. Thanks to the union, the NUJ, which still had some power left to wield, no newcomer could train in the head office of a national paper. The *Guardian* at that time sold around 180,000 copies and wanted to do better. Recent graduates were cheap to employ (though my starting salary of £1,050 seemed plenty to me, and translated into take-home pay of £16 a week, ample when my shared rent was a little over £3 a week, and beer was 10p a pint). We were also presumed to be able to spell, which was important since the paper's reputation for misprints – hence the *Grauniad* – rankled. It was due to a shortage of proof readers, who had to be paid union rates. Harry interviewed me in London. His main concern was that the recruits could write vividly. He mentioned a friend of his who had written of someone that they were such an inverted snob that they'd stopped smoking Wills Woodbine cigarettes when the firm used silver paper for the inside wrapping. For the rest of the interview I spoke entirely in metaphors, similes and allegories. It must have been like listening to a very bad experimental play. However, all the other people I'd applied to – the BBC, the *Scotsman* and the *Liverpool Echo* – turned me down, so I was hugely relieved when the offer from Manchester came.

~

If Harry liked you, you were fine. Some of his appointments, such as Michael Frayn, were inspired, the result of an ability to spot talent in the most diffident applicants. Some were no good at all. Some were very good indeed, but nevertheless did not ever win his affection, and disappeared – to London, or to another paper, or into other work altogether – as soon as they could. Harry had his rough edges and he also had a blunt charm, which I suspect is a northern phenomenon, a sort of velvet fist in an iron glove. When you brought your expenses to him, he covered the total with his hand before signing them, involving some contortion in a right-handed man. The gesture was meant to imply that no *Guardian* employee would dream of fiddling their expenses – a noble thought, though of course you could only have abused that particular system once.

Harry was especially proud of the paper's Manchester roots; indeed, to him, it was still the *Manchester Guardian*, though the name of the city had been dropped years before. There was a popular story in the office that may or may not be true; Harry has no memory of it, but it feels true.

He had been asked to come to London for some *Guardian* function where a rather grand woman expressed puzzlement. 'Doesn't the *Guardian* have more reporters in London now than it does in Manchester?' she asked.

'Aye,' said Harry, 'and there's more Jews living in New York than there are in Jerusalem. But where do they keep the bleeding Ark of the Covenant?'

~

Esther Rose, Harry's wife, came from a celebrated Manchester newspaper family. Her uncle, Henry Rose – effectively her adoptive father, since her own father had died when she was very young – was the football correspondent of the Manchester edition of the *Daily Express* which made him, to all intents and purposes, the leading sports writer in the north. He was killed in the Munich air crash of 1958. Among other mourners, almost the whole Jewish population of Manchester turned out for his funeral, and the family was proud that his cortège was longer than for any of the players.

Every week when Manchester United played at home, Henry Rose paid a man 10 shillings – several times the price of a terrace ticket – to stand under the press box before the start of the match. At the point when, with infinite grandeur, he took his place in the front row of the box, the man's job was to point up and, as if in awed astonishment, shout, 'There's Henry Rose!' and many people within earshot would cheer.

In those days football correspondents thought of themselves as persons of great consequence – unsurprisingly, since along the roads to the ground every lamppost would have on it a placard bearing their name and picture. 'Jim Figgis is at this match. Read his exclusive report in tomorrow's *Daily Mirror*,' or whatever. Inconceivable today; a poster saying, 'Simon Hoggart is at this debate. Read his exclusive sketch in tomorrow's *Guardian*,' would be only marginally more ludicrous, though perhaps even less beguiling.

~

Harry had – indeed has – a mind that is infinitely curious, always eager to spot social change, the unexpected, the bizarre. He was also proud of having married into a Jewish family, one of considerable standing in the city. Esther wrote the plots for *Coronation Street*, already established as much the most popular regular programme on television. Harry kept a collection of Jewish jokes in his head, which, like most Jewish jokes, were metaphors indicating a wider truth, about the world or at least about Jewish character and traditions. My favourite was about the young Jewish man who is on the Euston to Manchester train. He is opposite an older Jewish man who is reading *The Times*.

'Excuse me, sir,' says the lad, 'could you tell me the time?'

Silence from behind the paper.

'I wondered, sir, if you could tell me the time?'

This is met by an impatient rustling.

The young man pleads. 'Sir, you are Jewish, you can see that I am Jewish, can't you please just tell me the time?'

Finally the older man sighs and puts down his paper. 'All right, here's why I don't want to tell you the time. Like you say, I'm Jewish, you're Jewish. We start talking. You're on your way to Manchester; being Jewish, you probably live in Prestwich. I live in Prestwich. You seem like a nice boy. I invite you to my house for dinner, you meet my family, you meet my daughter; she's a beautiful girl, the two of you start seeing each other. Next thing I know she's coming to me, she's saying, "Daddy, Daddy, I want to marry this boy!" You think I want my daughter to marry some guy can't afford a *watch*?'

~

(Naturally Alan Coren, my Jewish fellow panellist on *The News Quiz*, also had a large store of Jewish jokes. One of his favourites depended on ambiguous Jewish feelings about sex. A man goes into an antiques shop where he spots an old lamp. He gives it a wary rub, and out pops a genie.

'I'm a Jewish genie,' he says, 'I can only give you one wish. What is it?'

The customer says he wants to bring peace to his homeland of Israel.

The genie sighs. 'Look at this map. You got Egypt, Syria, Iraq, Iran, they all hate us. And they're armed to the teeth. What's one genie to do? Make another wish.'

The customer pauses, then says, 'I'd like a nice Jewish girl who'll give me a blow job.'

The genie gazes at him for a moment, then says wearily, 'Let's take another look at that map.')

~

Harry attracted stories. One that I know is true came one Christmas after the paper moved from its ancient home in Cross Street – to some, still the true Ark of the Covenant. The new offices were dull and unexciting, so to cheer up the newsroom they bought a canary. In those days few papers were published around holiday periods, so if Christmas fell near a weekend, the presses would not roll for three or four days or even more.

Afraid that the canary might starve, or at least get lonely, Harry decided to take it back to his house for the duration. On his way he went down to the print room to wish Merry Christmas to everyone who worked there. A compositor asked what he was doing with the canary.

'Taking it home for Christmas,' said Harry.

There was a startled silence until someone said, 'Blimey, we're having a turkey.'

~

Harry had a lot of newspaper wisdom. After I had been there a few months it was decided the paper needed a correspondent to cover the northern universities. I was asked to do the job. I said I thought I wasn't ready for a speciality, and needed to learn everyday reporting first. Harry exploded. 'You need to realize,' he shouted, 'there is nobody on the *Guardian*, not one, who is lying awake at night wondering what Simon Hoggart is going to do next!' This is true of the rest of the world as well, apart perhaps from one's mother or those who depend financially on you. I did the job, and learned a second useful lesson: academics are the most thin-skinned people in the country. Politicians, by contrast, generally take their medicine like little soldiers. Academics will pursue a misplaced comma, or at least a vaguely displeasing paraphrase, until they – and the editor – are close to exhaustion. I soon preferred Northern Ireland, where even the most vicious terrorist rarely bothered to carp. In fact their reaction to something they didn't like was either to ignore it altogether or else threaten to kill you, with nothing in between.

~

Once, early in my stint in Manchester, I was sent to reception to meet a 'nutter' who wanted to sell a secret to the editor and to no one else. He was standing there with a brown carrier bag stuffed with documents, and was clearly displeased to be fobbed off with an understrapper.

'What I have here,' he said, pointing to the bag, 'is a secret of cosmic significance. I am prepared to sell it to your editor for £16,000', a curiously exact figure, which would have bought a large family house in one of the better parts of Manchester.

Luckily I had spotted the doodles at the top of the papers sticking out of the bag. 'I think,' I said conspiratorially, 'you have discovered how flying saucers remain stable after they have entered the earth's atmosphere.'

He gave me a panic-stricken, 'so-you're-in-the-conspiracy-too' look before fleeing.

After this I was always sent to handle the nutters. In the absence of a similarly useful clue, I found it simplest to ask if they had been to see the *Telegraph* which, I implied, took a great interest in space travel and the paranormal generally.

~

(Like all journalists, my colleague Martin Kettle gets many communications from people who are, perhaps, not entirely in touch with the real world. One summer he opened a letter from a man who claimed that the wine chain Bottoms Up was in league with the government to kill him. He had good cause: every time he went to the local branch in Highgate, London, he was knocked over in the street, sometimes quite painfully. Could Martin report on this scandal?

It was a quiet day, so out of curiosity Martin phoned the shop and, somewhat embarrassed, recounted the tale. There was a pause. 'Do you think your reader has a hearing aid?' It turned out that because of the hot weather, they had had to keep the shop door open, and dogs kept wandering in. So they had installed one of those whistles that humans can't hear but dogs find frightening. Some hearing aids were badly affected and could cause a shock to their wearer. It was a very – very – rare example of a nutter's story containing a degree of truth.)

~

It is hard not to feel sorry for these people. What depths of despair have led them to a newspaper, to a reporter they have never met and who probably has no knowledge of the field of their obsession in the first place? Huge envelopes plop on to one's desk, often decorated with drawings in felt pen and colourful stickers, as if we were likely to say, 'This looks interesting. I see the sender has taken the trouble to decorate his envelope to make it stand out. Must be worth a read!'

Inside there may be a hundred pages of correspondence between the writer and his local council, and covering notes from various professionals proving, yes proving, one's correspondent's case unanswerable. Once I came home to find in the porch a carrier bag containing a hundred A5 envelopes each stuffed with similar material. Whoever left it believed his brother had been poisoned while working for the government in some establishment. He asked me to distribute the other ninety-nine envelopes among journalists I knew. I wrote back suggesting that if there was a case, he should perhaps start with a lawyer. I got no reply, being just another lazy, heartless hack, who had failed to see a crying injustice and so would never become the British Woodward or Bernstein.

MPs get these complaints more often than journalists, and have developed a series of strategies which they share among themselves. Some work very well. 'I suggest that you wear rubber boots at home. This means that the deadly rays can't be earthed and so your brain won't be affected.' Like homeopathy, this can have a placebo effect.

~

In those days the *Daily Mirror* horoscope was written by a sub in the Manchester office. Some astrologers at least make a stab at studying the skies, apply what they imagine to be science, and produce 'charts' which are roughly as useful as the contents of fortune cookies. Many of them are no doubt quite sincere, and untroubled by the fact that all their colleagues disagree with each other. If it is a valid field of study, as they claim, it is like a branch of physics in which nobody can even agree on the boiling point of water.

I met Shelley von Strunckel, a well-known diviner of the cosmos for various newspapers and magazines. We were in a radio studio where I was protesting that there was no truth in what she did, and she insisted that there was. She promised to send me her predictions for the year just finished. This would demonstrate her remarkable foreknowledge of great events. When the sheet arrived – it had appeared in a proper newspaper, the *Sunday Times* – she had indicated her best prognostication in yellow marker pen: 'President Clinton will continue to skate on thin ice.' I felt at the time that 'US President faces tricky problems in coming year' could probably have been guessed without studying the position of Mars relative to the constellations. But all astrologers depend on similar vagueness, plus a handful of precise predictions which over the years provides them with at least one amazingly correct prognostication that they can boast about for ever.

According to a story, much loved in Manchester, the *Mirror* man got so bored with making up endless stuff about 'romance beckons' and 'be wary of those who do not wish you well at work' that one day he wrote: 'Gemini [or whatever]: all the sorrows of yesteryear are as nothing to what will befall you today.' Complaints poured in and the man was fired.

I always liked the cartoon that appeared in the old *Punch*. It showed a man listening to the radio, which is announcing: 'In a major leap forward for astrology, all persons born under the sign of Scorpio were yesterday run over by egg lorries.'

~

All reporting in Manchester was then overshadowed by the Moors murders. The trial of Ian Brady and Myra Hindley, held in Chester on the grounds that they could not get a fair trial in Manchester, had finished just two years before. The evidence was, of course, horrible beyond imagination, but the most unspeakable of all was the tape the couple had made of the abuse, torture and murder of Lesley Ann Downey. It included the little girl screaming in agony and fear, pleading for her mother. It also destroyed Hindley's claim that she had been an unwilling participant, dragged into being an accomplice by Brady's irresistible personality. Only a minuscule fraction of the public has ever heard the tape, though it accounted for much of the powerful campaign to prevent Hindley from being paroled. Reporters who heard it in court said that they had nightmares about it for years afterwards, and would wake up gasping with terror in the middle of the night. Few people in the trade were unaffected;

one close friend of mine had been on the local paper in Hyde, and was the first reporter on the scene after the police arrived to discover their last murder.

~

I did quite a bit of ordinary reporting, some of it very ordinary. Rawtenstall Co-op had a new general secretary. The Manchester Ship Canal was to run pleasure cruises for tourists. Granada TV was dropping a programme. When Michael Frayn joined the paper he was given the Miscellany column to write. It was full of similar material. Frayn found items such as 'The vicar of Saddleworth reports seeing a heron on his roof. Have other readers had the same experience?' dreadfully dull, and so turned it into the funniest newspaper column I have ever read, under the same title, Miscellany, but peopled with Frayn's own fictional characters: Rollo Swavely, the well-known public relations man; Christopher Smoothe, the minister for chance and speculation; Christopher and Lavinia Crumble, who are quiveringly aware of every new trend; and Horace and Doris Morris, who are helplessly behind the times. These people are still alive today.

~

I found that I was learning very little about the world, but a great deal about my chosen trade. I was sent to Aberystwyth to cover the Prince of Wales's arrival there as a student. My colleagues, from all papers except the *FT*, spent their day in the town's main hotel, waiting to be briefed shortly before deadline time by the prince's equerry. The atmosphere in the bar was fuggy, and the weather outside pleasant, so I went for a stroll on my own, only to see prince and courtier walking into a shop. After they had left I went in and asked what they had bought. Coat hangers. Had the prince himself paid? No, the man with him paid. I took a careful note, then back out in the street saw them leave a small grocer's. I forget exactly what was bought, but it was the usual stuff – tea, sugar, milk and so forth. A disappointing absence of lobster and caviar, I thought, but back at the hotel my account was seized upon like a bucket of fresh water on the raft of the *Medusa*.

When the equerry arrived he recounted the prince's day: meeting fellow students, tutors, lunch in the cafeteria, etc. He finished and was greeted by a grim silence.

'I think,' said someone, 'there is something you're not telling us.'

The equerry was, reasonably, puzzled.

'I think you are not telling us about the prince's shopping expedition!'

'Oh, that,' said the equerry, still puzzled. 'He just bought some odds and ends, stuff he'll need. I didn't think you'd be interested in that.'

Not interested? Was he mad? The very fact that the heir to the throne was having to buy his own tea and coat hangers like a normal human being was a source of intense interest and made page leads in the tabloids the next day. The newspaper world is similar in many superficial ways to the real world, but also deeply different. It's rather like those planets the *Star Trek* crew visit, in which the atmosphere is identical to ours, and for some reason everyone speaks English, except they breathe through gills, or have purple skin.

~

My companion on the Aberystwyth trip was a middle-aged photographer called Tom Stoddart, who had been on the paper for many decades. He had once taken a picture of a horse pulling a cart in the street near the office. It was also eating hay from the cart in front. It was apparently a charming picture, but the paper refused to print it on the grounds that the *Manchester Guardian* could not appear to condone theft.

Tom's great obsession was parking. It was always uppermost in his mind. On a journey to Liverpool he asked me where my family lived. Birmingham, I said. Ooh dear, he replied, that was a terrible place for parking. Had we always lived there? No, I said, before that we lived in Leicester. Ah, he said, parking was tricky there, but not as bad as Birmingham. And had we lived anywhere apart from those two cities? When I said that we had lived in Hull, a faraway gleam came into his eyes, and he said, 'Now, Hull, there's some great parking there!'

The mania never left him. He arrived in Aberystwyth after me. I saw him emerge through the hotel entrance and remarked to whoever I was in the bar with, 'He'll come in here and immediately start talking about parking,' and he did.

'Sorry I'm late, but it's taken me for ever to find somewhere to park . . .' he said.

~

I was rather lonely in Manchester, being incompetent at making friends, and my self-esteem did not allow me to scuttle off home to visit my family more than, say, once a month. So I took up reporting on football matches. This produced a little extra money and gave me something to do. The first match I covered was Blackpool v. Chelsea, in the old Division One. Chelsea were then top of the league, and Blackpool bottom of the division. Nevertheless, Blackpool scored three times in the first half, and the match looked to be over. But Chelsea rallied and scored three times after half-time, then won the game through an own goal. I went back to Manchester and thought long and hard about my report. This was going to establish me as the next Neville Cardus, the renowned cricket correspondent, a new star who combined an erudite range of learning with an extraordinary gift for bringing out the agonizing drama of a great sporting event. Finally, around Sunday lunchtime, I wrote: 'Like the heroes of a Greek tragedy, Blackpool took on the gods of Chelsea, and were cut down by their own hubris. And just as Oedipus put out his own eyes, so it was Blackpool's hapless left-back who completed the final destruction . . .' Or words very close to that.

I phoned it over, and apart from a courteous call asking me to add the names of the goal-scorers, there was no reaction from the office. But there, on the doormat, next day, at the top of the sports page, was my report, unchanged and uncut.

I went in to work with something of a swagger, expecting plaudits from my colleagues. Not one of them mentioned it, however, and I later realized that they were simply being kind. Then at around teatime the night editor, Joe Minogue, arrived, beaming happily.

'Read your football report, Simon. I enjoyed it.'

'Did you, Joe? Thanks very much.'

'Will you tell me one thing, though? Were they playing with a ball, or a bloody discus?'

~

By an odd coincidence, I heard another account of that same match, about thirty-five years later, when I preceded Ron 'Chopper' Harris, the former captain of Chelsea, speaking at a lunch. He said that the entire Chelsea team had been drinking and gambling in Blackpool until around 4 a.m. of the morning before the match. This had amply explained their poor performance in the first half. He also told a story about playing against Manchester United. The then manager, Tommy Docherty, had taken him aside and told him that United (never then known as 'Man U') had a very promising newcomer called George Best. 'I want you to take him out,' Docherty said.

'Boss, if I go for him too hard I might get sent off.'

'Put it this way, son,' said Docherty, 'they'll miss him more than we'll miss you.' (Best would drink with anyone, even *Guardian* employees, and could often be found in one of the office pubs, The New Grapes, knocking back Bacardis even the night before a match.)

~

At this time, the paper's Manchester United correspondent retired, and I briefly took his place while they looked round for someone new. Even then, their players were among the most famous and the most exciting in the league: Bobby Charlton, Denis Law, Paddy Crerand and of course George Best. I should have borne in mind Dr Johnson's dictum that you must read back your writing, select the finest phrases, and strike them out. 'The ball seemed to play around Best's feet like a loyal puppy'; 'Crerand served up passes from midfield like a waiter in an expensive restaurant flourishing a silver-domed dish.' Discomfiting to read now, but nobody at the paper complained. I suspect the people who might have taken me to one side for a quiet word did not, on the whole, read the sports pages.

After each United home match, the press were invited into the directors' room where there was a free bar and buffet for the following two hours. It was luxury almost beyond my understanding. Prawn vol-au-vents! Sausage rolls! Cream horns, and as much as you could possibly drink to swill it down. I would have suffered any number of 0–0 draws in return for such lavish hospitality. Now and again a player would arrive to talk about the match, usually Crerand, who was sharp and cynical and funny. United was the city's Roman Catholic team, and when a new manager was required, Crerand said, 'You'll see the white smoke coming up from Old Trafford.' City was the Jewish team, and those who were neither could make their choice.

~

I arranged to interview a young man, one of Manchester United's more promising players, whose claim to celebrity was being thought the only player for the club ever to have possessed a university degree, in economics. His name was Alan Gowling. I took him to lunch at a Berni Inn (being able to buy anyone lunch required advance permission and much planning). He was interesting, but perhaps slightly disappointing. I asked what his long-term ambitions were, hoping he might say, 'To score a hat-trick in the Cup Final and write a comparative critique of Adam Smith and Keynes,' but instead he said, 'I just want to do my best for Sir Matt and all the lads.' (Sir Matt Busby had returned briefly to manage the club.) Alan did score four goals against Southampton in one match I watched, but did not hold down a permanent first-team place, and ended up playing for different northern clubs in various divisions. He now runs a chemical plant.

~

Not all the matches I covered were in any way glamorous. I covered Oldham Athletic, where the popular local joke was, 'If Latics were playing in my back yard, I'd draw the curtains.' I once went back to Hull for some Division Four clash where, again, I learned something about my new profession. I forget the names, but at some point there was what was then called a goalmouth scramble. One of the Hull players scored, but it was almost impossible to see which. Urgent talks were held in the press box. A name was required, pronto. After about a minute's discussion, one was selected, and everyone agreed to stick to him – even those who had thought it had been another player altogether. After the match the player who actually had scored came to the press box to make sure we'd got his name. We hadn't. He was furious. One of the old hands patted him on the shoulder and said, 'Sorry, lad, you might well be right. But it's on the wires now, so it's too late.' Very occasionally I wonder how he coped with this injustice.

'Did I ever tell you kids about the time I scored against Hartlepool, and someone else was credited with the goal?'

'Only about a hundred times, Grandad.'

More proof that, in the newspaper world, what matters is not getting it right, but getting it the same as everyone else. Otherwise people might imagine you were wrong.

~

I also reviewed theatre productions in the north. There was a thriving rep scene, and I saw fine performances in Bolton, Sheffield, Leeds, Liverpool, Buxton and all over the region. But the big shows tended to be in the two great theatres in Manchester, the Opera House and the Palace. I had gone with a colleague to see a pre-London run of *The Good Companions*, based on Priestley's novel with music by André Previn. He was then married to actress Mia Farrow, and I still smoked, two circumstances that came together with almost fatal consequences. In those days – it seems astonishing now – you could smoke in some theatres, including the Palace, Manchester. Most people did. My friend and I were sitting in our seats by the aisle in the stalls when two striking young women walked towards us and sat in the row in front. It was only when they were a few feet away that we spotted that one of them was Mia Farrow.

She had long hair, before the days of her short-cropped gamine look. I was nervous at having a famous film star so close to me. The lights went down. Part of her long, shining hair cascaded into the ashtray in front of me, but it was dark, so I didn't see. I stubbed my cigarette out in the ashtray.

There was a noise. It must have been as loud as a flea snapping its fingers, but to me it might have been the crack of doom, or the Hoover Dam about to collapse. There was a smell, which again was sufficiently mild for her not to notice, but could have been a dozen stink bombs. I could see the ends of her hair glowing in the dark, but by some miracle she had no idea what had happened. Hair does not burn easily, unless it has been treated with certain chemicals, and thank goodness after a short time it went out. But I still wake up wondering what would have happened if she had used one sort of hairspray and her head had gone up in flames, as singer Michael Jackson's once did. It would, I think, have been hard to win a $1 million settlement in Manchester, especially in the 1970s, but I imagine she would have tried.

The show was not very good, and the tunes unmemorable. It had a short London run, and later the couple got divorced. Possibly that night, as they prepared for bed, he might have said, 'My God, Mia, what in hell happened to your hair?'

~

The northern editor of the *Guardian* was Brian Redhead, who was charming, extraordinarily talented, and probably the most solipsistic person I have ever met. He was a tremendous name-dropper, and somehow managed to drop his own name too – a trick I have rarely seen accomplished – in recounted conversations which revealed him to be relaxed and at home with the famous and powerful. Journalist Alan Brien used to describe the difference between name-dropping and reasonable conversation. If Moses comes down from the mountain and says, 'I've just been talking to God, and he's given me these Ten Commandments' – that's fine. If he says, 'I've just been talking to God, and I must say he's looking awfully well lately,' that's name-dropping.

Our assumption with Brian was that if you said, 'Nice day, isn't it?' he would reply, 'D'you know, I said exactly that to Margaret Thatcher this morning, and she said, "As usual, Brian, you're absolutely right." ' He used to tell people that he had appointed me, which might be technically true, but it was certainly Harry Whewell who made the choice. I suppose I should be flattered, but I am sure that even if the conversation had been on the lines of: 'That Hoggart, he's workmanlike, I suppose,' Brian would have seized what small degree of credit was on offer.

On my first day I was summoned to meet him in his office. What degree had I got? I said a 2.1. 'Why didn't you get a first? I did,' he replied. They were his opening words. I saw little of him after that, though I later discovered that he had got his first only in Part One of the tripos, therefore it wasn't a real first – an arcane point to be sure, but at Oxbridge it counts.

At the time, Alistair Cooke was the paper's United States correspondent, and a very good one too, though he was not a man stricken by anxiety about deadlines. He loved golf and boxing, and if there was a big match or tournament he would write a majestic, beautifully crafted piece. This would appear in the *Guardian* a day after the event had been covered everywhere else. But it was worth waiting for.

Once Cooke had reason to visit Manchester, a rare event. (He did affect a certain grandeur. When a new foreign editor took up his job, he took a whistle-stop tour of the world, visiting correspondents in Paris, Moscow, Bonn, Washington and also New York, where Cooke lived in a vast, rent-controlled apartment. Usually foreign correspondents are desperate to talk to the new boss, either to show off their matchless knowledge of the country, or to complain about the appalling conditions in which they have to exist, or both. Only in New York was the new boss told that he would have to wait until the correspondent could find time in his diary.)

Cooke was not comfortable on his own, so he phoned Redhead from the Midland Hotel, Manchester, and asked him to join him for a drink. Naturally Redhead turned up, and promptly. It must have been a magnificent clash of egos. At one point the waiter came over to their table with a menu. He said that his wife would never forgive him if he had had the greatest voice in radio in his bar, and had failed to get an autograph. So Brian took the menu, signed it, and handed it back. Game, set and match – or perhaps not. It is quite possible that Brian genuinely assumed he was more famous than the man who wrote *Letter from America*.

After a while it became clear to Brian that he would not become editor of the *Guardian* any time soon, so he went to edit the sister paper, the *Manchester Evening News*, whose slogan was 'Just a friend dropping in', which became Brian's nickname, since it was said to describe his relaxed management style.

Later, when he finally realized that he would never edit the *Guardian*, he took his considerable skills to the *Today* programme (he had chaired a Radio 4 discussion programme called *A Word in Edgeways*, so called, cynics scoffed, because while Brian was there it was so hard to get one). There is no doubt that he was a superb broadcaster. As his *Today* colleague John Humphrys used to say, he managed to turn any programme into a conversation with the listener – though, as in his face-to-face encounters, it was not always possible for the listener to take part.

I last met him when he interviewed me and a colleague from *The Times* for the *Today* programme at a party conference in Brighton. After we'd finished, he said, 'That's the last time I'll be interviewing either of you. I'm going to be a vicar.'

We expressed astonishment.

'I've always wanted to be a vicar,' he said, 'and if I don't do it now, I never will. You have to do a course, and there's one at Manchester. I was worried that I might not be able to manage it, but when I saw that the first two books on the reading list were written by me, I thought I could probably cope!'

Back in London, my then editor Donald Trelford asked me to write up this revelation. Redhead was a famous figure; his name would be well known to every *Observer* reader. I phoned the head of theology at Manchester and told him what Brian had said. There was an embarrassed pause, of the type you get when someone is trying to find a courteous way of saying something that might not be wholly agreeable. 'Yerrss,' said the professor, 'Brian has expressed an interest in doing our course, and I am sure we could take him. But his books are, umm, well, they're absolutely marvellous, of course, but rather for the layman. I don't *think* we would have them on our students' reading list . . .'

I feel churlish writing some of this. Brian's son died in a car crash in France – the present BBC political editor, Nick Robinson, was in the same crash but survived – and I have noticed that people who lose a child often have the light dimmed in their eyes. They can go on to have a rich, fulfilled life, but there is always something missing, a great, aching hole, that will never be filled.

After Brian died, the BBC ran a series called *Radio Lives* about celebrated figures in broadcasting. They asked me to contribute some anecdotes. I said I feared they might not be altogether favourable, and was that what they really wanted? The producer replied that they had lots of contributors praising Brian to the skies, and wanted a little vinegar to go with the oil. I heard the finished programme, but it turned out that I was kindlier than John Humphrys, who had umpteen more stories about Brian's fantasizing. Was Brian deliberately lying? I don't think so. Like many people who find themselves of great interest, he saw no reason not to make himself yet more fascinating, to gild the already gorgeous lily. Often such people are delightful, if somewhat wearing, company. They want you to share their liking for themselves, and find that the quickest way to achieve this is through boundless charm and persistence. They are like people who've discovered a new restaurant, and can't just tell you about it – they have to nag you until you agree to go, then nag you to tell them how marvellous it was.

~

Now and again I would be sent on the road with Bob Smithies, one of a long line of first-rate photographers who worked for the paper's northern office. These days reporters are desperate to get space for their articles to appear. Then the paper seemed constantly short of material, so they sent Bob and me out for a week at a time to find curiosities, amusing or intriguing items that might not be 'news' in any sense, but would fill space. Bob had been raised in Bury, in one of those cultured working-class families where huge store was placed on a love of the arts and literature. Bob knew more about music and books and the theatre than most Oxbridge graduates.

In his youth, the paper had helped fill space by sending him off to photograph L.S. Lowry in his studio. Lowry was known locally, though not yet nationally famous. But every year or so a picture would appear in the *Guardian*, taken by Bob, and captioned something like: 'The artist L.S. Lowry, at work on his latest canvas in his studio in Salford'. After some years, Lowry said to Bob that he was very grateful for all the interest he had shown. He wished to reciprocate. Would Bob like to have any two paintings on the walls, for £50? This would, I suppose, be the equivalent of between £1,000 and £2,000 now – though since most families, including middle-class ones, lived more or less from hand to mouth, it must have felt like far more.

Bob and his wife Mildred had agonized discussions, but finally decided to accept the offer and he brought the two pictures home. At this point Bob's life became a sort of terrifying roller-coaster. Lowry suddenly became famous, and the paintings were then so valuable that they could no longer afford the insurance. So they sold them, and used the money to build a holiday home on the North Wales coast, where they were wonderfully happy, until their son died in his early teens. He had had a weak heart, which had not been diagnosed, though as Bob put it, 'If we'd known we'd have wrapped him in cotton wool, and he'd have died a bit later, but he wouldn't have had a boyhood.'

Bob had to change his life, so he went to work as a presenter for the north-western programmes on Granada TV, where he developed a jovial and avuncular style subtly different from the man I knew, as if he had sprayed himself with a sort of TV patina. He was always courteous; if we happened to be in a public area, say outside a party conference in Blackpool, hordes of people would approach him. 'It is you, isn't it!' they would say roguishly, and he would always admit that it was, in a genial, self-deprecating manner, which seemed generally to please.

~

(As someone who appears very occasionally on TV, I too get approached, though normally by people who only vaguely recognize me and assume they have encountered me in some other part of their life. 'Did you go to Bradford University?' someone asked me. I was pursued down the street by a man in Edinburgh who was convinced that I lived near him in Penicuik, a small town a few miles south. He refused to believe that I had then never even heard of the place. And once, at a Tory conference in Blackpool, I was having a coffee with a colleague at a table shared by two northern men, one of whom glowered at me. 'Have I seen you on television?' he demanded, rather aggressively, as if I were a rapist he had identified from a photofit.

It gave me the perfect chance to use a line I had stolen from the American comedian, Emo. 'I don't know,' I said. 'I'm afraid you can't see through the other way.')

~

Bob's great love was compiling crosswords, which he had been doing on and off for decades. He worked frequently for the *Guardian*, and after he retired from Granada he became, I would guess, the second most popular of the paper's compilers, after Araucaria. His speciality was anagrams which cunningly incorporated the answer, such as 'Intrigue born in a Derry manger (11)': GERRYMANDER. The city was famous for its crooked ward divisions. His crosswords were collected in books, but his greatest pride was probably a postcard from Araucaria, congratulating him on one particular clue, 'Amundsen's forwarding address (4)', to which the answer was MUSH.

In those days, if you were out of the office, you sent your articles through the copytakers. They were a smallish group, intensely proud of their skills, and determined not to be taken for granted by correspondents. Some were astonishingly quick, and could type almost as fast as you could read the material. Others were much slower, and it was frustrating to hear them pecking out one word at a time while you stood in a phone box, fearful of missing the last train. Or there might be other people outside, waiting to use the phone, getting angrier as the minutes limped by. Once I was phoning something from a bar in Glasgow. I had been connected for a few seconds when a drinker came up to me and said, 'You've just got one minute on that phone, son, before I smash you in the face.' He might have been placed there by the tourist board, purely to meet visitors' expectations of the city. Saying to the desk, 'I'm sorry I was late, but there was a bloke here threatening to smash me in the face,' would not have been a remotely acceptable excuse, so I ploughed on. The man seemed to forget his threat and drifted away.

Copytakers had their favourite lines. 'Is there much more of this?' they would ask wearily, as what you had thought of as a superb piece of prose wafted into their headphones. This cry generally came before their break, which was sacrosanct and inviolate. Saying, 'I'm in Northern Ireland and a howling mob, armed with nailed staves, is advancing down the street in the direction of this phone box' (as was once the case) would never trump the break. 'I'm just handing you over,' they would say, and it was a matter of luck whether they managed to transfer you to the person at the next typewriter. They had their order of priorities. Towards the end of the evening there would be only one, or perhaps two, on duty. On one occasion I had phoned to give an account of some more mayhem in Ulster and begged to have my story taken down. The copytaker told me with strained patience that I should wait my turn; she had to take the report of a lacrosse match.

Some copytakers responded to what they were typing. Joe, one of the best, was extremely left-wing. 'That Tony Benn, he's a real enemy of the workers, eh, Simon!' he would offer in the manner of a pub bore, confident of getting agreement around the bar. One of the earliest events I covered in Manchester involved a little girl who was missing. It was an awful story, and indeed they found her body a few days later. In the meantime, mistaking the word used for professional waterproof clothing, I reported that 'firemen wearing rubbers searched the canal.' It was several minutes before the copytaker stopped laughing and resumed typing.

Others were nit-picking. One seemed to delight in making life difficult for the reporter. In the summer of 1980 I was in Washington, and since all our correspondents happened to be out of town, I was asked to cover the routine political news of the day. I managed to reach the copytakers, and got the stroppy one.

'President Carter—' I began.

'Spell that!' he barked.

Later I added, 'The President's national security adviser, Zbigniew Brzezinski . . . that's Z-B-'

'I can spell, thank you *very* much.'

~

Communications were always difficult. One of the most ingenious reporters was Harold Jackson, who won innumerable awards for his coverage of the world's most tumultuous places. Things were not helped by the fact that the foreign desk, as a last genuflection to the paper's northern origins, had been kept in Manchester. Phoning or telexing to London was relatively easy – foreigners had heard of London – but Manchester was tricky. Jackson was endlessly resourceful. He covered the Soviet invasion of Czechoslovakia in 1968, having somehow got past the border guards, and found a way of telexing his outstanding reports, vividly capturing the emotions and the horrors. One day was exceptionally quiet. He sent a thoughtful piece about the silence in the streets, the resentful populace going grudgingly about their business, the wary Soviet soldiers surveying each square from the turret of their tanks. Suddenly the piece lapsed into journalese: 'Machine guns answered the clatter of my typewriter as I watched the Soviet bear mow down peaceful protesters in the war-torn streets of Prague . . .' and much along those lines. The telex ended with the words, 'here Jackson petered out.'

It turned out that the *Daily Sketch* had finally decided to send a man on the story. He had just arrived and begged Jackson to let him use the telex line he had somehow wangled. Naturally the story was made up out of whole cloth – there hadn't been time actually to find anything out. But then to most papers it was the dateline that counted. If your man had managed somehow to fly into war-torn Filthistan, then it was thought quite legitimate for him to file an excitable piece from the airport bar. Serious research would begin with the *aperçus* of the taxi-driver who took him into town.

~

One reporter joined the paper at the same time as me. He was called Bill Hanley, and he came from a working-class family who lived in a council house in Birkenhead. His brother was a merchant seaman. Bill was one of the cleverest people I have ever met, yet quite mad. He had gone to the LSE, the first of his family even to dream of going to university. Occasionally he was convinced he was a changeling. He loved his family, yet found them very difficult – heaven knows how they found him. At times he displayed a curious and attractive naïveté, such as when his bank manager sent him a letter asking what he proposed to do about his overdraft. Bill asked me: 'I'll just send him a cheque, that'll do it, won't it?' I thought this was a joke, but it wasn't.

We shared flats and houses, with or without other young members of the staff, in various parts of Manchester. Now and then Bill would offer to cook, which was always a mistake. Once he announced with a great flourish that he was going to make breakfast: bacon and eggs. He put it on, then popped into my room for a chat, asking after a while, 'How long does it take to fry an egg?' The egg was not just burned, but had bonded to the pan, which we had to throw away. Another time he said we were going to have sprouts and risotto for dinner. The sprouts were uncooked, the risotto burned black. Bill was one of those people for whom daily living presents just too much of a challenge.

But I couldn't resist a spasm of envy when he got a story on the front page of all editions, in his first week. There had been some Liberal Party meeting in Manchester. Bill had approached the party elders after the event and explained that he was new to journalism; would they be kind enough to give him a leak? They kindly told him the name of the new president of the party, which would barely rate a paragraph now, but to a traditionally Liberal paper was then of some importance. The story appeared with an accompanying commentary by the political editor. Bill was up and running. It turned out that the first story of his career was also its high spot.

In retrospect it is clear that he was suffering from bipolar disorder. When he was high, he could talk brilliantly, dazzlingly, hilariously. Bill on form could keep a group of printers, late reporters and random drinkers in painful fits of laughter at one in the morning. When he was at the other end of the spectrum he was gloomy like a man carrying round his own personal thundercloud.

He was very proud of being on the *Guardian*. (Though as a cousin of my mother's said, being told by my mum that I had got the job, 'Well, he's got to start somewhere I suppose.') Christmas came round, and Bill decided to send a personalized card to all his friends. The printer told him that a run of two hundred would be the best value. The card had the usual four pages. One and four were a montage from the paper, printed in red, of Bill's stories and bylines. 'Liberals choose new president, by William Hanley', for instance. Page two was a big photograph of Bill on the telephone, helpfully labelled 'William Hanley'. Page three was the letterhead from the paper, listing address, phone and telex numbers, and, along the bottom, the names of directors. In the middle was the legend: 'Best wishes for Christmas and the New Year, from William Hanley.' Underneath he signed 'Bill'. His name appeared eleven times on the card.

Few people are on Christmas-card terms with a hundred people, never mind two hundred. Having sent a few to Birkenhead, Bill gave one to every single person employed in the northern office of the *Guardian*. Then he sent one to each of the children in the class where he had worked as a temporary teacher. Even so this left more than a hundred cards, which lay in drifts around his bedroom for several months.

He began to take time off for medical treatment. These days I suspect they would have known what chemicals to prescribe, but then nothing seemed to help. The paper reluctantly fired him, since it had become clear that he would rarely be in for work and when he was, he achieved very little. Bill went into a series of mental hospitals in the Merseyside area, from which he would send me short begging letters, for surprisingly precise amounts, rather like schoolboys do. 'The sum of £13.45 will allow me to go to Edinburgh where I have hopes of obtaining a job on *Scottish Field* . . . If you felt able to send me £7.70, I would be able to buy a pair of shoes to replace the ones I have, which are beyond repair . . . I hope you will not mind me asking you for a cheque for £5.45, this would enable me to join my friend on a trip to Blackpool.'

In the end I arranged a monthly standing order, so that he always had something for the occasional outing or the odd drink. There was an element of guilt in this. We were the same age, and had got the same job at the same time. He was, without doubt, cleverer than me, yet had been pursued by constant and unremitting misfortune. His condition grew steadily worse, and he died in hospital in 2008, watched over by a small but intensely loyal group of friends, who could still discern the surreal wit and even charm that were lodged inside his brain.

~

Northern Ireland claimed more of my time, and in early 1971 I went to live there. After nearly three years I felt that I had done enough, and wanted to cash in on the false but generally held belief that it was a dangerous place to work. I came to London and had lunch with the news editor, Jean Stead. She said briskly that she was happy to give me a job in the London office, but pointed out that I didn't know what job I wanted to do. Bizarrely I had not thought to make this important decision, so I said the first thing that popped into my head – politics.

She replied that the paper already had a full complement of political reporters, so I had better think again.

That night the political editor rang to say that the most junior member of the staff had announced that morning that she was leaving for the BBC. Would I like the job? Yes, I would.

THE GREEN ROOM

4

The Green Room

Enoch Powell & Bill Haley

Television green rooms are strange places, receptive yet frightening, each like a well-appointed condemned cell. You have generally been delivered there at least half an hour before you're due to appear – TV people have a desperate need to know that you are corporeally present and their running order is not going to be wrecked – so you hang about aimlessly for quite some time, exchanging embarrassed smiles with whomever else might be in the green room with you. There could be a last-minute reprieve – 'Terribly sorry, but with this plane crash we're running over, and we're going to have to drop your item. Thanks so much for coming in. Your car is downstairs . . .' – though unlike the prisoner you probably don't want the reprieve. More likely, the executioner suddenly arrives in the shape of the floor manager who deftly steers you to a sofa so slidy and yet so lumpy that Ikea would reject it; within ten seconds he has you miked up. (The executioner Albert Pierrepoint claimed he could have a man in the noose and hooded, then dead, just 7.5 seconds after shaking his hand.) You are aware of a magnificent set of teeth belonging to the presenter who is at a desk. She or he is flashing them in your direction. You also become aware that you cannot remember this person's name.

Suddenly they have swivelled round and are reading from an autocue. 'Once again, raffia table mats are in the news. One person who knows all there is to know on this topic is Simon Hoggart of the *Guardian*. Simon, raffia table mats – why are they so controversial?'

You stammer a reply, but it doesn't matter, because although their televisions are on nobody is actually listening at home, and also because the presenter isn't listening at all. I remember appearing on *Breakfast Time* with Frank Bough. I was promoting – much of *Breakfast Time* consisted of plugging BBC programmes – a programme I presented about a narrow-gauge railway that had been built to serve the Klondike gold prospectors in the Yukon, Canada. I had done it because I was asked and had enjoyed doing it. I liked the crew, and I thought the Yukon in autumn was one of the most wild and beautiful places I had ever seen. (We met a young man from Manchester who lived in the woods there, and survived on the one moose non-Indian people are allowed to shoot each year. We asked what the main drawbacks of living in the Yukon were. 'Mosquitoes,' he replied. We asked how big they were. 'Put it this way. They could steal your hubcaps.') The interview went like this:

Bough: What got you obsessed by railways?
Me: Well, I'm not really obsessed.
Bough: But something must have made you fascinated by trains.
Me: I'm not all that fascinated, but it is an interesting story.
Bough: Simon Hoggart, catch up with his love of railways tonight at 8 p.m. . . .

I don't blame him. He had people yelling in his ear which, like the voices novelist Evelyn Waugh described in *The Ordeal of Gilbert Pinfold*, were far more urgent and demanding than anything emitted from someone sitting in front of him. Except that Bough's voices came from real people. Or real-ish.

~

Once I sat in a green room early one morning facing a shortish, sandy-haired man. 'G'day,' he said with a warm smile.

I smiled back and resumed reading the papers.

Suddenly the executioner came for him. 'This way, Mr Laver,' she said.

I had been sitting opposite one of the greatest sportsmen of the last century. He can have no memory of this incident at all, but it still makes me cringe.

~

On another occasion I was presenting an experimental BBC2 programme called *Friday Night, Saturday Morning*. Among the guests were novelist Malcolm Bradbury and opera singer Dame Kiri Te Kanawa. I had known Bradbury for many years, since he was a colleague of my father at Birmingham University. It would be wrong to say he had dandled me on his knee – I was seventeen at the time – but he always took a kindly interest in what I was up to. I, in turn, took a kindly interest in his career, especially his two finest novels, *Eating People Is Wrong* and *The History Man*, which later made one of the BBC's best drama series, capturing perfectly the grasping idealism of the late sixties and early seventies. Like many writers, Malcolm liked meeting famous people and in the green room he made straight for Dame Kiri. After a short while it became clear that he was anxious to find a point of common interest, perhaps so that he could later tell friends, 'I said to Kiri Te Kanawa, and she agreed with me . . .'

He set about the task energetically and effectively and swiftly discovered that they and their families took their holidays in Portugal. The conversation went roughly like this:

Bradbury: It is the most beautiful country, isn't it?
Dame Kiri: Oh yes, it's very beautiful.
Bradbury: And we just love the food and wine.

Dame Kiri: Yes, we love the food and wine too.

Bradbury: And the people, they're marvellous!

Dame Kiri: They certainly are lovely people.

Bradbury: Do you know, they are the only people in history to have had a successful revolution in which not a single person died!

Dame Kiri (slightly puzzled): They had a revolution? Well, my husband and I mostly go for the golf.

To say I cherished the look on Malcolm's face would be unfair and unkind, though he did look crestfallen.

My career as an interviewer didn't really recover from the subsequent encounter on air with Dame Kiri. She was delightful, but hadn't really grasped that the art of being interviewed is to cooperate with your interviewer in a kind of cosy conspiracy, to be having a friendly chat, with the audience sitting at home as if waiting to join in. I had been told by the very efficient researcher that Dame Kiri had a wonderful story to tell about the first time she appeared at the Metropolitan Opera in New York. It was such a wonderful story that the researcher wasn't going to tell me what it was, because the producers would want the cameras to pick up the look of delighted astonishment on my face, quite unrehearsed.

The interview proceeded quite normally until we got to her trip to New York. 'Where I gather you had an astonishing experience at the Met,' I prompted.

'Yes, I certainly did,' said Dame Kiri with a reflective smile. She seemed disinclined to continue, and didn't. I still don't know why.

I had no idea what to do, which is why I have always been a hopeless interrogator.

~

At one stage *Friday Night, Saturday Morning* had embedded in it a prototype TV version of *The News Quiz*, with Ned Sherrin in the chair. Once I appeared with Nigel Dempster in the 'Street of Shame' team against John Wells and George Melly. There had been a technical delay which George filled by drinking a vast quantity of Campari, which struck me as the least cool drink someone as uber-cool as him might choose. When we came to do the quiz he was completely and happily drunk and had nothing to say at all. The other four of us kept up the usual predictable banter – a picture of men in white clothes trekking across snowy wastes was described as the Irish expedition to the Sahara Desert – but George sat there silently with an enormous and blissful smile on his face, until John Wells said in desperation, 'Can George have a point for not getting anything wrong?' The recollection may have been embarrassing for George, if he had a recollection.

~

Inevitably one came across these people in their other lives. Nigel Dempster once took me to lunch, purely, so far as I can judge, to boast. He told me that his gossip column in the *Daily Mail* was so popular that the paper could print it alone, with nothing else, sell for the same price and not lose a single reader. I knew that his column was well-read but not to that breathtaking extent; by the end it had become a sorry shadow of its past glories, all too easy to parody: 'Hortensia del Piero, second eldest daughter of Octavio del Piero, who recently lent one of his celebrated string of polo ponies to South American champion José Delgardo, and who has entertained Prince Charles at his *estancia* in the Pueblo del Mar, tells me that her close friend Lucia Hart-Bakewell, married last year to furniture polish heir Frederick ("Tripper") Blasco, who previously escorted playgirl the Hon. Drusilla Mars, may be pregnant . . .' The column had become an endless list of people virtually unknown to anyone outside the confines of the column. It is true that readers will enjoy gossip even about people they have never heard of – you can write gossipy paragraphs about a bus inspector in Devizes or a schoolteacher in Aberdeen provided the material is colourful enough – but none the less there are limits. I often feel the same about our coverage of politics. Does anyone care who is deputy chairman of the Commons Committee on Privileges, or is in charge of Labour Party recruitment? Yet we constantly write about these people as if they mattered, perhaps hoping that our mere interest will make them persons of consequence.

~

George Melly I knew slightly because he had been a friend, or at least a good acquaintance, of my father. He admired Dad's work, and Dad enjoyed the whiff of showbiz loucheness that George exuded. On one occasion my parents had taken us children and my mother's mother to a holiday cottage in Wales. It turned out to be close to where the Mellys had a house, and they invited us over for lunch. The conversation, about Soho, jazz, books and who was sleeping with whom must have seemed inexplicable and nightmarish to my grandmother, who sat bolt upright throughout, as if by keeping absolutely still she could make herself believe that the whole terrible event was not actually happening.

~

George had a day job, which involved helping Mark Boxer draw his pocket cartoons for *The Times*. I used to fill in when George was touring abroad. The task involved reading the day's papers, then having a conversation with Mark as to likely topics. Neither would actually write the caption, but together you would hope to tease out something that would work. If the cartoon reflected social change as well as routine headlines, all the better. For example, there was a story about African embassies having to move out of the more expensive parts of London because their governments couldn't afford the property prices. We agreed on a curtain-twitching couple looking out on to the street. 'I see the blacks are moving out. There goes the neighbourhood!'

My favourite, which I still have (Mark paid you £25 for your time, or else gave you the – far more valuable – original artwork), came after Michael Heseltine had been attacked by Greenham Common women who threw paint at him when he was giving a talk in Oxford. Mark drew, with his customary and astonishing economy of line, an anxious mother, a truculent-looking schoolgirl, and a psychologist, all horn-rimmed glasses and tufts of hair on either side of his bald head. 'She needs a channel for her aggression. Have you thought of pacifism?'

Another I liked more than Mark did, because he detested the cliché of two people walking past a news placard and commenting on it. But we couldn't see any way round this. The Duke of Devonshire had just announced that he was joining the SDP, then seen as the quintessence of *bien pensant* bourgeois politics. 'At least it gets rid of our middle-class image,' one of the men is saying. That night Rupert Murdoch sacked Harry Evans as editor of *The Times*, and at some point in the chaos the cartoon was lost and never recovered.

~

The first time I ever appeared on television was on *Face the Press*, a show in which a panel of journalists interviewed a public figure. We were to face George Woodcock, then general secretary of the TUC, and I had spent much time briefing myself. At the last moment he cancelled, and was replaced by George Mikes, the Hungarian humorist, whose work I had enjoyed. The half-hour was chaired by Ludovic Kennedy. He and Mikes went in for a little gentle Magyar one-upmanship.

It turned out they used the same Hungarian dentist. 'Alex recommended him to me,' said Kennedy. 'Alexander Korda.'

Mikes smiled. 'Arthur recommended him to me. Arthur Koestler.'

I was very nervous and found it difficult to ask questions that weren't entirely, demeaningly stupid. 'Where do you get your funny ideas from?' was one, I recall. 'Is it difficult being a humorous writer?' In the end I fell silent, until the floor manager walked past with a sign reading 'Wind up now'. For some reason I thought this was for me, and I said, as I had seen so many TV presenters say, 'Well, that's all we have time for.' I became aware of Kennedy's hand hitting my knee, very hard.

'Not you, me, you cunt!' he explained.

It was some years before I went on television again.

~

Breakfast with Frost was always a popular show to appear on, since you actually had breakfast with David Frost afterwards. On one occasion I had been on the terrible sofa talking about the day's papers, and soon afterwards found myself in a room near the top of Television Centre, being served a BBC breakfast. Others there included Sir John Major, Joan Bakewell, Moira Stewart – the newsreader later sacked for being too old, and one of the most genteel people I have ever met – plus Frost himself. The subject turned to a bill going through parliament the following week. Its intention was to give people who had changed sex the same legal rights as those of the sex they had adopted. Apparently there were some minor glitches in the existing law. I said that I had been surprised to learn from the debate that one-third of all sex-change operations turned women into men.

'What I want to know,' said Frost, 'is whether a man who has been a woman can ever' – here there was a long, Frosty pause, familiar from *That Was the Week That Was* – 'have an *erection.*'

I muttered something I had stolen from the comedian Jeremy Hardy – 'It's amazing what you can do with a lollipop stick' – but the joy for me was seeing the absolute 'Am I going to have to think of a reply to this, for God's sake?' horror on the faces of everyone there, most especially Sir John, but also Moira Stewart, and even Joan Bakewell, who I should think is almost unshockable.

~

Andrew Marr took over the show when David Frost moved to Al Jazeera, the Arab news network. ('Hello, good evening, and al-akhbar,' as Rory Bremner put it.) In its new format, the programme included interviews with people outside politics, such as actors and singers. Once I was on at the same time as Joan Baez, someone whose work I had enjoyed since boyhood when my father brought her LPs back from America. She turned out to be charming and chatty, and handed round signed copies of her CD to everyone at the table. My friend Brian Hollywood, who was number two on the production team, asked her if it was true that she had once hit Henry Kissinger. She looked appalled. 'I would never offer physical violence to anyone,' she said, somewhat primly I thought.

But she had met him, she said. She had once found herself in the same elevator as the celebrated butcher of babies. It was, she thought, her golden opportunity to tell Kissinger exactly what she thought of him and his realpolitik foreign policy. But the words would not come so the two of them stood in silence until Kissinger said, 'I love your music.'

'Why, thank you,' she replied, bewildered but courteous, the opportunity gone for ever.

~

ITN used to have its headquarters in Wells Street, off Oxford Street, which it shared with the studios used by several regional companies when they needed to run an interview from London. In those days Reggie Bosanquet was one of ITN's most popular newsreaders, not least because he usually appeared to be tipsy and sometimes plainly drunk. Viewers would watch and wait in delight for the slurred words, the strange and unexpected elisions, and the facial expressions which never seemed quite to match whichever emotion – sadness, delight, anger – a news item might be thought likely to evoke.

Bosanquet spent much of the day, between bulletins, in a wine bar across the street from the studios. I was once introduced to him in the green room. He then left carrying a large goblet of red wine in each hand. I asked where he was going. 'To read the news, of course,' I was told. He put the glasses on a shelf under the desk, and swigged from them during the filmed inserts in the bulletin.

~

In the first election of 1974 Enoch Powell said that he was going to vote Labour because Labour offered a referendum on our continuing membership of the European Community, as it then was. (Hard, sometimes, to recall how the two main parties have reversed their position on Europe.) I was to chat about the day's events on Thames Television's local London news programme. Enoch was also to appear, as was Bill Haley who, with the Comets, was making what turned out to be his final tour of Britain. He was wearing an extraordinary multi-coloured jacket which resembled your TV screen when the signal is lost – engineers call it 'noise'. It was hideous, but heart-warmingly appropriate for the first globally successful rock-and-roll singer.

An embarrassed young man, a researcher, had to introduce

the two men. 'Pleased to meet 'cha, Mr Powell,' said Bill Haley, pronouncing it as 'pole'. He clearly had no idea who Enoch was, and why should he? There was a moment of tension in the green room as we waited for the response.

'And I,' Enoch said in that familiar flat Black Country accent, 'am very pleased to meet you. I have always *wanted* to meet you!'

I had a happy vision of Enoch, in drape jacket, crêpe-soled shoes and a duck's-arse haircut, standing by the juke-box, tapping his feet, looking round for trouble.

~

Powell was well aware of the effect his presence produced – the fear, the awe, the resentment, the loathing, the admiration – and seemed at times to be floating outside himself, looking in, enjoying a sort of out-of-body experience as he judged the impression he was making on other people. Once in a green room, the journalist George Ffitch told a story about George Thomas, then Speaker of the Commons. It was a good, if slightly complicated anecdote. At the end, Powell said, 'But that cannot be true, because . . .' and explained why.

Ffitch laughed and said, 'There you go, Enoch, spoiling a perfectly good story.'

'But I have not spoiled it,' said Powell, very seriously. 'Because now, when you tell the story, you can add at the end, "And then Enoch said . . ." and you will have a *much* better story.'

~

I and some colleagues lunched with Powell during Harold Wilson's last administration. He ordered tripe. 'We shall be talking it, so I may as well be eating it at the same time.' We asked what he thought of the Labour government. 'I feel about them much as a father does about his children. He may not admire what they do, or even like them very much. But he cannot avoid responsibility for the fact that they are there.' Powell never, ever underestimated his own importance.

~

I think the worst experience I ever had in a studio was on radio, live. It was *Midweek* on Radio 4, then presented by Russell Harty, a man of remarkable diffidence and courtesy. He had an unusually thin skin for a celebrity, and was easily bruised by confrontation. (Most established TV presenters, with the exception of a few like Michael Parkinson, are a disturbing blend of arrogance and insecurity. The arrogance derives from being constantly recognized in the street and fawned over by waiters, shop assistants, passers-by and so forth. The insecurity comes from the knowledge that a few weeks of poor ratings, or a misconceived remark, can destroy a career. Never quite overnight, but the descent, from prime-time show to guest on daytime TV then opening small branches of supermarkets, is relentless.)

Russell was different. He was in a constant state of anxiety. I later learned that he took a tranquillizer before doing any programme, on radio or TV. Even he, however, must have thought that this particular show would be easy. I would give him no trouble, and the other guests, who included an amiable chap from *Nationwide*, an early-evening TV programme, the new head of the Salvation Army, Sue Ryder of Sue Ryder Homes, and Gregory Peck, would chat away merrily and unprompted. However, Gregory Peck and I had got off to a bad start. I had arrived at Broadcasting House just before he did, and the woman who was looking after him approached the reception desk just after me. Gregory Peck hovered some way back. The receptionist knew me, smiled, and called out to one of the uniformed sherpas – chiefly elderly and often disabled ex-servicemen – whose job it was to guide people through the impossible maze that was, and still is, Broadcasting House. 'Oh, John,' she said, 'would you take Mr Hoggart, and . . .' – she waved a vague arm – '*this* gentleman, down to the studio.'

The star was clearly thunderstruck at not being recognized, and indeed not recognized while some minor civilian whom he himself naturally did not recognize, was recognized. For someone who had been a leading man in Hollywood for decades it must have been brutal, like Michael Winner being told to take a bike to KFC if he wanted any lunch. He didn't quite recover. My attempts to chat were rebuffed. When the programme began he said as little as possible, speaking only when spoken to, and then very briefly.

Russell was by this time fairly flustered. He started by interviewing Sue Ryder.

'If I may,' she said, in a tone that implied that she most certainly might and no one could stop her, 'I would like to read out our statement of aims.' She produced a piece of A4 paper covered in close print.

Russell blenched. 'Perhaps just one or two?' he suggested nervously.

Ms Ryder favoured him with a little smile, like a governess whose pupil has just enquired whether he might learn only three irregular verbs. 'First, our intention is to provide comfortable and secure homes for injured ex-servicemen . . .' or words along those lines. Russell tried to stop her, but nothing could. She ploughed on, until I thought one of us might need to feign suicide in order to distract her. Finally she stopped, but that was almost all her allotted time used up.

It was Gregory Peck's turn. Russell began by saying that he had been born in the California city of La Jolla, which he pronounced, as any English person would, with a hard J, as in 'jam' and the double l to rhyme with 'collar'. After this introduction, Gregory Peck drawled, 'Well, we could begin this interview by deciding whether we are going to continue pronouncing the name of my home town "la joller" or give it its correct pronunciation, "la hoya".'

If a boa constrictor had chosen that moment to coil round Russell's legs he could not have looked more alarmed. The interview failed. Next, the man from the Salvation Army managed to make the work of that institution sound as fascinating as being honorary treasurer of a small golf club.

I then had to give a jokey summary of the week's news. I gabbled through it, to almost complete silence apart from some kindly chuckles provided by Russell and the man from *Nationwide*. The tabloids were obsessed by two stories at that time: the extreme youth of some female contestants at that year's Wimbledon, and the marriage of Fred Astaire to a woman literally young enough to be his granddaughter. At one point I said something like, 'Tracy Austin may be young, but she is positively wizened compared to the new Mrs Fred Astaire.'

There was another long silence. The atmosphere, already bad, now resembled a dinner party at which every possible social solecism has occurred, and the only reason the guests haven't made a break for the door is that they don't want to make things horribly worse for the hostess, who is about to cry.

Then Gregory Peck said, 'I do not like to interrupt that quick-fire summary of the week's news, but the new Mrs Robyn Astaire is a good friend of mine, and I can assure you that she is anything but *wizened*.'

The temptation to shout, 'No, you blithering idiot, that's the opposite of what I said, and in any case it was a joke, you stupid, stuck-up, self-important prannet.' But I didn't.

Russell looked shell-shocked after the show, most particularly because of the la joller-la hoya mistake, which he regarded as a terrible reflection on his professionalism. But nobody could have coped with that lot, the studio guests from Hades. I reckoned that he would have needed a tranquillizer after the show too.

~

Russell had a good line in self-deprecation. Of course we all prefer to deprecate ourselves rather than have others do it for us, but it's an attractive quality none the less. He used to tell a story about being in a shop in his home town of Giggleswick, Yorkshire. Two boys were in the shop and were whispering to each other.

'It is him, in't it?' one of them said.

'No it isn't, I don't think it is . . .'

The two went on at length until one of them plucked up the courage to ask, 'Mister, did you used to work in this shop?'

~

But Russell at least gave the impression of knowing what he was talking about. Richard Baker, who for a long time presented *Start the Week*, carried an air of great vagueness round with him, like a little cloud. Once I appeared to talk about humour in politics, an old chestnut of a topic, which over the decades must have earned me an average of, ooh, £13.76 a year. With me, to discuss political caricature, was Michael ffolkes, a superlative cartoonist who specialized in great rococo designs, often like a more erotic Ronald Searle. One of his full-page works could have sat happily in the Tate, I thought. It showed the hallway of a stately home. A peer, in tweeds and plus-fours, is walking upstairs, presumably for his afternoon nap. He has a chambermaid slung over his shoulder. The duchess, or at least the wife, is saying, 'Oh, Jasper, can't you just take up a cup of tea like anyone else?'

Michael was an alcoholic, which was a terrible shame. Goodness knows what he could have produced if the booze hadn't got him. I once sat next to him at a *Punch* lunch where the first course was avocado vinaigrette. He began shaking pepper on it. He shook and shook until the pepper pot was empty, and the avocado covered in a small, grey mountain, like a recently erupted volcano, with an avocado-shaped patch of clean plate beneath. Then he fell asleep in it.

At eight thirty on a Monday morning, none of us was feeling terrific, and Richard Baker had a line to make each of us feel a little bit worse. 'I'm afraid I haven't had time to read your marvellous book!' he said to me, leaving open the question of how he knew it was marvellous. 'I'm sure you'll tell us all the most interesting bits!' To Michael he said, 'I'm afraid I haven't seen your marvellous *Flook* strip in the paper this morning!' Since *Flook* was drawn by Wally Fawkes, who did do caricatures of politicians, it was by now clear that a mistake had been made. The show somehow proceeded, with Michael wobbling gently from side to side. Someone in the control room must have realized that he was in no condition to say anything, so Baker wound up the programme without addressing a word to him.

Later Michael apologized to me. 'I'm sorry I wasn't much use,' he said. 'You see, I hadn't had a drink.'

'But it was only eight thirty in the morning,' I said stupidly.

'Yes, well, I probably start drinking rather earlier than most people,' he replied.

Later I heard a *Start the Week* which included Peter Brook, the theatre producer. Richard Baker said that Brook was bringing to London his play *The Ik*, a horrifying drama about a Ugandan tribe so poor and so desperate that they ate their own children in order to survive. After a brief description of this ultimate human degradation, Richard Baker asked, 'So, Peter Brook, do you have the same fear of flying as the rest of us?'

The humorous interlude was generally provided by a chap called Kenneth Robinson, whose monologue was rarely interrupted by laughter. This was rough on him, but the reason was that guests realized they had three minutes or so in which they would not suddenly be asked a question for which they were entirely unprepared, such as 'What is the funniest thing that has ever happened to you on holiday?' and so felt able to switch off, entering for a few moments a state of pleasant near-unconsciousness.

~

If *Midweek* had been grisly, it was almost matched by my stint doing *The Jimmy Young Show* one week while Jimmy – a far more skilful broadcaster than his faintly disconnected manner implied – was at his holiday house in Florida. They took me for a training session in which I had to comment on the day's news. Princess Diana had spoken at a dinner for people with eating disorders. 'It was a formal do,' I said, 'nobody was allowed to throw up until after the loyal toast.' The producer groaned, obviously sensing a long week ahead. And so it proved to be. I was almost hopeless, and left with an enormous admiration for the people who can do the job smoothly and amusingly day after day. I kept referring to the listeners as 'readers'; interviews were marked by long pauses as I worked out what to say. They impressed on me the immense importance of getting the timing right at the top of each hour, so that the news could come in precisely at 0 minutes and 00 seconds. This would sometimes mean working back from the length of the record, leaving ten seconds to back-announce it and get people ready for the news, or the pips. This would mean that you had to stop talking at, say, precisely 56 minutes and 47 seconds. The lowest point came when I finished right on the button. 'Well done,' said the producer. 'You got it exactly on the second. Unfortunately one minute early. Just keep talking, will you?' By this point he had lost the will to live. It is a truism that happens to be true: the hardest job of all is to make a difficult job look easy.

~

Humphrey Lyttelton was much loved by all who worked with him, but was extremely private. When a member of the *I'm Sorry I Haven't a Clue* panel, of which he was chairman, phoned him at home, all Humph wanted to know was how he had got hold of his number. I watched him chair the show once, and was impressed by his distant detachment. He seemingly paid no attention to what the panel were saying, riffling through his notes, oblivious to the jokes. Whereas even Colin Sell, the much abused pianist, was roaring with laughter.

I wanted to talk to him while I was chairman of *The News Quiz*, and got the chance at a BBC Christmas party, which was held in the Radio Theatre under Broadcasting House. Most people were on the stage, but Humph was sitting alone in the middle of a row of stalls. I summoned up a degree of courage, and told him who I was and how much I liked the show. He was charming, if a little fretful. He also was a blend of the cool jazz trumpeter, used to late gigs, smoky clubs, crooked promoters and long drives home, plus an anxious old man, who reminded me slightly of my mother.

He said he was getting too old for all the touring the show involved. Why, they had been booked into Gateshead, and he had been given the name of the hotel where they were to stay. It was not in any hotel guide, but was on the waterfront. He had a vision of a cheap flophouse crammed with drunken seamen. But when they arrived it had turned out that the waterfront was rather pleasant, and the hotel brand new, which was why it hadn't appeared in the guides. He had gone up to his room, run his finger along the desk, and it appeared to be free of dust!

This was all slightly disappointing, from a man who once would willingly have grabbed what sleep he could on a filthy mattress in the back of a van as it cruised down the M1 at four in the morning. So I asked about the game, Mornington Crescent.

Ah, he said, people always asked about that. 'I say to them, you wouldn't expect me to explain the rules of chess in the interval at a jazz concert, would you? Well, Mornington Crescent is much more complicated than chess.'

It had been invented when the programme had a producer whom they didn't greatly like. They had been having a few drinks in one of their hotel rooms, and had heard him coming down the corridor. 'Quick,' somebody said, 'let's invent a game that he won't understand.' Which they did.

~

Humph's great ability was to sound as if he didn't understand the significance of the joke he was uttering – his tone implied that it was scarcely more amusing than the shipping forecast. I remember almost driving into a tree while listening to *Clue* on the radio. He told one of his cruel but funny jokes about Lionel Blair on the TV charades show, confusingly called *Give Us a Clue*. Blair is in fact happily married with children, but his camp manner made him a permanent target for the Radio 4 script-writers. 'Tears came to his eyes during the team's Italian tour,' Humph said in that flat, disengaged tone of voice, 'when he was unable to finish off *Two Gentlemen of Verona* without using his mouth.' Sandi Toksvig's whooping laughter went on for at least a minute uncut, an eternity in radio, and an unusual example of the laugh being even funnier than the joke.

IRELAND

5

Ireland

Ian Paisley & Other Statespersons

My favourite Northern Ireland story dates from shortly before the Troubles began, in the mid-1960s. It came from a colleague who worked for the Irish edition of the *Daily Mirror.* There had been a terrible storm in Belfast, and lightning had struck a Protestant church in the south of the city, bringing timber and masonry down on the choir stalls, just a few minutes after choir practice had ended. Nobody was hurt, but it was a remarkable escape. The reporter arrived soon afterwards to find the minister wandering about the rubble.

'Truly the Lord has been merciful to us tonight!' he said.

The reporter asked whether the church was insured.

'Ah well, no,' said the minister. 'Unfortunately we're not covered against Acts of God.'

~

Once I was sent to Baltimore, County Cork, where the IRA had, somewhat optimistically, announced that they were going to blow up a Royal Navy survey ship that had been working off the coast as a goodwill gesture to the Irish government. The phone exchange was operated by a Mrs O'Driscoll. I enquired whether, if the attack took place at night, we would be able to get a phone call through to England. 'Ah,' she said, 'we operate a twenty-four-hour service here in Baltimore. But you mustn't call us after nine o'clock, because that's when we go to bed.' Luckily the IRA thought better of it.

~

I worked in Northern Ireland off and on from the start of the Troubles, in autumn 1968, then lived there from 1971 to 1973. The first civil rights march in Londonderry (or Derry) was in October 1968, and the papers the following day had pictures of Gerry Fitt, a Westminster MP, with blood streaming from his head as a result of being batoned by a policeman. Later it was suggested that Fitt had deliberately arranged to be hit in order to create a dramatic picture. I have no way of knowing, though I do know that he was inventive enough to pull such a stunt but also brave enough to walk into a line of armed policemen.

I was a trainee, but was sent to join Geoffrey Moorhouse, a reporter who had been despatched from London. Moorhouse went on to become one of the country's most celebrated travel writers, producing books about Calcutta, New York and the Sahara Desert, which he tried to cross on a camel. He was unlike any reporter I have met before or since. His pieces were not really articles but compositions. Once I burst in on him with what I thought were thrilling quotes from the Protestants who dominated the gerrymandered Derry council. 'Oh, could you be an angel,' he said, 'and leave me alone?' You will find few of Fleet Street's most hard-bitten asking anyone to be an angel.

That night we went to dinner at a Berni Inn, again the height of extravagance at the time. He was morose and silent. I asked what he would normally be doing at this time while on an assignment. 'Normally, I would be in my hotel room with a sandwich and a book of poetry,' he said longingly. Again, you will meet few journalists for whom this is their notion of a grand night in.

~

Depending on how you marked the beginning and the end, the Troubles dragged on for a third of a century, five times the length of the Second World War. I used to write occasionally that the people of Ulster would do anything for peace except vote for it, a remark that infuriated some readers. It was certainly true that over the decades there was growing support for the more extreme parties – Ian Paisley's Democratic Unionists and Sinn Fein, allied to the Provisional IRA. The old Ulster Unionists and the moderate SDLP came to be seen as irrelevancies, as did the moderate and non-sectarian Alliance Party, which had a steady but inadequate vote from the well-meaning bourgeoisie. I guess that this hardening of the electoral arteries was more out of fear than from any desire for the violence to continue; people felt that if they didn't vote for the party that would put their view with the greatest fervour, then the other lot would, and so gain the upper hand. Protestants voted for the DUP because Catholics were voting for Sinn Fein and vice versa. It was, absurdly, a little like a water shortage: if a hosepipe ban is threatened, everyone feels they must water their gardens immediately, which in turn makes the hosepipe ban inevitable. They wanted to get their extremism in first.

~

The people of Ulster certainly enjoyed being covered by the media. I was in a Belfast city centre pub during the hostage crisis at the 1972 Munich Olympics. Nothing else appeared on the television news, and the clientele was getting cross, muttering that there ought to be more about Northern Ireland. Who cared about a few dead Israeli athletes in Germany, when there were bombs and shootings down the street? The *Belfast Newsletter*, then a militantly Unionist paper, did all it could to bring the horrors of its readers' situation to their attention, every morning without fail, even when, as on some days, the horrors were not particularly horrible. One day every mainland newspaper had as its lead story some crucial decision by the then Prime Minister, Ted Heath, on incomes policy. The *Newsletter* led with the story 'IRA blows up letterbox'.

(The *Newsletter* is much changed. They rapidly discovered that their readers were largely bored by politics. Whenever there was an election, the sales of the paper would fall. When they ran a front-page report featuring a picture of a puppy, with the headline 'Can anyone find a home for this dog?', sales increased sharply.)

~

Many people in Ulster could not envisage a world in which their preoccupations were of no importance. Liverpool and Everton fans sometimes find it hard to believe that anyone is indifferent to their great rivalry. During the great Blair–Brown wars in the Labour Party from 1994 to 2007 many protagonists assumed that everyone, including political journalists, was committed to one side or another. A Jewish BBC reporter once told me that he had been in the Shankill Road when an aggressive man had demanded to know if he was a Catholic or a Protestant.

'Actually, I'm a Jew,' he said.

'Aye, but are you a Catholic Jew or a Protestant Jew?' his interrogator insisted.

It is sometimes thought that this is an apocryphal story, but it isn't.

~

Because everyone they knew was on one side or the other, the people of Northern Ireland assumed the same was true of everybody in the world, including the London press, which had ignored them almost completely from the founding of the Free State until the growth of the civil rights movement in 1968. The *Telegraph* was thought to be the most reliably Unionist (which meant in effect Protestant or loyalist) and the *Guardian* was deemed to be Republican. This was in spite of the fact that our deputy editor at the time was John Cole, a Labour supporter working in London, but a Unionist on his home turf of Ulster. John was – and is – a very fair-minded man, but if he felt an article was liable to give aid and comfort to the Republicans it had to be proved beyond doubt. I recall hour-long phone conversations in which I had to persuade him that everything I had written was impeccably sourced.

The reporters agreed informally that any one of us could claim to work for whichever paper would be least likely to infuriate the people we were dealing with, who might well be armed, or be close friends with people who were. So reporters from, say, the *Express*, would say they were from the *Guardian* if they found themselves among angry Republicans.

On one occasion there had been a bomb, presumably planted by the IRA, on a Protestant housing estate to the south of Belfast. No one had been hurt, but it was a quiet news day and the assembled press decided to take taxis and investigate. We found the inhabitants, of what had been a fairly peaceful part of the city, in a state of considerable fear and annoyance. As we piled out of the cabs, the man from the *Telegraph* introduced himself. Then we all did the same (and I have forgotten the exact names): 'Jim Allen, *Daily Telegraph*'; 'Bryn Morgan, *Daily Telegraph*'; 'Brian Wanstead, *Daily Telegraph*'; 'Simon Hoggart, *Daily Telegraph*'. And so on down the line.

One man, clearly a sort of community spokesman, looked deeply suspicious. 'There seem to be an awful lot of youse from the *Daily Telegraph*,' he said.

Jim didn't miss a beat. 'That's right,' he said. 'When the news editor found out what had been done to you people here, he sent every available reporter!'

This answer, which meshed flawlessly with the inhabitants' sense of their importance in the national, even international, scheme of things, satisfied them perfectly.

~

The constant media coverage made the inhabitants almost instinctively practised in appearing in the media. They knew what was expected, and could provide it with smooth efficiency, like experienced waiters in an upmarket restaurant. On one occasion I and some colleagues heard about a Protestant march on Andersonstown, a Catholic suburb of west Belfast with a substantial IRA population. The march – actually it was more of a sizeable foot-borne assault – was in revenge for an IRA bombing at the Harland & Wolff shipyard where, many years before, the *Titanic* had been built. Nobody had been hurt, but H&W had an almost exclusively Protestant workforce, so the attack was seen as a form of economic warfare.

We arrived shortly after the police, having learned at the last minute about the descent upon Andersonstown, had routed the invaders. We met a woman in her home. The Protestants had burst into the house, and a group had seized her husband, forcing him to lie flat on his face in the back garden, holding a gun to his head, and promising to kill him. Meanwhile, another group had set fire to the bed in which her young son was sleeping. Then their assailants heard the police sirens and fled, releasing her husband and allowing her to rescue her child. She was immediately interviewed for the local BBC radio, and I heard the recording the following morning. A few moments after what must have been overwhelmingly the most terrifying event of her life, she spoke articulately and clearly, telling the story in a compelling fashion, which heightened the tension and provided fascinating if horrifying detail. But this was common in Northern Ireland. It was as if they were all actors who had trained for years in drama school, and had suddenly got their chance on stage.

~

I dated a beautiful young woman, a schoolteacher, who lived in Andersonstown, a few times. Like so many young people on both sides, she led a sort of double life. Her clothes, her hair, her favourite music and TV programmes were much the same as those of any other young woman of her age anywhere in the UK. Yet she was entirely committed to the culture and political beliefs of those among whom she had been raised. As it happened, her uncle was interned as a member of the IRA, her aunt was jailed for incitement to join the IRA and was later assassinated in hospital, her cousin blew himself up bombing a council office – and had rather pathetically left a 'Paisley for Prime Minister' ballpoint pen at the scene, which survived the blast but fooled nobody – and her brother was beaten up by British soldiers simply because of his surname.

She took me to places I would never have dared go on my own, where you could hear rebel songs performed with enormous gusto, and where fights would erupt suddenly and viciously, lasting a few seconds but generally requiring an ambulance. Sometimes, when we had both had a few drinks, she would abuse soldiers on the way home – as a gentleman, I felt obliged to take her back to her parents' house – and I feared they would respond with violence. But they never did; the sight of this slender, well-dressed and attractive young woman must have caused terminal confusion, and we were never attacked.

Once, she told me, she and a friend had dated two members of the support staff for a motor-racing team. The engineers had taken them out to dinner, then driven them home in a car transporter which they had parked outside her house while they enjoyed a snog. In the morning, word got round the estate that the IRA had delivered an enormous shipment of arms from a massive lorry outside their house. Even when she explained what had happened, many neighbours refused to believe her because the news was too good for them to relinquish.

~

I learned even more about the relationship between the media and real life, which is often a tenuous one. It was the practice of the night news editor on the *Newsletter* to send the late reporter out at around 9 p.m. to bring him a supper of fish and chips. One night the reporter, fed up with this chore, decided to drop in at the Europa Hotel, which was where most of the broadsheet correspondents stayed, and was always a good source for a few drinks, jokes and background gossip. After half an hour or so, he felt he ought to account for the absence of the fish and chips, so he phoned his boss and fibbed that he had been passing the Markets area – a small Catholic enclave near the city centre – and had heard shooting. He believed, he said, that a British Army unit had come under fire from the IRA.

The news editor phoned the army press office in Lisburn, County Down, about ten miles from Belfast. They had heard nothing about this incident, which was a serious matter, because it could mean the men were pinned down, wounded or dead. They immediately sent in an armoured car to investigate. As it rolled into the Markets area, it came under IRA fire. In such a way did life imitate artifice. Fortunately no one was hurt.

Dr Marten's yellow laces,
Wrangler jeans and clip-on braces,
We're the girls who slit your faces,
Dee Street Boot Girls!
– written up in the (loyalist) Dee Street area.

Fuck the next Pope
– planning for the future; graffito in the Protestant Shankill Road.

Northern Irish people have an extraordinary facility for the language. One popular story described two farmers watching a more prosperous neighbour riding to church on a fine new stallion: 'Look at him, you'd think his horse had just shat marmalade.'

A motorist trying to squeeze his car into a tight space asked a passing boy, 'Will you watch me park?'

'Why, are ye verra' good at it?'

'I'll sum it up in two words: ridick-lous' – old lady in Andersonstown, to reporters.

~

Martin Bell, who became even better known as an independent MP elected on an anti-corruption ticket, was a frequent BBC correspondent in the early days of the Troubles. His reporting did not find favour with Protestants, who at that time were convinced that all the media were against them. There may have been some truth in that; the first challenge to their authority came from the civil rights movement, which had drawn its inspiration, language and often music from the American equivalent. For a while the media were delighted to have our own equivalents of the great American struggles, and segregated lunch counters. Though when the army moved in to Derry, black soldiers were often objects of vilification, sometimes by the same people who had so movingly sung 'We Shall Overcome' a few weeks before. They would have been astonished if you had accused them of racism; why, it was they who had suffered from the British and the Ulster loyalists for centuries. Sending black soldiers to their neighbourhood was just another example of that historical oppression, or so many of them thought.

When Bell was covering Protestant rallies addressed by the Revd Ian Paisley, he would sometimes be pointed out to the crowd by the turbulent cleric. 'I see that Mr Martin Bell is present at this rally!' he would boom. 'I detest violence in all its forms, but I realize that I may be powerless to restrain your anger . . .' Bell survived, in part because for some reason people find it hard to attack someone they have seen on television – or at least they did then, before appearing on television became obligatory for almost everyone.

~

On one occasion, Bell and his crew were filming a riot in the Newtownards Road, a largely Protestant district. Protestant riots were fairly uncommon, in those days anyway, and the community regarded itself as far more inclined to be law-abiding than the Catholics. Oh, you might get the odd murder and bout of torture, but there was much less civil disobedience en masse. Bell was suddenly aware of an old lady hitting his arm, hard and repeatedly, with an umbrella.

'Madam, why are you doing that?' he asked.

'Because you're photographing things that aren't happening,' she replied.

~

Once a colleague and I were invited to the quarters used by the Blues and Royals, one of the poshest regiments in the British Army. They had a regimental roulette table and would be gaming that night. The officers were mostly tow-haired public school boys, charming, more socially confident than anyone has a right to be. They covered the Newtownards Road area and the night we were there a riot took place. We said that we ought to go out and report on this still somewhat unusual event. The soldiers looked at us as if we were mad – let a little thing like a few stones and petrol bombs interfere with the serious business of the night? We were ushered into the radio room where, we were told, 'Sparks' would keep us up to date with what was going on. So he did, though obviously from only one point of view.

It was clearly quite a serious riot, because now and again another tow-haired youth in uniform would arrive, often bandaged, sometimes still bleeding. They would stroll over to the *banque* operated by a sergeant and ask for, say, £20 worth of chips, then play with the same insouciance as they might have displayed on leave at Baden-Baden or Monte Carlo.

~

When people asked whether Northern Ireland was horribly dangerous, I replied that not one journalist had been killed except for a BBC man who got drunk at a party and drove his car into a tree. I also pointed out that even at the height of the mayhem, if you were an uninvolved civilian – that is, not in the army, the police or any paramilitary group – you were ten times more likely to be killed on Ulster's dangerous roads than you were to lose your life to a bomb or a bullet. Since nobody wakes up in the morning filled with dread that they might be killed by a car that day, there was no real reason why anyone should be especially anxious. What is frightening of course is the sense that civil order has broken down, and the normal assumption that someone is more or less in control is absent. While people might be suspicious of one newspaper or another, generally they treated us well. They were, I used to tell everyone at home, the nicest people in the world except when they were trying to kill you. Which, on the whole, they weren't.

~

One summer Saturday afternoon a group of us were watching an England football match in my room at the Europa Hotel. I had the only colour TV in the hotel. We could hear gunfire from the Turf Lodge area, which was between the city centre and the mountains to the west. The gunfire was still continuing when the match ended, and so Brian Woosey of the *Sun* and I decided to take a look. It was, perhaps, slightly beyond the call of duty since neither of us had to write for the following day. We arrived to find the streets deserted, and though we could hear the gunfire, there was no sign of where it was coming from or who it was aimed at. A woman, perhaps in her forties, came out of her front door and shouted at us, 'Come on in, you'll be killed out there!' So we took shelter. She was a widow with a ten-year-old son. Knowing the habits of journalists, she produced a bottle of whiskey which she said was left over from Christmas. We drank it while playing Monopoly with the boy. Finally the shooting died down, and we decided to drive back. We turned a corner and ran straight into an IRA roadblock, and that was the moment when I remembered that I had left my press card back in the hotel.

It was a bad moment. The two young men were waving rusty revolvers around. I didn't think they would kill me, though they would certainly be suspicious of someone my age with an English accent. Having longer hair than any soldier wouldn't help either; they'd simply assume that I was in Intelligence. I might expect to be incarcerated until lunchtime the following day, when they would be able to phone the *Guardian* to check if I was who I claimed to be.

But luckily there was no problem. Brian had his press card, and impressed the young terrorists by being from the *Sun*, which was not then available in Northern Ireland. They had heard that the paper's Templegate was the best racing tipster of all. Why couldn't they get his tips? Brian was as relaxed as if he were passing the time of day in a pub. He had good news: the *Sun* would be published in Northern Ireland in a few short months, and yes, Templegate was indeed the best. The IRA men were delighted with this news, and waved us cheerily on our way, pausing to warn us that there was a roadblock manned by the military – their word for the British Army – across one street on our route back. Naturally we drove straight towards it, in order to warn them about the IRA roadblock, but it had moved away.

I thought both small incidents – the solicitous widow and the easily pleased terrorists – showed the essential kindness of most people in the province. The kindness had survived any amount of danger, strife and social unrest.

~

Quite a number of reporters either made their names in Northern Ireland, or went to work there at some stage in a celebrated career. Max Hastings and John Sergeant are among the best known. Tim Jones worked for *The Times* and was a fine chess player as well as a resourceful reporter. His main problem as a chess player was finding anyone sufficiently challenging to play against. His boredom had resulted in some damage at the critic Bernard Levin's flat while he was playing him in the paper's chess tournament. In the tedium of waiting for Levin to play he took to rocking back and forth on a valuable Chippendale chair. Levin was, apparently, gracious about its broken leg.

Tim had been present at the early riots in Londonderry and was called back to give evidence to the Scarman Tribunal, held in the city itself. He had been told that his session would begin on a Monday afternoon, so he refrained from drinking. He wasn't called that day, so he abstained the next day too. By Wednesday lunchtime he was giving up hope, so had a generous and restorative lunch. When he had to give evidence that afternoon, things did not go entirely to plan. At one point the brief for the tribunal asked him if he could confirm that he had seen a rioter throw a brick – here he pointed at a map – at this location here, which had hit a soldier standing at that location there.

Tim agreed.

'Are you aware, Mr Jones, that that is a distance of one mile?'

That Friday Tim was flying back to London from Belfast with a colleague from the *Daily Mirror*, Chris Buckland. Lord Scarman was sitting a few rows in front of them. Buckland suggested it was a good moment to make his peace, so Tim went forward and was greeted with an ironic smile.

'Lord Scarman,' he said, 'I just want you to know that I envy you, but I don't admire you.'

He reported back to Buckland who said that the only thing for him to do was to catch up with him at the baggage carousel and say what he had really intended.

So he tried once more: 'Lord Scarman, what I meant to say was "I envy you, but by God I don't admire you!" '

Scarman scurried on his way.

~

Robert Fisk loved mayhem. Many foreign correspondents do. The late David Blundy, who worked for the short-lived *Sunday Correspondent*, died in El Salvador because he had gone to cover a gun battle, even though it was Saturday morning, and his article for the week had long been locked away. There was virtually no chance that anything he wrote would appear. Fisk, now the widely read Middle East correspondent of the *Independent*, then on *The Times*, hunted down violence wherever he could find it. I had to keep a close eye on what he was doing, as he was my opposite number on the paper usually regarded as our leading rival, and we often worked together. He arrived in Derry later than most people, but was determined to make up for lost time. Once after days of rioting the city seemed calmer than it had, and most of us decided to take a relaxing break. (Occasionally the press pack would declare a 'national holiday' which meant that nobody was allowed to write anything, unless a very serious event occurred.) Fisk, however, discovered that a small disturbance was taking place in front of the RUC station. He burst into the bar, and breathlessly told me that thirty-five young men were rioting. I was annoyed, but fearing he might write it up as an important development, decided that I ought to file a paragraph, if only to cover my back. As I phoned, the door of the booth was wrenched open. It was Fisk, looking as if he had that minute arrived in Aix from Ghent, bearing vital tidings. 'Simon, Simon!' he cried. 'The police have just revised their estimate! It's now forty young men!'

~

Nothing held back Fisk's relentless pursuit of the news. On another quiet day, the only conceivable story was the distant threat of a strike by the Police Reserve. It seemed unlikely to grip readers of the paper, so I was snoozing in bed when the phone rang. It was Fisk. 'Simon, I *must* talk to you,' he said. 'Meet me in the coffee bar!'

When I did, he said solemnly, 'Simon, there is one thing I want more than anything else in the whole world.'

I asked what – a million pounds, perhaps, or a good woman to love?

'No,' he said impatiently, 'I want those quotes from the chairman of the Police Reserve Federation.'

~

We often ate in the Europa's restaurant, which featured 'Royal Barge Feasts', beef Wellington and the like. As in American movies the waiters could bring the phone to your table and plug it in, which looked quite sophisticated, though generally implied little more than some minor query from the office. I read in a paper that fine clarets were now so expensive that diners in London were having to pay an astonishing £25 a bottle for, say, Château Latour. This featured on the Europa's wine list at £5 a bottle. I decided it was my duty to save the paper £20 a time by buying it for guests. Fisk discovered that word got around – 'Simon Hoggart bought us this delicious wine, I wonder if you might get the same' – and soon the cellars were cleared out. Even in my part-time career as a wine writer, I have not had Latour before or since, except once at the château itself, where I was offered a barrel sample, which tastes of nothing at all except to a palate more sensitive than mine. But Ulster was not wine territory. Invited out to dinner one night, I decided to take some, and went to a pub. They sold me two bottles of 'Mundy's South African Wine, bottled at Shipquay St, Londonderry'. After the first glass we decided this was the precise and exact opposite of the Château Latour, so threw it on the fire, where it flared vividly in most colours of the rainbow.

~

The Europa was frequently bombed, and one bomb, placed in the bus station behind the hotel, blew in several windows, and injured a photographer who had been looking out when it exploded. Colleagues carried him to the lift where he lay groaning. The lift stopped, and Fisk got in. He looked at the photographer, blood pouring from his head, and remarked, 'Well, at least we've got our intro for today.' I don't think he was being callous. To Fisk life consisted entirely and exclusively of stories and of course in Belfast they lay all around.

~

I liked him, in spite of his hyper-energy, which left me rather washed out. Dinner at his house, with his wife Judy (after five years she could take no more, divorced him, and married a delightful and of course very brave weapons and bomb expert), was almost nerve-racking. One evening he spent the entire time on the phone to *The Times* trying to persuade them to run his story on page one, and did not stop until he had succeeded.

He was also present on one of the most idyllic days of my life. The Fisks, plus Renagh Holohan of the *Irish Times* and I rented a boat on Lough Erne in County Fermanagh. It was a bright, sunny day in May, and we floated from island to island, one of them covered in an almost sinister way with bluebells, another dotted with early Celtic remains and we picnicked there. There were no other tourists, except for one boat containing a Swiss family.

~

We often collaborated. Once Gerry Fitt, the SDLP MP for West Belfast, told us both that the army was trying to blackmail a young man who lived in the Catholic Falls Road and who worked as a waiter at the Europa into providing them with information about his neighbourhood and gossip picked up in the hotel. The soldiers told him that if he didn't they would pass information round that he had been sleeping with the wife of an internee. He was terrified, but Fitt was delighted. He summoned Fisk and me, and phoned the number the young man had been given, pretending to be him. The awful truth was confirmed, and the then Prime Minister Ted Heath had to tell the Commons that such tactics would not be used again.

~

Fitt was an extraordinarily brave man, who had the Ulster 'dander', a sort of rolling, slightly swaggering gait. His principal enemies were in the Provisional IRA, who loathed and detested the idea of a moderate party drawing support away from them. In the end they burned him out of his home. He drank a great deal of gin. At the Commons, he liked to stand on the terrace in summer, raise his glass to the tourist boats passing, and yell, 'And it's all free!' to the annoyance, presumably, of anyone who believed him.

In the early seventies I attended a conference in Oxford devoted to Northern Ireland. On the Sunday morning, after it was over, Nick Ross of the BBC offered me a lift back to London in his car, but warned me that Gerry and his two detectives guarding him would be with us.

'Jesus, boys,' said Gerry, as we set off. 'I have the most terrible hangover.'

'Yeah,' said one of the detectives, 'we realized you was in a bad way this morning when we woke you up and you offered us a fiver to get you a cup of tea.'

'Y'see,' said Fitt, 'I'd been drinking whisky last night instead of gin, and it always gives me a terrible hangover.'

'I know now why you're a Roman Catholic, Gerry,' said the other detective.

'Why's that?'

'Because you get so close to death every time you fall asleep.'

~

After he lost his seat, Gerry was made a peer. It is customary for peers who have just 'taken their place' – that is, been sworn in – to hold a party for family and friends. It is also customary for Black Rod, the chief administrator of the House of Lords, to put in an appearance, naturally in his full Tudor uniform, with tights and a sort of lace bib round his neck, as if about to be shaved. Lady Fitt turned to her husband with tears in her eyes, and said, 'Oh, Gerry, I didn't know you'd booked a band.'

~

The other important figure in the SDLP was John Hume, who was quite different from Fitt in almost every way. Belfast is essentially a British industrial city, like Liverpool or Glasgow, and Gerry the kind of political fixer every such place contains. He would have been entirely at home in Tammany Hall in New York.

Derry is mistier, more rural, more obviously a part of Ireland. I once gave Hume a lift from Dublin to Derry. Soon after we had crossed the border into the North, we saw ahead of us an Ulster Defence Association roadblock. This was bad news, for although the UDA was a legitimate organization, formed to replace the hated B Specials, many of them had connections with various shady, less legal Protestant groups, whom they might possibly warn that Hume was on his way. I needn't have worried. With the air of one well practised in necessary subterfuge, Hume took out his handkerchief, placed it over his face and pretended to have a ferocious coughing fit. Meanwhile I put on the most upper-class English accent I could manage, stressing the London in Londonderry, always the mark of a Unionist. (In the same way, you can usually tell a Washingtonian's politics by whether he talks about National Airport – Democrat – or Ronald Reagan Airport, Republican.) We were waved on our way and had no trouble. I thought it odd that the part-time soldiers hadn't asked to see my passenger's face, though they might well have assumed that I was with the army.

~

I never met Marcus McCausland, though he had unwillingly an important role in the Troubles. He was a landed gentleman, living in a nineteenth-century stately pile near Limavady called Drenagh, who had converted to Catholicism, which in that place at that time was almost unheard of. He was an eccentric, and a great enthusiast for the modernization of farming methods. Once he gave a demonstration of crop spraying from a light aircraft, but he had mounted the sprayer the wrong way round, and drenched the farmers who had been summoned to watch with fertilizer. He reckoned he could save money on shotgun cartridges by making his own, and began by drying the powder in the Aga: the resulting explosion almost destroyed the kitchen.

McCausland thought it a good idea to act as a go-between with the government and the IRA. In those days the 'Officials' or Official IRA, were strong in Derry. They were known as 'Stickies' because their Sinn Fein badges were stuck on, unlike the Provisionals, who used pins, but who were only briefly known as 'Pinnies' or 'Pinheads' before becoming universally known as 'Provos'. The Stickies were Marxists, unlike the Provos, who favoured a straightforward, traditional blend of Irish nationalism and lethal violence. The Stickies also had a hopeless notion of public relations. Among their victims was Ranger Best, a boy from the Bogside in Derry who had joined the British Army and was murdered while visiting his family at home. In 1971 the Stickies also grabbed Marcus McCausland from his car and shot him. The revulsion created by these two murders, plus a few others, caused the Stickies to declare that they would take no further part in the violence. I was invited to stay at Drenagh a year or so after McCausland's death, and it was impossibly romantic and evocative of Ireland. Bits were falling down, and the gardens were full of damp rhododendrons. When I read J.G. Farrell's novel *Troubles*, the Majestic Hotel, a metaphor for the crumbling British Empire, was in my mind's eye Drenagh.

~

Jim O'Sullivan was an IRA man who had been on the run, but within Belfast, for many months. He moved round in disguise, which worked well until a car in which he was travelling with three other men was stopped by Scottish soldiers. Afraid of being recognized, O'Sullivan was reluctant to get out of the car. 'You too, Jimmy,' said one of the soldiers. He didn't know that 'Jimmy' was for many Glaswegians the routine form of address for any male stranger, so assumed he'd been spotted, and ran. As he fled his wig fell off, and he was quickly caught. This story delighted the army, feeding as it did stereotypes of Irish fecklessness, stupidity and ignorance, though the IRA had proved quite adept at holding the British Army at bay for many years.

~

For many soldiers, Ulster was a tremendous shock. They had been used to media that took their side on almost every occasion. Now, up against an enemy that was articulate – and articulate in English, as well as being familiar with the media that was reporting them – they found their actions and statements constantly questioned. A soldier might shoot a civilian. The civilian's friends, families and neighbours would insist that he had been completely unarmed, was a peace-loving lad whose only mistake was to be in the wrong place at the wrong time. The army for their part would declare that the youth had drawn a gun and fired it at the soldier who subsequently shot him. It was generally impossible to decide who was telling the truth, since the soldier would be terrified of the consequences of shooting an unarmed civilian, and if he had enough bravura would convince the interrogating officers of his story. A day or so later it was sometimes possible to form a judgement after a study of the Catholic, nationalist newspaper, the *Irish News*, which carried a host of In Memoriam ads for every IRA man who perished. Faced with the choice of enjoying a propaganda victory – British military oppressors gun down innocent man in cold blood – or commemorating a brave volunteer who had given his life for Ireland, they would always choose the latter. For, as many people have acknowledged, in Irish mythology the land must always be nourished with the blood of its martyrs. To be an unacknowledged martyr would be a waste of one's whole life.

~

The officer I admired most was Major George Styles, a bomb disposal expert, and an incredibly good one. He also had a dry sense of humour, a considerable scepticism about the army's top brass, and an enormous relish for his job. He defused two huge bombs outside the Europa Hotel in the space of two days. The devices were designed primarily to kill the person trying to defuse them and were fitted with delicate booby traps that cause the slightest movement in any direction to detonate them. Often the most sensible thing to do was to clear the area, and shoot at the bomb until it exploded. However, it was essential to recover this delicate and sophisticated device intact in order to learn how it worked. (And to save the Crown, the pub opposite the Europa, which may be the most beautifully decorated pub in the United Kingdom. It has recently been restored, and is more magnificent than ever.)

A bomb is as characteristic of its maker as his face or fingerprints, and the man who made these was known as the Castlereagh bomber, since that's where the first had been planted. Styles thought of himself as being in a duel with this man, though a lopsided duel, since it was most likely to end with his own death. The bomb maker might be found and arrested, but would probably keep his life unless he literally hoist himself with his home-made petard. You could say, I suppose, that Styles was the ultimate winner, since he died peacefully in 2006, unlike seventeen other bomb disposal men who died in the course of the Troubles.

~

If you lived in the Europa, as I did, you got used to the bombing and thanked the heavens that the IRA generally made a practice of phoning warnings. On one occasion a bomb was planted down a street at the side of the hotel. The RUC evacuated the street, and sealed it off. Keith Graves, a BBC reporter often sent to Belfast, was determined to get his camera crew down there. The police were determined to stop him. So, to make his point,

Keith grabbed the senior officer by his lapels and shook him. I have never seen anyone do this before or since.

~

The hotel was frequently evacuated. My colleague Derek Brown once managed to sleep through the hotel alarm one Saturday morning (Saturday being our day off, it was the morning for a lie-in). Assuming the building was now empty, someone turned off the alarm. Derek rose, took a leisurely shower, and looked out into the street, where he saw staff and guests assembled behind a police line some distance away. He got dressed with remarkable speed. Another time an American reporter was fretting about a letter in his pigeon-hole. The hall porter, an unflappable man called Tommy Dunne, declined to let him re-enter the hotel until the all-clear. 'Anyway, sir,' he said, 'in a moment or so you'll be getting it airmail.'

~

On Bloody Friday, 21 July 1972, nine people were killed by IRA bombs planted almost at random around Belfast. It was quite terrifying to be in the city at that time. Walking past any parked car called for genuine reserves of courage, on which I was permanently rather low. Like most people I fled to the safety of the familiar, which in my case meant the Europa. I was having a cup of tea in the coffee bar when the kitchen staff came running out yelling that there was a bomb at the back. Nerves were stretched and people panicked, all at once, like a virus passed from one victim to another at astonishing speed.

I was determined not to be infected. People flung themselves into the revolving door at the centre of the lobby. It quickly jammed. So I walked down the line of swing doors to either side, carefully unlocking them. 'Use the swing doors!' I ordered, with an authority I did not know I possessed. People stopped hurling themselves at the revolving doors, and crashed into the swing doors – which unwittingly, but very carefully, I had locked.

Now and again, though rarely these days, sympathizers with the IRA, or at least the Republican cause, complain – quite legitimately – about Bloody Sunday in January 1972, when civil rights protesters were shot by the British Army. I point out that at least we have had two enquiries into the events, the second costing nearly 200 million pounds. I then gently ask if we have had the results from the IRA's (non-existent) enquiry into Bloody Friday. They generally go away muttering something about it being 'irrelevant'.

~

A year or so later I was asked to take part in a debate at Trinity College Dublin on events in the North. My principal opponent was Rita O'Hare, who was the spokeswoman for Sinn Fein. To my delight and surprise, the students were almost entirely on my side. Trinity College Dublin used to be exclusively Protestant, but of course is no longer. These students regarded the IRA as the embalmers of a long forgotten, outdated mythology. It was heartening. Ms O'Hare insisted that the British were holding on to the Six Counties for imperialistic reasons. I pointed out that there was nothing the British would like more than to get rid of the whole expensive, dangerous and debilitating problem. If that meant a united Ireland, that would be just fine. On the other hand, the last thing the Irish government wanted was to incorporate a million angry Protestants who had just learned that politically motivated violence pays very well, plus half a million Catholics who knew a great deal about politically motivated violence and might think to deploy it again.

Ms O'Hare said that Britain wanted to keep Ulster for strategic reasons.

'What?' I asked. 'In case the Canadian Navy sails up the Foyle and seizes Derry?'

This got a huge laugh, and I quote it not to boast, but to say how encouraging the reaction was.

The people of the South found the North vaguely threatening and insufferably dull. Some years before, I had attended the destruction of the British embassy in Dublin in the wake of Bloody Sunday. I met nothing but kindness and consideration from the crowd that had gathered to watch the spectacle. One man offered to find a cab to take me back to my hotel. Round about the same time, the IRA attacked the Irish Army base at the Curragh, near the racecourse. They used wire cutters to break the perimeter fence and began to swarm in. But I still remember the air of calm that prevailed. The major who was looking after the press asked one of the guards if he had had his tea, and offered to replace him until he had.

NEWS QUIZ

6

News Quiz

Alan Coren & Linda Smith

The greatest fan of the radio show *The News Quiz* in the mid-1980s was a woman called Joyce, who must have been in her eighties. Her hair was wild and straggly, and her teeth were much the same. Every week, without exception, Joyce would be first in the queue for seats at the Paris Theatre in Regent Street. (This was the venue where *Round the Horne*, *The Goon Show* and *Hancock's Half Hour* had been taped. It would be nice to say that the ghosts of comedians past infused the atmosphere, but they didn't; the BBC had cleared out almost all the evidence.)

She was sometimes accompanied by another elderly woman, called Ethel, who appeared to look up to her and to whom Joyce graciously condescended. Once the doors were opened, the pair would march in briskly and take up their traditional position in the centre of the front row.

Joyce had an extraordinary laugh. These days almost every outdoor event in Britain ends with a firework display. There is one type of rocket that emits a banshee screech very suddenly; the noise lasts a few seconds, then ends just as abruptly. Joyce's laugh was like that – it began and ended without warning. Sometimes it was unrelated to how funny a remark had been. But Joyce realized that somebody was trying to make a joke, and responded accordingly. It was generous of her, and encouraging to newcomers who would inevitably be nervous. Their first attempt at humour might be met with silence, or an almost inaudible murmur of the faintest possible amusement, but then, like a surprise assault in the trenches, Joyce's laugh would break out and fill the theatre. It could be quite alarming; you wondered at times if she might literally die laughing, or at least stun someone sitting nearby.

She never hung around after the show and never tried to chat to the panellists, but simply disappeared. We had no idea where she came from or what she did, though she must have been a pensioner, and Alan Coren once said he had seen her in the National Portrait Gallery, another free attraction.

Then the BBC tried to ban her. They had had complaints. Listeners had written demanding to know why the shrieking woman was allowed to make so much noise. She was spoiling their enjoyment of the programme. She should be made to stay away. The panellists, the producer and I were appalled and felt we could not desert our most tenacious fan. The thought of Joyce having to sit at home while the show was being recorded was too painful to contemplate.

Christmas was coming, and we decided to show her how much we at least appreciated her loyalty and enthusiasm. We got a card, and over the weeks everyone who appeared on the programme signed it. We bought a bottle of sherry. In those days there was a separate recording of the show in late December which covered news of the previous year and was broadcast during the holiday period. Joyce would be in the front row; the card and the sherry were ready for us to present at the end. But she didn't come in that night.

We never saw her again and never discovered what had happened to her. Later we found that someone had stolen the sherry.

~

I first appeared on *The News Quiz* in 1980. It was a disaster. Nothing I said was remotely funny, or seemed remotely funny to the audience, who maintained a courteous but chilly silence. Even Joyce's screech seemed muted, and especially hollow in the surrounding silence. I had been nervous at the start, but not so nervous as to account for my failure; I couldn't do it. In the end I was just miserable. I gave up mentally, and began to form a list in my head of people who had lived rich, fulfilled lives without ever succeeding on *The News Quiz*. For some reason, the only two names that came to mind were Mozart and the Nobel Prize winner Albert Schweitzer. It was in this mood of blank resignation that I heard my next question from Barry Took, who was then the programme's chairman. It concerned a remarkable story. A postman in East Anglia used to enter events at paraplegic games, even though he was perfectly fit and able-bodied. I suppose he just liked to win things, even if it involved reckless cheating.

Once, unsurprisingly, he won several events at a paraplegic games held somewhere in the UK. His local paper printed a picture of him, sitting in his wheelchair, proudly wearing the medals. As it happened, one of his jobs was to deliver the paper along with the mail, so, fearing discovery, he cut the picture out from every copy before pushing it through the letterboxes. The people with mutilated papers compared notes and he was quickly exposed.

I can't remember what I said, except that it started something like 'By day he was a postman, but at night he entered the twilight world of paraplegic games . . .' It made no sense, but I was past caring. Barry, however, started to laugh. When he laughed hard, he used to claim that it made his ears hurt, and he would tug on them to relieve the pain. The audience laughed at him laughing, which took time and gave me the chance to think of something else. 'The locals were first tipped off when they saw him walking down the path on his hands, pushing the letters through the flap with his teeth,' or something similar. Barry kept repeating that his ears hurt, the audience laughed at that again, and from then on they laughed at everything I said, even when it wasn't meant to be funny. A remark like 'My points, I think, Barry,' would be met by gusts of hilarity.

At the end of the show, the producer came down on to the stage and said, 'Great stuff about the postman, but I'm afraid we can't use it. The switchboard would be jammed – protests from the disabled lobby. Can you do it again, Simon, but straight? Thanks.'

Two days later I listened to the broadcast. For the first half of the show you heard my limp replies to the questions and the audience's near silence, followed by a dull, workmanlike answer to the question about the postman. Then for a reason that must have been entirely inexplicable to anyone listening, the audience hooted and howled at everything I said.

~

The show was very different in those days. For one thing it was generally peopled by journalists who, it was hoped, might raise a laugh talking about stories they were familiar with. Often they failed to raise even a titter. Sometimes they would affect a certain strained jollity. 'I suspect this question might refer to our beloved Prime Minister!' they might say, or some such. The audience would chuckle faintly. On one occasion there were not even faint chuckles. A group of several dozen Swedish radio trainees had been given tickets – the BBC sometimes has a bewildering ability to mismatch programmes and audiences – and they sat in the middle of the regulars, emitting waves of Nordic incomprehension, for while their English was probably perfect, their knowledge of British public figures and events was not up to the demands of a satirical programme about current affairs. Their presence cast an air of crepuscular gloom over the auditorium.

In any case, a typical audience was a few dozen people, the Paris Theatre being usually in those days perhaps a quarter full.

~

After the show we would often go round the corner to eat at Cohen and Wong, not a fusion restaurant, but one that offered both Jewish and Chinese food at the same time, though cooked and served separately. It was not a good concept and the food was undistinguished, but we liked it because the idea was so silly. It didn't last long.

~

In 1983 Barry Took went into television – vastly better paid than radio – to present *Points of View.* It was not, perhaps, the best use of his talents. His style was harshly parodied on *Not the Nine O'Clock News*: 'If you would like to write praising the BBC to the skies, the address is . . .' But Barry was a comic writer of near genius. He co-wrote *Round the Horne*, in my view still the funniest show ever on BBC radio, with Marty Feldman, though Barry liked to imply that there was only one person who did the real work in that partnership, and it wasn't Marty. He also drew together the *Monty Python* team and, even more difficult, persuaded the BBC to give them a first series, and yet more difficult than that, to give them a second series.

Both of those achievements made this country, and in the case of *Monty Python* the world, a much happier place.

Round the Horne was the object of study, even abroad. Barry delighted in getting letters from a student in Tokyo, who was writing a thesis about it. 'Please explain what is the significance of "a club in Paddington"?' This was the kind of place that Julian and Sandy might frequent. (BBC rules had for a long time prohibited any reference, direct or indirect, to homosexual activity, which was then illegal. These sketches were not sailing close to the wind, but heading for the eye of the hurricane. Many of their jokes are still told today:

Julian and Sandy are lawyers, and Kenneth Horne asks them for help with a civil case: 'Can't 'elp you, Mr Horne, we have a criminal practice that takes up most of our time.'

Or Julian and Sandy are down below, on a ship that's in danger of sinking. Kenneth Horne asks, 'Did you drag yourselves up on deck?'

'Ooh, no, there wasn't time. We just went casual like, sweater and jeans.')

When Barry died there was a memorial service for him near his home in St John's Wood. John Cleese spoke and was very funny. There ought to be a statue to Barry somewhere, or perhaps a plaque in St Paul's Covent Garden, the theatrical church.

~

I took over as chairman from 1983 until we went to live in America, in 1985. The show chugged along, with the best moments being provided by Alan Coren, sometimes in partnership, or rather rivalry, with Richard Ingrams. Coren never really liked Ingrams, partly because *Private Eye*, which Ingrams then edited, was always rude about *Punch*, which Alan then edited. There was also an undercurrent, involving an ambitious, clever Jewish lad from north London who cared desperately about winning, up against a languid public schoolboy who made a point of not having the remotest interest in the score. Winning really mattered to Alan. Once while he was appearing in the daytime TV show *Call My Bluff*, I asked him whether his or Sandi Toksvig's team was ahead in total games won. Oh, he said, it really didn't matter, it was a game, who cared who was ahead, and so forth, adding, 'Actually, I'm leading, 86 to 83.' Or some similar figure. Richard Ingrams sometimes bailed out of the show when he felt that he had been snubbed or insulted. This was a shame, since the double act – Ingrams claiming to know nothing at all ('If it wasn't in the *Telegraph* I probably wouldn't have seen it') and Coren as the swot who knew everything – worked wonderfully well and was loved by the audience. It was rare for Coren to get an answer wrong; almost as rare for Ingrams to get one right, or at least admit to knowing the answer.

Quite often we relied on Alan to say something – anything – that was funny. When he was on form, it felt as if you had inserted a roll into a pianola, and the thing would go on churning out jokes without conscious effort on anyone's part, perhaps not even his. I recall one particularly dull round in which nobody had said anything amusing. The whole recording had the excitement and buzz of a doctor's waiting room, without any of the tension. Then Alan got the last story, about a man who had offered to give his brother one of his kidneys. The surgeons discovered that, astonishingly, he had three. 'And when they opened him up, it was like Dewhurst's shop window in there . . .' He would keep going for several minutes, the bubble of hilarity bouncing and glittering off the audience, often rescuing the round and the entire show.

That was important; sometimes if you had one really good gag, it would be remembered and passed around, fine word-of-mouth publicity for the programme. A story cropped up that one in seven flat-dwellers in Birmingham had complained about the noise of their neighbours having sex. Barry: 'Police were called after a woman reported that she could constantly hear someone in the next flat shouting, "Yes! Yes! Oh, y-e-e-s!" but ended their enquiries when they discovered it was only Tony Slattery's agent.' An in-joke: the comedian was known for never turning down any work.

~

Alan was responsible for one of the two funniest gags I recall from my later spell as chairman. The first came in 1997. We tend to forget that Princess Diana was rapidly losing public favour at the time, since after her divorce she seemed to spend much of her life on yachts with various playboys, many of them foreign. *The News Quiz* audience was a good bellwether of middle England, being for the most part middle-aged, middle-class Radio 4 listeners. Any joke about Sarah Ferguson, Prince Andrew's wife, would get a laugh, whereas, up to 1996, cracks at the expense of Princess Di were met with a certain whey-faced disapproval and even hissing. By 1997, however, the halo was badly in need of buffing. She was always wonderfully sensitive to the tides of public opinion and had taken up the cause of landmine removal. Often she was depicted in the newspapers wearing white security clothing as if she herself were risking her life by leading the hunt for the infernal devices.

Alan got the question. 'You're asking the wrong bloke,' he said. 'I don't know anything about landmines or Princess Di.' He paused. 'Except you'd be mad to want to poke either of them.'

There was a short interval which I recognized as the moment when members of the audience turn to each other and ask by words or gesture, 'Did he actually say what I think he said?' Then there was a great shout of laughter.

The programme was broadcast, the joke included, on the Saturday lunchtime. The repeat was scheduled for Monday evening, but that Saturday night there was a crash in the Tunnel de l'Alma, and we all woke up to the frenzied grieving that the media informed us we were engaged in. (Over on Radio 2, Michael Parkinson and his producer were told that theirs would be the first normal programming of the day, starting at 11 a.m. But would they check the playlist first? It's lucky they did, as the planned opening record was 'Putting on the Ritz'.)

The producer of *The News Quiz*, meanwhile, went into Broadcasting House, extracted the tape from wherever it was, and locked it in a safe, so that the joke could never, ever be broadcast again, even by accident.

~

When we returned from the United States, in late 1989, the show had changed greatly. It changed even more the following year. *Have I Got News For You* was the last in a long line of attempts to transfer the format to television, and the only one that worked. The producers understood that it wasn't the news that made the show, or even witty remarks about the news, but the interaction between the panellists. On *The News Quiz* nobody is given the questions in advance (it might sometimes sound as if they are, but that's because the panellists aren't stupid and can predict at least half the stories that are likely to crop up). On *HIGNFY*, by contrast, there is a 'rehearsal' at which all the pictures are shown, giving the panellists an hour or so to work out their jokes – though not of course the banter among them.

So it soon became clear that *The News Quiz* was going to have to perk up and become funnier. The producers did this by clearing out most of the journalists, except Francis Wheen and of course Alan Coren, and replacing them with comedians, some of them very witty indeed. Andy Hamilton and Jeremy Hardy were astoundingly inventive and often miraculously funny. Meanwhile Barry Took had returned from television and found himself tugging his ears more and more often.

~

Barry retired in 1996, and I took over the chairmanship for a second time. It was a far easier job than being a panellist, since the chairman and the newsreader are the only participants with a script. I would start each show with an attempt to warm up the audience – though sometimes they would be cooled down – by reading clippings sent in by listeners which for the most part could not have been used in the broadcast programme. One of my favourites was a report from the *Yorkshire Post* about a China v. England football match in Beijing. 'Though Gascoigne and Shearer probed early, England had difficulty finding any chinks in the home defence.'

~

Soon afterwards Linda Smith became a regular panellist. She began by being extremely nervous (I think one or two of the questions might have been leaked to her beforehand, if only to calm her nerves) but very soon grew to be adored by the audience. When, before a recording, I told them that she was appearing there would be a short sigh of pleasure, like a wave rolling on to a shingle beach. When she wasn't on, the temperature seemed to drop a few degrees as disappointment made the audience slightly chilly. She could create wonderful lines: 'I come from Erith. It isn't twinned with anywhere, but it does have a suicide pact with Dagenham.'

Her great ability was to take the raw material of news stories – distant, alien events that we know are important, yet which often seem to have little to do with our own lives – and weave them into our day-to-day existence. Take her routine about the weapons of mass destruction in Iraq. She felt sorry for Bush and Blair, she said, hunting for them everywhere. 'It's like my scissors. I can never remember where I've put them.' (Pause for audience to enjoy the weird juxtaposition of Linda's scissors and battlefield nuclear weapons.) 'On the other hand, I do know my scissors exist.'

All comedians need timing, but Linda could do something more: she could ride a laugh, knowing exactly the right time to interrupt it, like a surfer judging the perfect moment to leap into a wave.

Take my other favourite joke from the programme. The question was about the new French version of Viagra, which was claimed to last for twenty-four hours – roughly twenty-three hours and forty minutes longer than most men would need it, I felt. Alan had his Viagra joke ('Can you get it over the counter? Only if you take two') which was so well known to the audience that he did not need to recount the punchline.

This time Sandi Toksvig chipped in that it was National Condom Week, and she had been surprised to get through the post a sort of measuring device, a piece of flat plastic that helped you select the size of condom that would fit. It had three holes, marked 'large', 'medium' and 'trim'. It was, she said, similar to those things you used to measure how much spaghetti you need to cook – family of six, family of four, etc.

I asked if this, so to speak, measured the spaghetti before or after you put it in the boiling salted water. At this point, Sandi, one of those comedians who is generous with her laughter at other comedians' jokes, which is not something you can say about all of them, began to lose it. She was chortling and whooping and yelling, and the audience joined in, as if singing along at a rock concert.

Linda waited until the laughter was just beginning to subside, and with deft precision she chipped in with, 'I think Simon is asking if it's *al dente.*'

~

Linda was not without malice, but it was malice saved for the powerful and the rich. When someone said that we should deny novelist Jeffrey Archer the oxygen of publicity, she said tartly, 'I'd like to deny him the oxygen of oxygen.' But she had a wonderful ear for the way people really talk. In that way she was a sort of working-class Joyce Grenfell. She knew from observation what it was like to be the sort of person who finds life almost too difficult to cope with. Sometimes she would drift into a fantasy where she was visiting Alan in an old folks' home: 'I'm sure the nurses aren't stealing your clothes, dear. Isn't she marvellous, that one over there. She comes to see her nan every week, and it's two buses you know.' We would often bring friends along to watch the show being recorded and afterwards, over drinks, they would all want to meet Linda, who would not only come over and shake hands, but chat to them, find out something about them, discover interests in common. She was never Lady Bountiful, never acted the star greeting her adoring fans.

~

She loved talking about her own background. Though she had been to Sheffield University, and most of her early success as a performer had been around South Yorkshire and Derbyshire, she often returned to London and would always see her mother in Erith. She'd explain why she was coming down – she had a gig in the West End on Saturday, but would pop over on Sunday before returning to Sheffield for another gig . . . After some years of this, her mother dropped into that voice all children, of whatever age, dread hearing from their parents, the voice that means 'I am about to ask a very serious question which I haven't liked to ask for a long time, but now I need to know . . .' What was it going to be? Probably 'Why don't you marry and settle down?'

'What I want to know,' said her mother, 'is what is a *gig*?'

~

Linda died of ovarian cancer. In its early stages I had crassly admired her new hair-do, and my wife had to point out that it was a wig, the most obvious sign of chemotherapy. She was determined not to be identified by her illness, didn't want articles saying 'brave Linda Smith, the comedian battling against ovarian cancer'. I do not know the moment she registered that death was inevitable. I do know that she kept coming on to the programme, and we could see her fading, slowly, like the light fading at dusk. One time she came on, and was tired. You could tell that the mind was still working, but the jokes came more slowly. When she died millions of people suddenly realized how much they missed her, how much they had taken her extraordinary gifts for granted.

~

There was a small family funeral and cremation, then a few days later a celebration of her life at the Theatre Royal, Stratford East. Linda was president of the Humanist Association, and firmly believed that there was nothing after death but absence and disintegration. Still, her friend Mark Steel, who MC'ed the event, began by saying, 'Linda didn't believe in the afterlife. But, just in case she's wrong, and she's looking down on us now, let's give her a great big cheer!' Several hundred people erupted with laughter. It set the tone perfectly.

~

Her partner, Warren Lakin, then set about commemorating her life in as many ways as he could manage. For a long time, her death became his life. There was a special edition of *The News Quiz*, broadcast the weekend after her death (I will not forget the BBC apparatchik who wanted to have a normal show that week: 'It's what she would have wanted.' Nonsense: she'd have wanted a tribute, all of us would. And in any case, neither I nor any of the panellists would have taken part in a 'normal' show). Later there was another Radio 4 compilation of her best work from several shows. Warren put together a book containing recollections and much of her best material. Then there was a second book, a memoir called *Driving Miss Linda*, about their life together. He organized a massive tribute in a West End theatre, with many of her favourite performers, and live stage versions of the radio shows she'd appeared on. Readings of her work were put on at various venues. Along with Warren and others I took part in two tribute events at literary festivals (she loved going to the one in the Lake District, Words by the Water, asking the audience, 'Where do the people of Keswick go to buy their indoor wear?'). We all turned up for her posthumous induction into the Radio Hall of Fame. A group of Labour MPs held a lunch in her memory at which Warren read more of her work. Warren continued to commemorate Linda's life long after he had acquired a new girlfriend, a charming young woman who didn't seem to mind the permanent and ghostly presence of her predecessor, like the second Mrs de Winter, without the scandal.

~

I left the show in 2006. It had become clear that they wanted a more showbizzy air to the programme (if anything, since the death of Alan, there are even fewer writing journalists appearing) and if I hadn't decided to go, I'm pretty sure they would have sacked me in a year or so anyway. Sandi Toksvig took me to what she described as 'the best Danish restaurant in London' – it was a delicious if somewhat herring-intensive meal – and she chairs it with far more ad lib wit than I ever managed. I almost always catch the show now, especially when Andy Hamilton, Jeremy Hardy or Fred Macaulay are on.

MEETING THE FAMOUS

7

Meeting the Famous

Princess Di & Dallas

Journalists sometimes get to meet famous people, and it usually isn't too intimidating, especially if the famous people are in the line of business you write about. It would be a callow sports reporter who became nervous in the presence of Andy Murray or David Beckham, and a useless political correspondent who was tongue-tied on meeting the Prime Minister. Actually, politicians tend to be more agitated when they encounter journalists, to whom an indiscreet word is so often a mistake and occasionally a disaster. Most politicians have in their heads the equivalent of the seven-second tape delay used by radio stations for phone-in programmes; if anyone says anything obscene or libellous it can be stopped before it's broadcast. Pols have the same quivering sensitivity to anything that might do them lasting harm.

The trick, if you're in a social situation such as a reception or a dinner, is to put the famous person at their ease, much as the Queen does. You can do this by asking them about something that has nothing to do with their professional world. If they like opera, or cooking, or genuinely support a football team rather than merely claim to, you can talk about that. And almost nobody, asked how their children are doing, is going to reply, 'Mind your own sodding business.' At a reception in Windsor Castle, my colleague Peter Oborne burst into the group surrounding the

Queen, demanding, 'What's your tip for the Derby, ma'am?' Her face lit up and she launched into a long discussion of form.

~

(This was the same reception, held for the press to mark the Queen's golden jubilee, at which the Duke of Edinburgh approached a group of journalists from the *Independent*, the newspaper that had started life by ignoring royal news altogether. The three were all wearing name tags.

> Duke: *Independent, Independent, Independent.* What on earth are you lot doing here?
> *Independent* hack, somewhat braver than the others: Well, for one thing, sir, you invited us.
> Duke: Well, you didn't have to come.)

Sometimes people are so famous that I, at least, get lockjaw. Or at any rate say something so stupid that, even if the celebrity forgets it a moment later, it lingers in my mind for decades, a little nugget of embarrassment, like a morsel of bacon that you can't get out of your teeth.

There was the time, in happier days, when Charles and Di went on an official visit to Australia. I had always wanted to go to Australia, and my then editor, Donald Trelford, was enthusiastic about sending his staff on royal stories. I suspect he was under the impression that this would, at some point, translate into a knighthood for himself, though such honours are mostly in the hands of government ministers, who would neither notice nor care if a royal tour was reported at length or ignored completely.

The trips usually begin with a cocktail party for the accompanying press. The notion is that the reptiles will be so impressed and honoured by hobnobbing with these notables that they will be kindly in their coverage, omitting small acts of foolishness or slips of the tongue. It works only occasionally.

The couple arrived – with, amid some ersatz controversy in the media, their newly born son William – in Alice Springs. The temperature was above 40°C, or 105°F. I had called into a hotel for lunch, and had been offered a choice of roast beef, roast pork, roast chicken or roast lamb, with roast potatoes, vegetables and gravy, all washed down with hot tea. Or cold beer. I suspect that to ask for a salad would have been seen as a sign of effeminacy. Outside it was so hot that you had to leave the car's air conditioning on for several minutes before it became possible to touch the steering wheel.

The reception began. I had been chatting with Andrew Morton, who was then royal correspondent for the *Daily Star*. The two of us were introduced to Prince Charles, whom neither of us had met. The prince praised a series of witty captions Clive James had added to pictures of the Queen during her American tour that had appeared in the *Observer* magazine, and which Donald Trelford feared might be seen at the palace as an example of *lèse-majesté*. The prince, however, pronounced them 'very funny'. He then turned to Andrew Morton and asked why he had gone into journalism.

'Because I wanted to write,' he said.

Charles replied, 'In that case, why on earth did you join the *Daily Star*?'

I thought this was rather rude, unintentionally or not, and tried to explain that writing for a tabloid was more difficult than writing for a 'serious' newspaper, since you had to compress the information into brief paragraphs using only short sentences and demotic language. The prince looked slightly taken aback.

Andrew Morton went on to be Princess Diana's confessor, and published her version of the regrettable marriage in his book, *Diana*. I sometimes wondered whether Charles's throwaway but demeaning remark might have made Morton all the more willing to cooperate in a scheme designed, successfully, to humiliate the prince.

~

Charles, I fear, has always lacked charisma, or at least the amount required in a modern celebrity royal. He often seems to suffer from reverse charisma, which I think of as *amsirac*. People with charisma get served first in crowded theatre bars, and when they wave an umbrella in Bond Street at the height of a wet rush hour two taxis screech to a halt. Those with amsirac can't get served in an empty pub until the barman has finished polishing a dozen glasses; if they do manage to hail a cab, the driver says, 'King's Cross? Nah, mate, outa my way.' Charles is aware of this, and a friend of mine, a diplomat who at one time worked closely with him, suspects it may have helped destroy the marriage. On a tour of Germany, he could not be found for a morning event. In the end he was discovered kicking a tin can round the courtyard of the *Schloss* where they were staying. 'They only want to see her,' he said, meaning Diana. 'They're not interested in me.' On this Australian tour the pair would walk down streets lined with cheering crowds, switching from one side to the other as if performing in a very slow barn dance. As he greeted a new group of well-wishers, he would often say something like, 'I'm afraid you've drawn the short straw,' meaning that they were not getting Diana. Sometimes he said it genially, sometimes grumpily. Most of the crowd did not try to hide their disappointment.

~

In the Alice Springs hotel I was steered towards Diana, and suddenly found myself talking to her on her own. I was petrified. I assumed, wrongly, that she would try to be both grand and distant. My short meeting with her husband five minutes earlier was the first time I had ever met a royal personage. She turned out to be pleasant, and conversational, so I found myself blithering. We had a longish chat about the problem of travelling long distances with small children, how they were always awake when you wanted to get some sleep, and vice versa. It was only after this heart-warming display of fellow-feeling that I remembered that I myself didn't have any children, and also that she had been travelling with an entourage of thirty-five people, any one of whom could have helped with the baby.

~

It is sometimes hard to recall the extent of Diana's worldwide stardom. Even those Australians who had a grumbling resentment against the very existence of our royals as their first family of state turned out in hordes to see her, doubtless adding to her husband's annoyance and frustration. Every minuscule detail of what she did and said was pored over by the media, in the manner of the old Kremlinologists interpreting a single paragraph in *Pravda*. A young housewife who talked to her for a few minutes was tracked down and suddenly found dozens of reporters and cameramen on her doorstep, demanding a verbatim account of the conversation. The room they occupied in Alice Springs was equipped with a whirlpool bath, giving one of the tabloids the headline 'Rub-a-Dub Tub', for the thought that the royal couple were at it at every opportunity was never stated, but often implied.

One British photographer, a woman who had gone to Australia with her young son to start a new life, overheard on a police radio that security was being increased at the hotel swimming pool. She suddenly realized she might get the Holy Grail all photographers yearned for then – Di in a bikini. At that time, none had ever appeared. It would have an incredible value, half a million pounds, maybe more. So she sneaked into the hotel grounds, took cover in a wooden shed by the pool where the equipment was kept and hid under a tarpaulin. She kept herself going by thinking of the house in Sydney she would be able to buy for herself and her son once she had sold the rights.

The heat was unbearable, which is perhaps why Charles and Diana never appeared at the pool. Maybe they were frolicking in the whirlpool bath. Most of the entourage did turn up, but a picture of a lady-in-waiting in a swimming costume would not have sold for anything at all. Later the photographer told me that the worst of it was the knowledge that, having missed the snap that would have changed her life, she had to wait hours before leaving the sweltering shed so as not to risk arrest.

Everywhere she went and however she was dressed, Diana managed to look impossibly glamorous, especially in some of the less impossibly glamorous locations where the tour took her. I meanwhile enjoyed the Australian use of the English language. They seemed to have two forms of communication: monosyllabic and rococo. So you might ask someone how he was, and he'd reply, 'Good.' And the wife? 'Good.' Had he fixed the problem with his car? 'It's good.'

But they could construct wonderful idioms, something caught by Barry Humphries in his Barry McKenzie strip for *Private Eye*. One evening Diana had attended a dinner in a provincial hotel, and the guests had naturally dressed up. One woman appeared looking remarkably attractive in an electric-blue gown that emphasized the most striking parts of her figure. An Australian photographer with whom I had struck up a drinking friendship said, 'I wouldn't mind having her, Simon!'

I said I thought that was her husband coming through the door behind her.

'Well, I'm sure she'd rather have my blue-veined junket pump up her,' he replied, as if it were the most natural thing to say.

Later I was with friends at lunch in a beach-side restaurant in Sydney. Some worked for ABC, the Australian equivalent of the BBC, and they were discussing a British TV star who had come out and behaved with the kind of intolerable grandeur Australians used to associate with the British, and which confirmed all their stereotypes of us. Finally a woman in our party ended the conversation by saying, 'You know what she can do with the rough end of a pineapple,' again, as if it were a common phrase in everyday use, as I later discovered it was, in Australia at least.

~

I encountered the princess again when she and her husband came to Washington. It was 1985, and already stories were appearing in the papers implying that all was not well in the marriage. One of their first engagements was at the British embassy for lunch. She had been placed between the British ambassador, Sir Oliver Wright, and one of his senior staff, John Kerr, later head of the Foreign Office. That night the royal couple were to meet members of the United States Supreme Court, and Sir Oliver, not a man in whose company conversation ever flagged since he was able to provide so much of it himself, decided to explain the working of the court, the role of the Chief Justice, some important recent cases, and so on, at very considerable length.

After he had finished, Diana said, 'Thank you, Sir Oliver,' then turned politely but quickly to her other side and said, 'Now, Mr Kerr, can you tell me what has been happening in the latest episodes of *Dallas* and *Dynasty*?'

Kerr explained that there were *Dallas* households and *Dynasty* households; his was a *Dallas* home, and he would happily bring her up to date on that series, but could not help with *Dynasty*.

~

(It is sometimes hard to remember how important *Dallas* and the timing of its broadcasts were in those pre-video days. The late Frank Johnson, the *Daily Telegraph* sketchwriter, once described going to a dinner party at the large Sussex house occupied by the right-wing journalist Andrew Alexander. The other guests included Mr and Mrs Enoch Powell. To his utter embarrassment, the young woman Frank had taken to the dinner suddenly remarked, as the meal was about to be served, 'Oh, *Dallas* is on now. I can't possibly miss it.' Andrew Alexander looked furious, but Enoch Powell said, 'Let us all watch this programme that is so important to the young lady,' and grudgingly the television was wheeled into the dining room. They ate the meal in near silence interrupted only by Powell asking questions, such as, 'Where is the psychiatrist? All Americans have psychiatrists,' or 'Why is that man wearing a hat indoors?'

'Because he's Texan, dear,' said Pamela Powell crisply.)

~

The party for the travelling hacks was also held at the British embassy. I was with a small group of people when we saw the press attaché walking past with the princess. I gave him a look that easily translated as, 'If you don't bring her over here, we will not only never invite you to our house again, but will probably leave diseased racoon corpses in your mailbox.' She came over and was introduced. I was struck once more by how much the camera likes women with big features: her face seemed as familiar as those of one's own children, since it had appeared on several thousand magazine covers, yet strangely different: her jaw was longer than I expected and her nose larger. I have noticed the same phenomenon with several women who photograph wonderfully – opera singer Kiri Te Kanawa and actress Diana Rigg among them. By contrast, Christine Keeler, of the Profumo Affair, who was breathtakingly beautiful in real life, had small, precise features and did not photograph well. Even the great photographer Jane Bown could not make her look other than mousy, especially if she wasn't wearing make-up. (To Christine Keeler it was never the 'Profumo Affair' – the war minister had been a marginal figure to her. She saw it as the 'Lucky Gordon Affair'; he was the pimp who had ruined her life.)

Someone in our party, a fashion correspondent, asked what the princess was wearing for the White House dinner that night. 'It's a little black number,' she replied. (I'd like to think she said 'little black numero', but I think that would have been sub-Sloane.) 'It's the last new thing I'm wearing on the whole tour.'

'So, it's sweater and jeans from now on, is it?' I asked, and suddenly she gave me the kind of look that had caused so many men to feel as if someone had whacked the back of their knees, very hard, with a baseball bat. Once on the Great Wall of China some workmen had offered me a drink from a bottle that I had assumed contained beer. In fact it was a powerful rice spirit, so the generous glug I hurled back made me suddenly realize, physically, that my brain was indeed composed of two hemispheres. Diana's laughter had a similar effect. The most famously beautiful woman in the world wasn't just laughing at my pleasantry; it might have been the funniest thing anyone had said since Oscar Wilde popped his clogs, and to judge from her astonished delight, certainly the wittiest remark she had heard for quite some time.

They say that with royalty it is fatal to become complacent, to feel that you're getting along so well that you might as well try to be even more relaxed. Diana had gone into a rather touching description of how nervous she felt at official functions. Her point was that she might be placed next to, for instance, a famous scientist. He would be tongue-tied talking to her, not realizing that she felt just as nervous talking to him. I said, 'Well, with any luck, they'll put you next to Clint Eastwood tonight, and you won't have to say a word.'

The reference to the laconic film star didn't work for her, and she gave me a blank and disappointing stare. But I can still see the iridescent smile from a few minutes before.

~

I was aware of the lockjaw effect again some years later. Near the row of west London Victorian semis where we live is a superb early Georgian terrace of large houses, mostly named after eighteenth- and early nineteenth-century admirals, a few yards away from a fine park. The largest house is at the end and used to be occupied by Alfred, Lord Tennyson, as a blue plaque confirms. When we moved in it was the home of Pete Townshend of rock band The Who. I had often wondered what I'd say if I bumped into him, perhaps in the pub. Maybe it would be a typical neighbours' conversation, about those bloody speed bumps, or have you tried the new Thai place that's just opened? Or I would say, 'Hi, thought you wanted to die before you got old. Well, you're looking a bit peaky . . .' though of course he must have heard a thousand variants on that one.

However, he kept himself to himself and I only came across him on one occasion when I saw him marching down his front path pushing a youth in front of him with an angry finger; local gossip identified the lad as his daughter's boyfriend. Then one weekend I was teaching our son to ride a bike in the park. There was a rustling in some bushes, and with a parent's peripheral vision I caught sight of a shambling tramp-like figure in a dirty anorak emerging.

''Ello,' said the tramp. 'I'm teaching my son to ride his bike too.'

I noticed first that there was another boy of a similar age to mine on a bike, and then that the man who had addressed me was no vagrant but one of the greatest rock legends of the century. I hadn't a clue what to say. My brain froze as if it had been dipped in liquid nitrogen. Finally I stuttered, 'How old is your boy?'

'Seven,' he said cheerfully. 'How old's yours?'

At this point I lost it altogether and heard myself calling to our son, 'Richard, how old are you?'

Soon afterwards they revived *Tommy* on Broadway, and the royalties allowed Townshend to buy The Wick, a superb house that had been the home of Sir John Mills, the actor, and which overlooks Petersham Meadows, one of the finest urban views in the country, so we never see him now.

~

It is important to tease politicians. They don't get enough teasing. Abuse they have by the bucketload, and sycophancy too, but teasing they can't really handle. James Fenton, the poet, was, surprisingly perhaps, once the political correspondent of the *New Statesman* and was adept at making politicians ill at ease. One day we were walking down the committee corridor and we were passed by David Owen, then foreign secretary. 'What a busy foreign secretary he is!' said James. 'Hurry scurry, hurry scurry, Foreign Secretary!' Owen looked round and grinned uneasily. It wasn't a witty remark, but it created a disturbing sense of anxiety. What could Fenton have meant? Was there some sinister secondary meaning?

~

James and I covered a Liberal conference in Llandudno, when David Steel was expected to be the next leader of the party. Fenton had an aunt who lived in the hills above the resort, and she had invited Steel, an aide, her nephew and me to dinner one night. Steel had just been reading Schumacher's modish book *Small Is Beautiful* and had been greatly taken by it.

'I cannot think,' he declared in the car, 'of any circumstances in which small is not beautiful.'

'Oh, I can,' said James.

Steel asked what.

'Well, for example, a gin and tonic,' said James.

There was a considerable kerfuffle around this time about the register of members' interests. It seems astonishing now that MPs should not have been obliged to list the sources of their extra-curricular earnings, but at the time the suggestion aroused the usual complaints: 'threat to democracy', 'only the rich will be able to afford to be MPs', and so forth. James suggested a register of members' sexual interests, and asked as many as he could find what their sexual interests were, though without much success. Sir William van Straubenzee, the Tory MP for Wokingham, was a man who could sound dreadfully pompous but who was in fact of a liberal and kindly disposition, who loathed only his own party's right-wingers. (Of Airey Neave, whom he disliked intensely in spite of his heroic escape from Colditz, he said in tones of lip-curling contempt, 'This man, this man, who has *crawled* out of every prison in Europe . . .') Van Straubenzee replied: 'Hedgehogs, tightly curled hedgehogs. They present such a challenge.' He was alarmed when Fenton printed this drollery in the *New Statesman* and claimed that some of his constituents had taken it seriously.

~

One of Fenton's favourite butts (he was always scrupulously courteous in his manner, which made it harder for the politicians to protest or often even to realize that they were being teased) was a Tory called Spencer le Marchant, a landowner from Derbyshire. Spencer was a whip, a job that normally requires a considerable low cunning, though few would ascribe that to him. He had an affable and agreeable manner, and was immensely generous: when I first met him he offered me a drink. When I asked for a pint, he had a word with the barman, who handed me a silver pint mug filled with champagne. However, life's more cerebral demands were sometimes beyond him. His lack of organization and fondness for a drink made us imagine that when he went home, he should have a label round his neck, like unaccompanied children on planes, marked, 'Please put this whip out at Buxton.'

It was generally agreed that it was his geniality that had won him his job. For instance, if a committee was sitting late at night on some dreary piece of legislation, the members would often hear a clanking in the corridor, and Spencer would arrive pushing a fully equipped drinks trolley.

In October one year Fenton asked Spencer where he had been for his holidays.

'Florida! Big-game fishing!' he replied.

Fenton enquired what he had fished for.

'Marlin! Huge buggers! Can take you hours to reel them in!'

'And what do you do when you've caught them?'

'You throw them back, of course. Can't eat 'em!'

'Do you know, Spencer,' said Fenton, 'you may just have hit on the solution to the Cod War.'

There was a long pause while Spencer mulled this over. Finally a light went on in his mind. 'No, James, you see it's quite different . . .'

~

John Sergeant and I had covered both Ted Heath's election campaigns in 1974. John was much the wittiest of all political correspondents, though in those days, as a BBC news reporter, he was never allowed to be funny on air. There was always a certain boys-on-the-bus air of mild hysteria among those of us following the Prime Minister (and later, leader of the opposition), not least because Heath stumped the country making the same speech time and again. In his main evening speech he might include some policy announcement packaged for the evening news, but for the rest of the time we were taking part in a travelling *Groundhog Day*, listening to the same words again and again. The February election took place during the three-day week as the miners were on strike. Heath, who had gone to the country with the slogan 'Who governs Britain?', decided to claim that the general chaos and misery had brought a heart-warming unity to the nation. 'But why, oh why, oh why, do we always have to have a crisis before we can work together like this?' he would ask, several times a day. At the end of the tour the travelling journalists clubbed together to buy him a copy of Gilbert O'Sullivan's hit record 'Why, Oh Why, Oh Why'. Heath didn't seem to find it at all amusing.

~

We found various ways of entertaining ourselves to lighten the tedium. One was to shout out meaningful slogans. Everywhere Heath went he would be met by jeers from a few ill-wishers, and considerable if vague encouragement from others. 'Good on yer, Ted,' or 'Good luck, Mr Heath!' Tory sympathizers would shout. There wasn't much variety. So John and I would hide behind cars or hoardings, and as he came near we'd stick out our heads and yell, 'Say "no" to a redefinition of the M3 money supply, Mr Heath!' or 'Resist the call for import surcharges on the Italian model, Ted!' We would look just long enough to register the mingled surprise and alarm on his face before pulling our heads back in, like meerkats.

~

During the next campaign of 1974, when Heath was fighting to unseat Harold Wilson for a second time, we travelled in the back of his plane. This had been provided by Dan-Air, a now forgotten airline which was never much loved by its passengers.

The chief flight attendant hated us, reasonably enough, because the press were rowdy, demanding, often drunk and always disinclined to follow her instructions. We called her Rosa Klebb, which was unfair but satisfying.

One day we were taxiing down to the runway at Glasgow airport when John reached up to press the orange button. Irma was down the aisle in a trice. 'Do you realize,' she almost screamed, 'that while we're taxiing, that button lights the emergency light in the cockpit? *What*, might I ask, is the emergency?'

John smiled at her calmly. 'My friend,' he said, waving in my direction, 'needs a drink.'

'That is not an emergency!' shouted Rosa. You could almost see wisps of smoke coming out of her ears.

'I'm sorry,' said John, 'but my friend is an alcoholic. When I say he needs a drink, I mean that he *needs* a drink.' His tone grew calmer, more understanding. 'To be precise, he needs a gin and tonic.'

At this point Rosa gave us both a furious glare and stormed towards the cockpit.

As she went, John called, 'And while you're up, would you get me one?'

Amazingly, after we had taken off, she did get our drinks. I sometimes wonder if she voted against him on *Strictly Come Dancing*.

~

Kingsley Amis I met only a few times, chiefly when he was at the bar of the Garrick Club, where I was occasionally taken by friends who were members. He seemed somewhat adrift, not a fish out of water exactly, but someone slightly distanced from his milieu, and by 1.55 p.m. – five minutes before last orders in the club's various dining rooms – dependent for conversation on whoever was left there, while having a fourth or fifth pre-lunch sharpener.

He famously said that the worst seven words in the English language were 'Shall we go straight to the table?'

I first met him when his publisher suggested that the *Guardian* might like to interview him about his novel *Russian Hide and Seek*, a paranoid fantasy about the Soviets occupying Britain. It was not his finest work, and for someone like me, who regarded *Lucky Jim* as the funniest novel of the post-war period, deeply disappointing. Still, it would be intriguing to meet him, and in December I phoned the number I had been given to make a lunch appointment.

With Christmas on its way this proved difficult. Finally we settled on 2 January.

'Oh, that's no use,' he exclaimed. 'I shall have a hangover.'

I thought for a moment, then pointed out that the heavy drinking was on New Year's Eve, so the suffering came on 1 January.

You could almost hear him pulling himself up to his full height at the other end of the phone. 'Some of us,' he said with great dignity, 'have hangovers that last *two* days.'

~

I was at King's College in Cambridge at the same time as Salman Rushdie. This was before he became an unofficial spokesperson for the wretched of the earth, those crushed under the iron heel of imperialism. (Years later I read an article by him in the *Observer* in which he complained that Britain was endemically racist. At the same time, the radio was carrying a report about the massacre of around one thousand Bengalis who had crossed into Assam looking for work, and had been slaughtered by the locals who did not wish to lose those jobs. The term 'racism' is usually used to mean racist speech and behaviour directed against black or Asian people. It is also used by those of any colour or creed who feel that others are biased against them.)

Unlike most of the public school boys at King's, who were well aware of changing times, and who made a point of being affable to those of us who had been educated at the public expense, Rushdie seemed somewhat aloof, even arrogant. He had been to Rugby (where it seems highly likely that he would have suffered some racist abuse) and most of his friends had attended private schools of one kind or another. My friend David Leigh, the grandson of an immigrant Jewish tailor, was the first member of his family to go to university, and he was determined to work – a task made more difficult by Rushdie's socializing in the room immediately above his. Leigh recalls the playing of loud music and popping of champagne corks, though there may be some rankling class resentment in this recollection.

Leigh repeatedly asked Rushdie to keep the noise down, and was – as is the way of most students – repeatedly ignored. So he bought an air pistol, and next time the row began he marched upstairs and shouted, 'Come on out, Rushdie, I've got a gun and I'm not afraid to use it.' Being a sensible fellow Rushdie declined, so Leigh fired a couple of pellets into the door to make his point, making him probably the only person ever to get a shot off anywhere in his general vicinity.

Years later I told this story at a college reunion for my contemporaries. Rushdie was not present, but I assumed several of his old friends were, so I embarked upon the tale in gingerly fashion. I need not have worried: it was received with delight.

He has subsequently said that this event never occurred. Leigh insists that it did. I cannot be sure who is right, but Leigh's memory is sharp and clear on the subject, and we all tend to forget events that embarrass us at the time, so I suspect it may have slipped Rushdie's memory. In any event, he behaved very prudently at the time.

~

As we all prepared to graduate, Salman produced a novel called *Grimus*, his first, which then as now was little read. I thought no more of him till around six or seven years later when I attended a debate at the Friends' Meeting House in Euston Road, London. The discussion was on race relations, and I had gone in support of a friend who was speaking in favour of laws banning racial prejudice, or at least banning its various manifestations. I need not have bothered; the hall was filled with well over a thousand people, the great majority of whom appeared to be on my friend's side.

Just before the speakers were to begin, to my great surprise Salman Rushdie appeared and addressed us. This was some time before *Midnight's Children* and many years before the *fatwa* against him resulting from *The Satanic Verses*. He introduced himself as an advertising man (he had worked for two large companies), and said he wanted to show us a cinema commercial that had shocked him.

It turned out to be one that would have been familiar to any cinema-goer in the mid-1970s and was a spoof of the film *Zulu*, advertising Silk Cut cigarettes. In it the Zulu army overwhelmed the British garrison, but instead of killing them, offered them packets of Silk Cut. 'It takes two weeks to get used to the new mild taste of the Silk Cut cigarettes,' said the Zulu chieftain, 'and two weeks is all you got, white man.' After a fortnight, the Zulus returned to find the British relaxing and enjoying the low-tar fags.

Inconceivable that such a commercial could be made today, even more so since the Zulus were played by white actors in black-face. The commercial had been skilfully shot and cunningly edited, so there were sniggers in the audience, even among those who might be inclined to share Salman's anger. After it was over, he told us how appalled he was, and informed us how appalled we were too. It was typical of the British advertising industry, he said, that black people could only appear either as joke figures, or else as villains. They were never allowed to take part in advertisements as normal members of society.

Unfortunately a number of people who didn't agree with him at all were scattered through the audience. They were mostly elderly, and from their accents, I guessed came from east London. I assumed they were either members or at least supporters of the National Front. They decided to take issue. (I cannot remember the exact examples they gave, but the point remains accurate.) 'Smith's crisps!' shouted one of the elderly persons.

'All right,' said Salman, 'Smith's crisps. But the very fact that you can remember the one example of a black person appearing as a normal man or woman in a TV ad makes my point.'

'Start-rite shoes!' said another.

'Well, the fact that you can remember the only two instances—'

'Smarties!' 'Electrolux!' 'Brentford Nylons!' were shot from various corners of the room.

'The fact that you can remember each example shows just how rare—'

But the horrid old people didn't stop. 'Admit it, son, you lost!' one of them yelled.

What struck me was the way that people with strong views are often incapable of viewing anything dispassionately. Salman was so convinced that the British advertising industry had decided to conceal all people of colour that he never noticed any of the – admittedly infrequent – times they appeared. Meanwhile the East Enders, quivering with fury at the integration of black people into British life, could spot a dark face appearing for two seconds in the background of a sweetie ad. Both sides saw only what they expected to see, and both were disgusted.

~

(The horribly embarrassed, walking-on-eggshells terror that afflicts many American people when it comes to race is often demonstrated on National Public Radio, whose staff and broadcasters would rather cut off their own noses than make a remark that might conceivably be interpreted as prejudiced in any way at all, to anybody. NPR is based in Washington, where a white city employee was dismissed for describing someone as 'niggardly'. The fact that the word has no connection at all with 'nigger' was not deemed an excuse, though he was finally reinstated when he pleaded that, as a gay man, he also suffered from oppression. An immigrant from Spain was refused work in a California fire department which operated a quota system on the grounds that he was not 'Hispanic'. And a British friend living in the US told me that she heard a woman on NPR describe herself as 'a person of gender'.

The quintessence of this gnawing anxiety came a short while after Jesse Jackson had decreed that the term 'black' was no longer acceptable; it was to be replaced by 'African-American'. Virtually every media outlet adopted the term, almost overnight, to the extent that when Nelson Mandela visited the States for the first time after his release from prison, a reporter addressed him: 'As an African-American yourself, Mr Mandela . . .'

Offering a friend a coffee in the States, I asked if she liked it 'black or white'. She shushed me, then said quietly, 'We say "with cream" or "without cream" now.')

~

I first met Alan Coren in 1979, when he was editor of *Punch* and asked me to write a political gossip column. It was a wonderful commission, as the arrival of Mrs Thatcher had made British politics not only fascinating again, but also slightly crazed. She was mistress of the follies but – and this is what made the whole situation so beguiling – she took the whole thing with incredible seriousness. She didn't do jokes, and could barely recognize one. This raised the standard of the jokes that centred on her. I could have filled the column most weeks with little else.

~

Working for *Punch* meant that you got invited every month or so to the famous *Punch* table with its incised initials. Sitting there was almost like taking tea with Walter Scott on the Scott Monument – though, in truth, there were not all that many famous names. Alan had invited some members of the royal family, such as the Duke of Edinburgh and Princess Anne, who had carved their names or their initials into the wood. There were also some utterly forgotten names, for – apart from a handful of great writers – nobody is more swiftly consigned to oblivion than a humorous writer whose time has passed. One of the few lasting people to have carved their names was Thackeray, who managed to chisel out 'WMT'. Mark Twain later declined to add his name, saying that two of Thackeray's three initials would suffice for him.

The meal finished, Alan would hold court. The first time I went, he announced that everyone wrote books about what would have happened if the Germans had won the war, but nobody ever wrote about events if the Italians had won. He soon spun off into the surreal – Nelson's Column would be replaced by a gigantic pepper grinder, for example – and I reflected that he was one of those rare people who put as much effort into their conversation as they do into their writing. Half of Alan's jokes were, essentially, written on water, or in the case of the *Punch* lunch, mediocre claret. Sometimes I suspected that they existed in a state of half-truth, stories or conversations that almost existed, or had occurred but required a little bottled relish to bring out their full flavour. For example, he used to describe being invited to lunch with the Queen. (Like many people from immigrant stock, he put great store by the royal family, and was disproportionately delighted when the royals came to the lunch.) He was late, and was driving at some speed towards the palace, when he was stopped by a policeman who enquired what the hurry was.

'Well, officer, you might not believe this,' said Alan, 'but I'm going for lunch with the Queen.'

In his story, the policeman eyed him suspiciously. 'What are you, sir, some kind of humorist?'

~

All *Punch* lunches were funny, and sometimes I wished that the jokes could have been canned and served up in the magazine which, even under Alan, still had the faint whiff of inter-war suburbia. It had lost its crusading touch – Thomas Hood's 'Song of a Shirt', on the wretched conditions of the workers, first appeared in *Punch* – and had deliberately ignored the satire boom. In any case, it would have been pointless to compete with *Private Eye* and it never tried. But there were no better comic writers in the land than Alan himself and, say, Keith Waterhouse. Waterhouse specialized in nostalgia for the north, though he himself lived happily in the soft south, mostly in a flat in Earls Court where he was ministered to by a succession of kindly ladies, some of whom he married, others whom he didn't.

Keith's output was quite extraordinary: novels, plays, non-fiction – one of my favourites is *The Theory and Practice of Lunch*, a topic on which he knew a great deal – two weekly columns for the *Daily Mirror* and articles for a host of other magazines. 'I don't like recessions,' he told me once, 'you don't get all those commissions from magazines like *Popular Caravanning*.' He managed to cram all his work into the mornings. At noon, or just after, he would take a glass of champagne, then go to lunch and the rest of the day was free for drinking and conviviality. Apart from food, drink and a fine seafront flat in Brighton, it was hard to see where he spent his money, of which there must have been a large amount. *Billy Liar* alone had been a bestselling novel, a successful film, and went on to be a musical and an ice show. (I greatly liked *Billy Liar on the Moon* in which Billy has grown up and become an executive for a dreary local authority in a dreary Home Counties new town. It has the sharp ring of truth on every page, and I often wondered how Keith contrived to keep up with so much of modern life without ever having to go there.)

For years I declined to meet him, since he was my hero-journalist, and I feared he might turn out to be unpleasant, or at least dislike me, which would have been a hurtful blow. In the event, he turned out to be delightful, and always up for mischief, whether drinking more champagne than was good for anybody, or picking a verbal fight with anybody who fancied one. He used to visit the Labour Party conference occasionally and one night, around midnight, after he had been drinking fairly steadily all day and through the evening, he joined up with a colleague who suggested they went somewhere else for another drink. 'Very well,' said Keith, 'just a little *apéritif* perhaps.'

I was present at a conversation he had with Roy Hattersley, who had just gone into the northern memorabilia trade himself. Keith was, half-humorously, half-seriously, trying to guard his territory. 'I'm keeping trams,' he told Hattersley. 'I invented trams. You' – he paused as if making an immense concession – 'can have gobstoppers.'

I mentioned Gerald Kaufman, who was trying to win a niche with his recollections of Leeds, and the pair of them looked at me with disdain, as if Spain and Portugal, having carved up South America, were to be told that Andorra would like some of the action too.

~

Alan died in 2008. He had been on holiday with his beloved wife Anne at their house in France when he felt a sharp prick, as if from a thorn or an insect sting, and reported feeling ill. She was an anaesthetist and familiar with serious illness, so called a doctor immediately. An ambulance rushed him to hospital in Nice where doctors closed down all his systems, rather as a computer closes itself down, program by program. He was suffering from necrotizing fasciitis, a flesh-eating disease. After several weeks he was flown back to London, and more or less recovered in hospital. But he was left horribly weakened so that when he contracted lung cancer, it ripped through his body like the Wehrmacht – an image he would have found satisfying, for the last war was the touchstone and origin for much of his humour. Coming into an empty radio studio where I had earlier left a briefcase, he said, 'I see von Stauffenberg is here already'; if I wore a leather jacket to *The News Quiz* we would suddenly be in an RAF briefing room in 1943: 'Must be the ball-bearing works at Schwendigen tonight . . .'

He used to chain-smoke during recordings; now and again he would try to give up but failed until the BBC banned smoking anywhere indoors. He knew the risks and talked about them, but of course if it hadn't been for the earlier illness he might have been alive today.

He was buried in Hampstead cemetery, by a liberal rabbi with an upper-class English accent. His great friend Christopher Matthew remembered some of his funniest lines. (The CIA said they wanted their operatives to work for longer before they retired. In response, Alan began an article: 'Bond tensed in the darkness, and reached for his teeth.')

PRIME MINISTERS

8

Prime Ministers

Macmillan to Cameron

It might be unfair to call Harold Macmillan a fraud, but he certainly loved acting a part, usually that of an elderly statesman, long past his prime, dependent on the kindness of others. He played the part while he was still Prime Minister but really only rounded out the character and elaborated the schtick after he had retired. The late Robert McKenzie, the political scholar and broadcaster, would interview him for BBC television at intervals, and Macmillan would affect a weary disdain for all events that had occurred since his time in office. Once McKenzie and the crew arrived a little early at Birch Grove, his home. They walked round the house and, peering in through the library windows, saw Macmillan up a ladder, taking a book from an upper shelf. When the butler showed them into the same room a few minutes later, they found him buried in an armchair, covered in blankets, apparently fast asleep. These sessions, in which the great actor-manager recounted some of his past triumphs and reflected on the inadequacies of those who were treading the boards after him, usually lasted a whole day. McKenzie, the crew and Macmillan himself decided to go to a local pub for lunch. 'Shall we go in Mrs Thatcher?' he asked, before explaining, 'It keeps talking at you, telling you to close the door properly and put your seat-belt on. It's a very bossy car.'

~

Macmillan regarded tweaking Mrs Thatcher as an important part of his job in retirement. At a time when she was in office, and there were five former Prime Ministers still alive (himself, Home, Heath, Wilson and Callaghan) he found himself at a state function with Heath and Callaghan. There were so many of them they could, he suggested, form a government of their own. 'And we wouldn't have any women in it, would we?' he said, to approving chuckles.

~

One time I covered him giving a talk to Young Conservatives. He arrived on stage very slowly, walking with two sticks, as if about to collapse and die. He had a warning for the eager, youthful, glossy faces in front of him: 'The arrows of ambition are plumed with the feathers of death,' he said. Or possibly, 'The arrows of death are plumed with the feathers of ambition.' I don't recall. I have never tracked either quote down, and am still not entirely clear what they might mean. Nor did he explain what he meant at the small session he had afterwards with the press. I would call it a 'briefing' but that implies that there was meaningful information to be passed on briskly. It was more like a gentle amble down memory lane. After he had wearily raised himself to his feet and shuffled gently away, his grandson, who had been looking after him, said that he was really quite sprightly and had only taken the sticks immediately before he walked on stage.

~

Macmillan had a wit drier than a manzanilla sherry. He once asked his friend Lord Carrington about Edmund Muskie, who had been Jimmy Carter's Secretary of State. 'You must remember him,' said Carrington. 'He's the fellow who lost his chance of running for President when he cried in public.'

'Why did he do that?' Macmillan asked.

'Because a newspaper in New Hampshire had accused his wife of being an alcoholic.'

Macmillan thought about this for a while and said, 'What an extraordinary reason for breaking down in tears.'

'I don't know,' said Carrington. 'What would you have done if a newspaper had said that Lady Dorothy was a drunkard?'

'I would have said, "You should have seen her mother," ' said Macmillan.

~

Ted Heath was the Conservatives' chief whip in 1963, when Macmillan fell ill shortly before he was due to speak to the party conference in Blackpool, so turning the conference into a prolonged leadership campaign. Heath had been to visit him in hospital, and in his bluff way had told him that he was looking well. (It was, perhaps, typical of Heath not to realize that there are times when people don't want to be told they're looking well. They wish to know how ghastly they appear.)

'Oh, no,' said Macmillan, 'I have died and returned to life.'

'Come, come, Harold,' said Heath, 'what on earth do you mean by that?' (Or words to that effect; I am relying on Heath's account.)

'I was lying here,' the Prime Minister continued, 'when I became aware that two men had come into the room. I cried out, "Who are you? What do you want?"

'Then one of them said, and his voice sounded as if it came from beyond the grave, "We have come to take away your scrambler." And that was when I knew I had died.'

~

Sir Alec Douglas-Home I met briefly, long after his short premiership (he had, after first renouncing the title of Lord Home to sit in the Commons as Sir Alec, resumed his peerage in order to sit in the Lords. The man changed his name roughly as often as some people change their cars). I cherished one story about him which illustrated his extraordinary diffidence. I have met quite a few shy, nervous politicians, who scamper away from the limelight like woodland creatures scuttling from the flapping of an owl's wings, but none who has made it to the very top. Lord Home, as he was for the second time, was in the first-class carriage of a train going from London to Edinburgh. A colleague of mine was sitting in the same compartment. Two middle-aged women walked past, looked in, did a double-take, walked further up the train, then returned and gingerly opened the door.

'Excuse me, but are you Sir Alec Douglas-Home?' one of the women asked.

He said that he was. The woman said that it was wonderful to meet him.

'We always say it was a great tragedy for this country that you were never Prime Minister.'

He smiled that curious smile, half-courteous amiability, half death's-head, and replied with great civility, 'As a matter of fact I was. But only for a very short time.'

He had that extraordinary toff's ability to express himself in such a way as made it perfectly clear what he thought without actually saying it. For example, after he left the Commons his seat was taken over by Sir Nicholas Fairbairn, one of the most extraordinary Tories ever to sit in Westminster. It was a surprise to many that Sir Nicholas was chosen as Sir Alec's successor. During the election, Sir Alec did the decent thing and helped the Conservative cause. The chap who was driving him was in some embarrassment as he found a convoluted way to express his own disapproval of Sir Nicholas. There was a long pause, broken when Sir Alec said, 'Yes. I heard that he campaigned in Crieff wearing lilac gloves.'

Fairbairn was a toper, and used to keep a hollow ebony cane with a silver, screw-on cap, which he kept filled with whisky. In those more innocent days he was permitted to take this on board the Edinburgh-to-London shuttle plane, to refresh his morning coffee. He also made his own clothes, including tartan trews, which he wore to debates.

Some years ago the Liberal Democrats were mounting a campaign against something they called 'secondary drinking'. I asked Ming Campbell, one of their front-bench spokesmen, what this might mean, and he told me a story about a court case in which he and Fairbairn – both advocates, or Scottish barristers – had been briefed to defend a man who had gone into a crowded Glasgow pub and fired two shotgun cartridges into the drinkers. It was an open-and-shut case, but they went for a few drinks to discuss it, then had some more drinks over a lavish lunch. They worked out the best defence they could, and took a taxi to the prison to meet their client.

After they had outlined the defence, such as it was, they asked if he had any questions.

'Aye,' he said. 'Sir Nicholas, would ye mind breathing on me again?'

~

Harold Wilson came to power two years after the Beatles' first hit. Sir Alec had succeeded almost exactly a year after 'Love Me Do' arrived, and when 'She Loves You' was still high in the charts. It is almost inconceivable that Sir Alec would have met the Fab Four, as they were known – to headline writers at least – as Wilson did, nor famously award them MBEs. The notion that rock singers (or pop artists as they were called) might appear on TV's *Question Time* or be invited to address party conferences to give their views on poverty, or the environment, as they routinely do now, would have been quite unimaginable then.

~

There were two Ted Heaths, the good Ted and the bad Ted. It was pure chance which you got. The late William van Straubenzee MP lived not far from him, and had been invited to his splendid home in Salisbury Cathedral Close on several occasions. 'I feel I ought to invite him back, but I'd be afraid of inflicting the bad Ted on the other guests,' he said.

Once he decided to take the risk and did have him to Sunday lunch. It was a semi-formal occasion, the men in jacket and tie, but Heath turned up in a Miami Dolphins turquoise and lime-green sweatshirt. He was a great fan of American football, and rarely missed a Super Bowl. This is one of those facts that you assume has been invented as a joke, but it hasn't.

~

Heath could be breathtakingly rude, in a fashion that did him great harm. For instance, John Nott – later defence secretary during the Falklands War – was number two at the Treasury during Heath's time in office. He was worried about signs that indicated that inflation was about to rise sharply, so he bearded Heath in the Members' Lobby and asked if he could see him for a word.

'If you want to resign,' Heath barked, 'put it in writing.'

Heath's friends, and they existed, said it was a joke, but Nott was deeply offended. In such a way did Heath let his support trickle away like water spilling onto sand.

~

Heath had got his first party appointment during the 1945 parliament. Sir Walter Bromley-Davenport was a Tory whip at the time, and had a brusque, no-nonsense approach to his job. Seeing a Conservative MP leaving the Commons when a vote was imminent on a three-line whip, he ordered him to stay. The man refused. So Bromley-Davenport kicked him, hard. Unfortunately he was not a Tory MP but the Belgian ambassador. Bromley-Davenport was obliged to resign, allowed to leave on the pretence that he needed to nurse his – solid Tory – constituency. Heath, whose own majority was actually lower than the communist vote, replaced him.

~

I saw the good Ted during 1974. At eve of poll in the second election he was supposed to go canvassing in his Bexley-Sidcup constituency. (The journalists covering him had eaten at a splendidly named restaurant, the Maharajah of Bexley.) He had clearly given up any hope of winning, and instead chatted to a couple of us in a pub, while people played darts nearby. He told us a story about negotiating with the then Irish Prime Minister, Jack Lynch, at Chequers, our Prime Minister's country home. It was the first meeting between the leaders of the two countries since the partition of Ireland. The talks had gone badly, and just as they were about to retire for the night, a civil servant whispered to Heath that they had laid in a case of Paddy, Lynch's favourite whiskey. This was brought out and instantly the mood changed. Everyone went to bed in a much better frame of mind. Next morning the talks resumed. Heath asked jovially if the Irish team would like some more of the Paddy, and to his astonishment they said yes. The talks had gone swimmingly after that.

Not long after this agreeable session we'd had in the pub with Heath – he happily bought his own round, which not all politicians do – he made a remarkable extempore speech in the Commons. Bumping into him at a reception, I said how effective it had been. He turned on me a look of sour distaste.

'I expect you'll find something unpleasant to say about it,' he remarked, before turning on his heel. At least Dr Jekyll had to drink a potion to become Mr Hyde; with Heath it seemed the result of some internal chemical process.

~

He always disliked Margaret Thatcher, and greatly regretted having to keep her in his Cabinet. (Those were the days in which some MPs were thought too weighty and significant to be left out; Thatcher herself changed all that with the mass sackings of people she called 'wets'. This came to mean liberal or left-wing, at least in Tory terms; in fact she meant originally those who always saw insuperable difficulties, with, say, the trade unions. Like most insults it became a badge of honour for those at whom it was aimed, like 'The Old Contemptibles', or, these days, 'queers'. Of Sir Ian Gilmour it was once said as high praise: 'He is so wet you could shoot snipe off him.')

After she had, to his horror, replaced him as leader of the Conservative Party and later as Prime Minister, Heath never missed a chance to make his loathing plain. When in 1990 she was forced to resign, he was quoted as saying, 'Rejoice, rejoice!' A reporter asked him if it was true that he had said this. 'No,' he replied gravely, 'what I said was, "Rejoice, rejoice, rejoice!" '

~

It was his practice to give a dinner for the more serious type of political correspondent every year at the Tory conference. Once he was holding court in Brighton, and the reporters had bought, as a jokey present, a chocolate model of Margaret Thatcher they had found in a seafront confectioner's. They placed it on the table in front of him, and with a big, satisfied grin, he picked up a knife and smashed it to pieces.

As Heath grew older he tended to fall asleep, without warning, in the middle of meals. At one of them he was recounting, at interminable length, an almost verbatim account of a meeting he had held with Fidel Castro in Cuba. Castro, a tyrant at home, had a tremendous gift for charming world leaders, who frequently came away thinking that someone so affable and hospitable must be a fine fellow, grossly traduced by the Americans.

On and on Heath's disquisition went, being almost as long as one of Castro's speeches. Suddenly he fell fast asleep. The startled guests didn't disturb him, and after a while began chatting among themselves. Then, with no more warning, he woke up and immediately resumed his account of Castro's conversation – from precisely the point at which he had fallen asleep.

~

Heath had, like all Prime Ministers, ended up in the bunker. Not the Führerbunker, of course, with which Number 10 is often compared, but there are slight similarities. Problems come not in single spies, but in battalions. You are surrounded by the only people who are desperate for you to succeed. Even many of your party colleagues are simply waiting either their own turn, or for the success of someone they support and from whom they expect sponsorship. Opposition is confined to the press, who can be largely dismissed as *parti pris*, or the formalized engagements of Prime Minister's Question Time, or on occasion a noisy crowd glimpsed outside the airport perimeter fence. In Number 10 your staff are not yes-men, but facilitators, the people whose job it is to say, 'Yes, I can see how we can manage that . . .'

In this airtight world, the trivial distractions of the A303 dualling or the inadequate medical care given to some MP's constituent can seem annoyingly trivial when you are embarked on the grand plan for a new high-speed railway, or yet another overarching reform of the NHS. Foreign events loom even larger.

At European or G20 summits everyone behaves with formalized courtesy. When the world banking system is being debated, few people can be troubled by the closure of a primary school hundreds of miles away. Inside and outside the laager, the rest of the country comes to be seen as a tedious irrelevance. Faced with a peeved backbencher, who would not rather take a call from Obama, or Sarkozy, or Merkel? In 1979 Jim Callaghan came back from Guadeloupe, to meet reporters pestering him about the multitudinous crises in the UK. He said that at the summit meeting he had seen no signs of mounting crisis. This created the headline, 'Crisis? What Crisis?' that did as much as anything to lose him the election later that year. He had forgotten the crucial facts that elude almost all Prime Ministers: foreign leaders do not have a vote in British elections, and British voters do not care two hoots what they think.

~

Margaret Thatcher was, in the end, no different. But she was lucky to have Bernard Ingham as her press officer. Being Margaret Thatcher was a very demanding, twenty-four-hour-a-day job. Nobody could possibly keep up the pace for seven days a week. So she had this male clone who could actually be her when she was too busy or too tired. Most of the time he did the job very well. He knew what she thought without having to consult her. Doctors threatening a strike? Ha, they would soon learn just how intransigent she could be. Wets in the Cabinet threatening a revolt? Let them.

Sometimes it went wrong. On one occasion, knowing her belief in the infallibility of the markets, he declared off the top of his head that she was indifferent to whether the pound fell to below parity with the dollar. This naturally caused a run on the pound, since speculators assumed that Britain would not defend the currency. The papers were full of suggestions that Bernard would have to be sacked. Of course not. Thatcher was perfectly capable, like most politicians, of simultaneously believing and not believing the same thing. She was convinced that the pound should find its natural level. She also believed that it should not fall to an unsustainable rate. In either event, Bernard was safe. She might as easily have sacked herself for making the wrong judgement call. A few days later she attended the annual party given by lobby journalists for the Prime Minister of the day. She towed Bernard around with her like a big loyal dog. 'Have you met Bernard?' she kept asking. 'Bernard is *marvellous*!' The fact that everybody present met Bernard on almost every weekday seemed to have passed her by.

~

I have always rubbed along with Bernard, at least on the rare occasions that we meet these days. There is a sort of unspoken fraternity of people who have worked for the *Guardian*, and for a long time he was one of the paper's Yorkshire correspondents. He was originally a Labour supporter, and famously once stood as Labour candidate for his local council. He was always a loyalist. On one occasion Harry Whewell, the *Guardian* northern news editor, visited him and his boss, Michael Parkin, in Leeds. They went to a pub where, according to Harry, Bernard spoke so vehemently against Labour supporters who did not give their backing to Hugh Gaitskell that his false teeth flew out of his mouth and across the bar. Later Bernard specialized in industrial relations and was disappointed – perhaps somewhat embittered – when the top job in the field went to Peter Jenkins, a man whose expertise and expenses were both sources for his colleagues of mingled admiration, envy and resentment.

(The paper has always had a deeply frugal side, and Alastair Hetherington, then editor, found Jenkins's bills for entertainment particularly hard to stomach. He asked him to trim them.

A day or so later Jenkins lunched the German ambassador. As the meal ended, it was pouring with rain outside, and the ambassador offered the use of his car to take him back to work after it had dropped the envoy at the embassy. As Jenkins was whisked down the Embankment, alone in the back of the vast ambassadorial Mercedes, he spotted Hetherington walking through the rain and asked the driver to pull up. As the editor climbed in he expostulated that this time Jenkins had really gone too far . . . But then Peter always believed that nothing was too good for the workers, or at least for the man whose job it was to write about the workers. I recall him asking me, a trainee, how he could get to Liverpool from Manchester. I told him which station to go to, and how frequent the trains were, but he brushed all that aside. He needed a taxi. He certainly couldn't be bothered with finding stations.

He was, on the other hand, very kind to young persons, and gave me much valuable help. The last time I saw him he had joined the *Independent* and was lunching alone at a French bistro in Battersea. It was a Thursday and he had all the day's papers, plus the two main political weeklies. As he worked his way through these he drank a gin and tonic, then ate a three-course meal washed down with a bottle of claret, topped off with a cognac. If that was how he treated himself, I thought, what feasts must have been laid before his contacts, who included many of the most powerful in the land.)

~

Bernard Ingham decided that Jenkins's preferment marked the end of his own time in journalism, and he left to join the civil service as a press officer. In the mid-1970s he worked for Tony Benn, who was energy secretary, and had made a puzzling speech. I couldn't work out what hidden meaning it contained, and phoned Bernard at the Department of Energy. He said he could tell me what it all signified, but he would have to kill me if I ever let on who had passed on the information. Or at least he would want to kill me. He made me swear that I would never, ever reveal him as the source. Would I give my most solemn word? I did. He had, he stressed, a wife and child to support. If he were named as the person who had passed on these astounding tidings, he would be thrown out of his job immediately. Thrilled beyond measure at the prospect of a world-shattering exclusive, I made every pledge he demanded. (Later events, I decided, made this promise unnecessary and so inoperative.)

'The reason that the Secretary of State made this speech,' he began, before demanding yet more vows of secrecy, 'is that the Secretary of State is stark, staring mad.'

The revelation didn't make the paper.

~

Bernard was at his finest during the Falklands War of 1982. In the afterglow of victory we tend to forget that many people were alarmed by Margaret Thatcher's decision to go to war. It seemed a remarkably risky venture for what seemed then a modest reward. She, however, had no doubts. The Argentine invasion was an outrage, and for Britain to tolerate it, or even accept it as a basis for negotiation, would be a source of continuing national shame. When, seven days after the invasion, Bernard held his usual court for the Sunday papers in the bow-fronted press secretary's room on the ground floor of Number 10, you could almost see the salt spray on his face as he – in spirit at least – sailed through the Atlantic with the task force. Many of my colleagues from the various Sundays seemed swathed in the Union Jack themselves, their job to rally to the colours as vigorously as any soldier receiving his call-up papers. In particular the man from the *Sunday Express* appeared to regard himself as a key part of the propaganda war. I asked if the Prime Minister was aware that quite a few of her Conservative colleagues had serious doubts about the enterprise. 'So!' said Bernard. 'It's come to this. She really is the only man amongst the lot of them!'

The man from the *Sunday Express* then asked if the Prime Minister had seen the 'disgusting' propaganda pictures of General Galtieri on the Falklands – '*eating* a penguin!'.

At this point Michael Jones of the *Sunday Times*, who had had a good lunch, and if not asleep was giving a fairly convincing portrayal of someone who was, stirred himself and remarked, 'Nothing wrong with that. Fellow probably likes a chocolate biscuit with his morning coffee.'

Not the most Wildean shaft ever made, of course, but perfect for puncturing the pompous, militaristic mood.

~

(Mike Jones had a gift for deflation. He was once nobbled at a reception by Lord Gladwyn, a Europhile of deeply held and persistent views. For some reason, Gladwyn addressed him with great passion in German, a language that Jones did not speak or understand. Jones reported: 'After about twenty minutes he said something that was obviously a question, so I said, in English, "I don't know, I think you just go to the bar and help yourself." ' Apparently Gladwyn looked furious and turned on his heel.)

~

Like many people held in the grip of their own convictions, Thatcher had trouble understanding the thoughts and words of others. She was, and no doubt is, a kindly woman. Staff were always pleased when she remembered their birthdays, even more when she remembered their children's birthdays. She could be tolerant of other people's way of living, even when she did not understand or sympathize with it. However, if she had a sense of humour, it was well hidden. There are many stories about this. When the Liberals adopted a sort of stylized yellow bird as their logo, one of her speechwriters produced a passage based on *Monty Python*'s parrot sketch – 'this parrot is no more, it has shuffled off this mortal coil and gone to join the choir invisible . . .' She had to be persuaded that the lines were funny, and would be recognized by the audience. She had one other concern: 'This Monty Python, is he one of us?'

Peter Jay, the son-in-law of the then Prime Minister Jim Callaghan, had said that Callaghan saw himself as Moses, leading his people after long travails into the promised land. It was a silly thing to say, and Thatcher's people seized on it. They wrote a line for her party conference speech: 'My message to Moses is, "keep taking the tablets".' But she didn't get the joke and tried to change it to 'keep taking the pills'. Only after it was carefully explained to her did she agree to the proper version.

~

She was none the less the source of much unwitting humour. Just as, in an early silent movie, when you see a man up a ladder with a pot of paint, you know with near certainty that the star is going to walk under the ladder at exactly the wrong moment, so with Thatcher. When a double entendre appeared in the offing, you felt she was certain to utter it. However she never reached the heights attained by the mistress of the ill-judged phrase, Dame Irene Ward, who had been Tory MP for Gateshead, and made it her business to defend the interests of our fighting men and women, mostly the women. She kept nagging successive defence ministers about delays in providing new uniforms for Wrens. The minister finally replied that these would follow once male sailors had got their replacement uniforms. 'Is the minister saying,' Dame Irene boomed, 'that Wrens' skirts must be held up until all ratings have been satisfied?'

I recall Thatcher being asked in the Commons about pacifists handing out leaflets outside an army barracks. 'I'm sure soldiers will know exactly what they can do with those leaflets!' she said, to outright laughter from the Labour side and surreptitious giggles from the Tories.

At a training centre in Putney she was introduced to an extremely large youth who was, as it happens, black. He was working with a giant wrench. 'Goodness,' she said, 'I've never seen a tool as big as that!'

Best of all Thatcher saved for her victory tour of the Falkland Islands. She was taken to inspect a large field gun, basically a ride-on lawnmower with a barrel several feet long. It was on a bluff, overlooking a plain on which another Argentine invasion might one day materialize. She admired the weapon, and the soldier manning it asked if she would like to fire a round.

'But mightn't it jerk me off?' she replied.

Chris Moncrieff of the Press Association, who was covering the visit, recorded the manful struggle of the soldier to keep his face, indeed his whole body, straight.

~

If Gladstone addressed Queen Victoria as if she were a public meeting, Thatcher tended to speak to people as if they were members of her Cabinet. I ran into a BBC reporter in the early days of her regime. He had just filmed an interview with her. She'd learned from him that his next assignment was to cover an OPEC meeting. 'If you want to help the British economy,' she told him sternly, 'persuade them not to put up the price of oil!'

The reporter looked fazed by this instruction, though not his Cockney cameraman, who said cheerily, 'Orright, darlin', I'll do my best!'

~

On one of her walkabouts, she met a young woman wearing an orange sweater. 'Do you know,' she said to the baffled girl, with every appearance of great interest, 'the curtains on our bus are exactly that colour!'

~

Every year at Christmas the House of Commons press gallery holds a party for reporters' children, and they generally also invite a few dozen deprived children from the Westminster area. Quite often a senior politician turns up to cast their lustre upon the occasion. This time Margaret Thatcher had come. I know the story to be true, because I had it from Father Christmas, or at least the reporter playing the part. Mrs Thatcher was in a relaxed mood, smiled and chatted to the children, and even those who knew who she was and felt rather awed were put at their ease.

Everybody seemed happy except one small boy, who was crying into his bowl of dessert. As the Prime Minister passed he looked up and said, 'Miss, Miss! They've given me blancmange and I don't like blancmange.'

'That,' she said, smiling sweetly, 'is what parties are all about: eating food you don't like!'

I felt at the time that this told us a lot about her style of government.

~

(My colleague Terry Kilmartin, the literary editor of the *Observer*, lived with his family next door to the Thatchers in Flood Street. They often heard the family in the garden. She was unnervingly calm. Once they heard her say, as if admonishing her son to clean his teeth properly, 'Now don't poke Carol in the face with that stick, Mark, because she won't grow up to be a pretty little girl.'

One time the Kilmartin children were invited round to share the twins' joint birthday party. Mrs Thatcher had personally made and iced a cake, a scale model of Windsor Castle.)

~

This failure to sense other people's mood and concerns extended to the royal family. Every summer she had to go to the traditional weekend at Balmoral. This is a source of some embarrassment and social difficulty for Prime Ministers and their wives, and presumably for the royals as well. Cherie Blair memorably described in her book how she hadn't realized that servants unpack the guests' suitcases, and so had found her contraceptive equipment. The royals' visit to Balmoral is relaxed – just them, a few close friends, monuments to their ancestors, and around ten million midges. Every year they have the traditional outdoor barbecue, and afterwards the Queen goes to a little hut to wash up. It is the one time in the year that she washes up, and so has much the same importance as opening the Christmas presents does for a small child. But Thatcher could never believe that anyone could do any job better than she did herself, whether governing the country or doing the chores. Why, it was the images of herself in Marigolds, washing up at home, that secured her image as a housewife and mother and helped to win her the Tory leadership in 1975. My informant said that she insisted on doing the washing-up. The Queen overruled her. She insisted again. The Queen, inevitably, won, but the interesting fact is that Thatcher thought she was offering to do her a favour, and did not realize she was proposing to deprive her monarch of one rare and valued contact with the real world, as lived by her subjects.

~

Thatcher could be charming when she had the time. At a formal dinner at Chequers a Wren who was one of the waitresses tripped and spilled lamb casserole into Geoffrey Howe's lap. Mrs

Thatcher was on her feet instantly, rushing round to comfort not the Chancellor of the Exchequer but the serving girl, hugging her and saying, 'Don't worry, my dear, it could happen to anyone.'

~

Mrs Thatcher had to be in control. All the time. Towards the end of his spell in office, Jim Callaghan recorded that at their occasional private meetings, she used to wag her finger at him. 'And I'm the Prime Minister!' he said wonderingly. For Neil Kinnock she had a degree of (in my view, unjustified) contempt. He certainly loathed what she was doing to the country, so their private meetings were fraught. He described one. 'She cannot ever give way, on anything,' he said. 'I arrived in her office once and she said, "I expect you'd like a cup of coffee."

'I said no, I'd just had one, and didn't want another.

'But she insisted. "You *must* have some coffee!"

'Again, I told her I didn't want any, but that didn't stop her summoning a secretary and instructing her to bring me a cup of coffee.'

~

Yet there was the odd softer side. Mike Elliott, now the European editor of *Time* magazine, used to work for her as an adviser. He had presented a policy paper. She tore it to pieces, raging about how second-rate it was, how hopelessly unfit for the task, until Mike simply wished for the floor to open beneath him, or for armed paratroopers to seize him and lead him to safety. After she had finished her harangue, she smiled sweetly, clasped his hands in hers, and said, 'You must *never* let me do that to you again.'

~

Not everyone was so lucky. As her power and authority seemed more assured, she felt it unnecessary to spare the feelings of those she did not need. The instances of chilliness, sometimes outright rudeness, became more frequent. One Tory MP I knew and liked decided to try to win her favour by complimenting her on her appearance. She generally liked that, especially from younger men.

'Prime Minister, you look ravishing,' he essayed.

'And when do I not?' she barked, walking briskly away.

Almost every Cabinet minister was insulted in one way or another. It was Geoffrey Howe who proved to be the worm that turned. Thatcher's constant, casual rudeness, the way she ignored him at meetings, all combined to create in him a tremendous fur-ball of resentment which he finally coughed up. His resignation speech in the autumn of 1990 marked the beginning of her swift defenestration. But if that was the proximate cause, things had been set in train by her then Chancellor, Nigel Lawson, who also found he could not tolerate her offensive and supercilious behaviour.

People often tell you that politics is about policies, or values, not about personalities. They are wrong.

~

She once met Barry Took (q.v.) who was no Thatcherite. But she had been told that he wrote comedy, so she explained that she needed some humour in her speeches. 'Now I want you to write two hundred funny things for me to say, and send them to me,' she told him.

~

Denis Thatcher was a man who believed in loyalty, at all times and in all circumstances. It became fashionable – it still is – for political leaders to hold press conferences with a claque at the back of the room. Their job is to demonstrate wild enthusiasm for what the leader says. This doesn't fool the media, of course, but it does sound better on television and radio. So she would make some perfectly workaday remark, and while the press wrote it down in a dutiful kind of way, a loud burst of applause and 'hear hears!' would come from Denis. Those who knew them best say that this loyalty had the effect of bolstering whatever mood she happened to be in. If, say, she was upset with one of her ministers, he would make her more upset. If she was determined to pursue some ill-advised policy, he would make her more determined.

Unlike her, he had a sharp eye for a refill. (She didn't do refills. A friend of mine, the late Douglas Johnson, a great expert on modern French history, was once summoned to Chequers as part of a group who were to brief her on recent events in France and interpret what they meant for British policy and interests. At around eleven or so in the morning, coffee was brought in. She however had a large tumbler, filled to the brim with whisky. The assembled academics were astonished, though she sipped it very slowly for the rest of the morning, and didn't finish the last drops until the end of lunch.)

~

Her staff became very careful about Denis. On her many tours abroad he would sometimes go down to the back of the plane where he could hope for a chat and something to drink. Unfortunately he tended to say exactly what he thought, often complaining about the country they had just visited. 'Canada,' he once remarked, 'is full of fuck all.' Another time he was asked what he had made of China. He thought for a moment, then averred, 'China is full of fuck all.'

One morning he and his wife were flying to Scotland. The flight attendant asked what he would like to drink, and he said firmly, 'A gin and tonic.'

'Isn't it a bit early for a gin and tonic?' Mrs Thatcher enquired.

'It is never too early for a gin and tonic,' he said.

Discretion sometimes won. Jim Naughtie of the *Today* programme recalls chatting to Denis on the landing at Downing Street during a reception, standing next to a large potted plant. Denis was drinking gin and tonic. One of the Prime Minister's detectives approached him and whispered, 'The Boss is here, sir.' Denis deftly poured his drink into the plant pot, then reached out to embrace his wife.

~

I had lunch with Tony Blair in 1992, when he was still home affairs spokesman for the Labour Party. I worked for the *Observer* at that point. He kept asking me what I thought about various matters, Labour policies, John Major's policies, everything. I'd ask him his opinion, and he would match by asking me mine.

After a while I wanted to yell at him, 'Look, the *Observer* is paying for this lunch because they want to know what you think. What I think, they already know because they pay me to tell them.' But I didn't.

Was it a form of flattery? Did he think I would go away and boast, 'I believe, and I can tell you that Tony Blair agrees with me . . .'? Perhaps it was simply a way of avoiding the question, a means of not committing himself to anything that might prove embarrassing later. Possibly a bit of both. But later I saw an interview with Sir Christopher Meyer, who used to be our ambassador in Washington. He was asked why Blair, who had got on so well with Bill Clinton, got on equally well with George W. Bush, and he replied that Blair was rather like a radio, searching for a signal, then suddenly locking on to it. Once he identified the signal Bush was sending out, he knew exactly what to say. On a far lower level he had wanted to find a signal from me, a potentially helpful journalist.

~

In 2003 I had gone to MC a charity dinner in Salisbury, held in a marquee in the Cathedral Close. It had been organized by a couple, former neighbours of ours, whose son had a rare form of blood cancer. They were the kind of people who could not passively accept such a circumstance, and wanted to do more for their boy than ferry him to and from Great Ormond Street Hospital, so they had decided on a huge event, shortly before Christmas, to raise money for children's cancer charities. The marquee was actually two tents stitched together, they had booked the choir of Salisbury Cathedral, and there were two auctions (on occasions such as this it is vital to offer as much cheap or free booze as possible, since a combination of liquor and vanity will make people pay extraordinary sums for items for which they might not normally want to pay the regular retail price).

I thought it was odd that we were searched by armed police officers when we arrived – this is not common at cathedrals – and then we saw the table plan which indicated that we were to sit with the Prime Minister and his wife, who, it turned out, were acquaintances of the organizers and had spent time with them at neighbouring houses in southern France. Somewhat to my relief Tony Blair, no doubt deciding he would be more relaxed if he didn't need to worry about having a journalist at his table, sat at the next one over.

His wife, however, seemed to relish the challenge. Every now and then I had to bob up and introduce the next speaker, or an auctioneer, or the choir, then return to the table and resume eating. In conversation I said that I had been looking at the silent auction. The first lot was from a hospital in Salisbury, which had offered 'mammogram or vasectomy – choice of one only, please'. I tried a small joke: 'I hope I don't win that one; I wouldn't know which to pick.'

Mrs Blair gave me a stern look. 'Men can get breast cancer, too,' she said. 'There are three hundred cases a year in this country.'

'I know,' I fibbed. 'I feel my breast in the shower every morning. But that's only to make sure I still have a heart.'

'Of course, you don't,' she said tartly. 'You're a journalist.' Then, to the rest of the table, '*Guardian* journalists are the worst. And *Guardian* sketchwriters are the worst of all.'

I thought it was going to be a long evening. So I introduced the Dean of Salisbury, and resumed my meal thoughtfully. Conversation turned to teenagers. Euan Blair had recently been found, drunk, lying on his face in Leicester Square. I said that our children were coming up to the same age as their two eldest, and we were beginning to cope with some of the same problems. Her face expressed distaste and disbelief. '*You* have children?' she asked, as if appalled that such a ghastly person could propagate the species.

At this point, something in me snapped and I said, 'Oh, stop it!'

She looked startled for a moment, then a broad smile appeared. Cherie had a very broad smile. Then she took up her cracker and handed me one end to pull with her. After that she could scarcely have been more charming.

This was not a naturally Labour crowd, but Cherie made a short speech about the cause which entirely won them over.

After the dinner, her husband, with guitar, joined a pick-up group with friends who had played together a few times. He looked happy and relaxed. It was the end of the year of the Iraq invasion, and to have nothing more to worry about than the next chord in 'The Midnight Hour' must have been an hour of blissful relief. Someone standing next to me said, 'I saw them in France. But they won't play "Summertime Blues" this time. It's got that line, "Gonna take my problem to the U-nited Nations".'

A day or so later I told the story to a colleague who knew Cherie Blair much better than I did. 'It's a Scouse thing,' he said.

'They go on challenging you. If you just get all huffy, they look down on you. But if you tell 'em where to get off, they like that.'

~

It is easy to depict Tony Blair as a liar. The important thing to remember is that he is a faithful and practising Christian, specifically a Roman Catholic. In the absence of empirical evidence, belief in the Church's tenets requires an act of faith, a sense that what you *feel* to be true is more important than what is demonstrably true. Blair also believes, and has said so, that he will be answerable to God when his life ends. I suspect that he sees God as an authority figure, not unlike a bank manager, who will tot up the pros and cons of his life, the good deeds and the wicked ones, and reach a conclusion. This is why his gut instinct to help invade Iraq overruled any number of weapons inspectors coming back with their negative reports, their facts and their figures. One million people, or however many there were, marching against the war was not an irrelevance, but it set up a choice between what they demanded and what his heart told him God wanted. He could imagine the conversation that might have ensued at the pearly gates. 'Are you seriously telling me that you let yourself be swayed by these demonstrators, when you knew what *I* wanted?' God would say in his sternest, most Godlike voice.

When Blair explained the invasion by saying, 'I believed it was the right thing to do,' he wasn't implying, as the rest of us would, 'but I could have been wrong,' as in: 'I put our life savings on Space Hopper in the 3.20 because I believed it would win.' Belief always trumps objective facts in Blair's mind. This is why the various enquiries into the Iraq war – Hutton, Chilcot and the rest – have failed to faze him at all.

Do I know this is true? Pretty much. You can gather it all by going through his quoted statements on Iraq, and on many other topics. His celebrated conference line, 'at our best when we are boldest' means, deconstructed, that when you *know* what has to be done, you should always do it, and ignore the doubts and caveats from your colleagues, the voters, or the people who will be affected – 'stakeholders' in the tedious modern jargon. Margaret Thatcher by contrast knew when to back down, at least she did right until the end, when the poll tax destroyed her.

~

Blair also had – as I learned during my first chat with him – an ability to sense very quickly what other people wanted to hear, and where possible he would provide it for them. This could have worrisome results. Foreign Office diplomats would prep him for, say, the visit of the President of Filthistan. They would tell him that Britain wanted to pay no more than £500 a tonne for Filthistan's radioactive sludge, or whatever. Then the President would emerge from Number 10, smiling merrily, and it would turn out that Blair had offered £550 a tonne. He could hardly bear to tell people what they didn't want to hear.

~

The most painful example came after the death of the Labour leader John Smith, when the Labour Party mourned in public and plotted frantically in private. It soon became clear that Blair was overwhelmingly the most popular candidate. His old friend Gordon Brown, however, had always been the senior partner in their relationship, being intellectually better equipped than Blair, and with far more experience and knowledge of the Labour Party. It had usually been assumed by them, and by those who knew them, that in the fullness of time, probably after Smith had been Prime Minister, Brown would inherit the leadership and Blair would follow.

When Smith died, what Blair should have said to Brown was, 'Look, I think I can win this and become Prime Minister after the next election. If you want to run too, that's fine.' Brown would either have not run at all, or, if he had, lost humiliatingly. This would have left Blair unchallenged in his position. But Blair couldn't bring himself to say it. Instead, either at the celebrated meal in the Granita restaurant, or in other conversations, he told Brown what Brown wanted to know – that after being Prime Minister for a spell he would step down in his favour. Brown heard: 'I will let you have the job before the end of a second term.' Blair meant: 'I will step down at some point, but only when I'm good and ready.'

~

Brown found himself in the position of the eldest son of a duke. The old man dies, and the family solicitor pays him a visit. 'I know you expected to inherit the title, the house, the land and the money. But the family have had a conference and we've decided that your younger brother looks better on television. So he's getting it all. But he will let you have it, some time in the future, when he feels like it.'

Few people could recover from such a humiliation. And Brown, like many people who can treat people brutally, has a very thin skin himself.

~

I found myself chatting to him at a reception in Downing Street. I had recently had an emergency eye operation, of the kind that makes people's knees buckle if you provide too detailed a description. I knew he had had a similar operation after his rugby accident at school, so I asked him about it. He was clearly quite proud of the fact that he had had the first laser operation on a detached retina ever performed in Britain and talked about it at some length. As a fellow sufferer I was fascinated, though I think anyone else overhearing would have disappeared, sharpish.

I asked him if he had had any further trouble with the eye.

'I've had no complaints,' he said cheerily.

'That's very encouraging,' I replied.

'In that case, will you write something nice about me for a change?' he said.

I thought it was very uncool for a Prime Minister to admit to reading critical articles, and even less cool to complain about them. The correct pose is to be standing aloof and above any such trivia. Thatcher and Blair never admitted to reading a newspaper, and in fact probably didn't. They had people to do it for them.

~

But Brown also lacks a certain *simpatico*, which is not the same as being unsympathetic – it merely suggests that he sometimes finds it hard to understand what's going on in people's minds.

The first press conference he gave in 2007, shortly after he became Prime Minister, came at the height of severe flooding in the West Midlands. He had flown out by helicopter to inspect the damage and see the rescue work. 'I would like to pay tribute to the wonderful work being done by the emergency services,' he said, which is fine, except that it sounds stilted and formulaic. Tony Blair would have found a fireman who had been working for forty-eight hours without sleep, and was just about to go home when a little girl had asked him to rescue her kitten from a rooftop. The tabloids would have lined up the fireman, the girl and the cat within half an hour and it would have been plastered all over the paper. As with 'the people's princess' on the day Princess Di was killed, Blair would have found, or been provided with, a phrase or an image that summed up the national mood.

When Brown met a member of the public facing a difficulty, he would say something like: 'We have recently launched a tripartite initiative designed to address this problem.' By contrast, a more well-tuned politician will, first, say what an awful problem it is and how deeply he feels for the sufferer. He will then scribble something on a bit of paper, which he passes to an aide. (It might say, 'Bloody hell, do these idiots think I am some kind of genius who can solve all their problems?' but that wouldn't matter.) He then should say, 'We have started to tackle the problem, which so many people experience, but clearly we haven't got it right yet. I'm going to ask for a full investigation into what's gone wrong in your case.' He may not mean it, and the problem might be forgotten the moment the bullet-proof limo leaves. But no damage would have been done, on screen at least.

~

Yet paradoxically the public did not seem to mind Brown's grumpiness. A book published early in 2010 purported to describe his foul temper. Pundits explained that this would be hugely damaging to Brown's chances in the coming election. In fact his poll figures nudged slightly upwards. When he made offensive remarks about Mrs Gillian Duffy in Rochdale, it was deemed that he had destroyed any chance he had of winning the election. In the event, Labour won Rochdale from the Liberal Democrats. The public clearly took a more realistic view of the pressures on a Prime Minister.

~

And he was never more popular than when he resigned in May 2010. His two boys, John and Fraser, who had been hidden entirely from view to the extent that if their bodies appeared on television their faces were fuzzed out, were suddenly brought before the gaze of the public, which fell in love with them, their cheeky smiles, and their obvious delight at being with their father. Brown has three smiles, starting with the real one, used unconsciously in the way we all do when telling a joke or meeting a friend. Then there is the adoring beatific one, bestowed upon family. And finally the terrible grimace, deployed to accompany a remark containing no humour whatever, with Brown's mouth apparently operated by an incompetent ventriloquist. It was the second of those smiles that appeared on the day he announced his resignation, and you could almost hear people around the country thinking, If I had known he was like that, I might even have voted for him.

~

David Cameron has the faultless courtesy of many Old Etonians. This is combined with a nervous awareness that having been to the school is no longer the same guarantee of social and financial privilege it once was. Many Old Etonians have stories about being treated almost as social pariahs, finding for example that some Oxbridge colleges are actively opposed to admitting them. Like Tony Blair, Cameron seems to have a terror of giving offence. He led the Commons in a round of standing applause when Blair finished Prime Minister's Questions for the last time. This was greatly resented by many older Tories who had suffered Blair for a decade, and saw no reason to break centuries of tradition to applaud him. When Cameron became Prime Minister, he stood outside 10 Downing Street and actually praised the Labour government for making the country more open at home and more compassionate abroad. These phrases mean little, but they evidently expressed some inner Cameronian need to promote warmth and friendship rather than rivalry and mistrust.

He is also remarkably competitive. This is a trivial example, but I have recently asked the questions at an annual charity quiz in Notting Hill, the area of London near his home. I first did this in 2005, shortly before the election. Everyone knew that Labour was likely to win once again, and that Cameron had a good chance of leading the party after Michael Howard had been defeated. Quizzes are usually hard fought, but Cameron, as the captain of his table, was incredibly determined, nagging his team-mates until the very last second to get crucial extra answers. In the end, I had to threaten that anyone who didn't get their reply sheets in within ten seconds would lose all points for that round, adding, 'Ten, nine, eight . . .' While I counted, Cameron flew from his table, barged to the front, and banged the paper down on the desk just as I shouted, 'One!' I reflected then that it was the last time I would ever be able to issue him with orders.

USA

9

USA

Ronald Reagan & Mt St Helens

It's fun being a Brit in America. For the most part, they like us. There is even a residual sense that we are the parent country – a pretty tenuous view now, but still there, like a pentimento on an aged canvas. When my wife had our first baby, she went to earnest classes and was advised of the great importance of natural childbirth. Caring fathers designed computer programs to time their wives' breathing patterns ('ah hah, ah hoo!'). Then reality hit her with its agonizing pain – they say that if women could remember what the experience was like from one child to the next, no one would ever have brothers or sisters – and she asked for a something, anything, to kill the agony.

The anaesthetist was a Filipino, Mr Gonzales, who evidently believed it was part of his job to chat cheerily to the husband, as if he were cutting my hair. 'Where you folks from?' he asked.

'England!' I shouted, for I was actually more worried about the screaming woman on the bed than keeping Mr Gonzales in light conversation.

But a faraway look came into his eyes. 'Ah,' he said, 'the old country!'

It was a touching moment. A faint nostalgia for Britain came with becoming a true American, like a love of the flag, baseball and hot dogs on the Fourth of July.

~

All British people are used to being told, with great courtesy, how much Americans adore your accent. Though if you don't sound like Prince Charles or Hugh Grant, they tend to assume you come from another Anglophone country – usually Australia – or else from Boston, where the inhabitants are thought to have strangulated accents like a British aristocrat might once have had. (I always liked the joke about the Bostonian love of 'scrod', which means baby cod. Go to baseball spring training in Florida to follow the Boston Red Sox, as thousands of people do, and you'll see signs outside cafés and diners declaring, 'Yes! We have scrod!' The joke involves a very grand Bostonian woman getting into a cab in New York and saying, 'Take me somewhere I can get scrod.' The driver replies, 'Lady, I heard it called a lotta things, but never in da pluperfect subjunctive.')

~

The success of British television programmes and British actors means that our accent is much less unfamiliar now, though as any visitor knows we can still be seized by lockjaw when asked 'to say something in that wonderful British accent'. I developed a handy all-purpose defence. Told that someone just loved my accent, I would smile gratefully and say, 'Why, I love yours too!' Sometimes they would grin, but twice people replied, puzzled, 'But I'm American – I don't have an accent.' (British actors sometimes complain that they are always obliged to play the villains in American films and on TV. This is not because Americans are prejudiced against us; it's because the British remain the dominant ethnic group, which makes them painless to stereotype. For years Italians complained about mobster films, Arabs complained about

Middle Eastern heavies. For a spell Hollywood went for southern rednecks – *Deliverance, My Cousin Vinny* – but there were even complaints about them. But there is no Anglo-American anti-defamation league. Yet.)

~

In 1972 I went to America on holiday and found myself with friends in Disneyland, the one in California. No one wanted to join me on the Space Mountain, the rollercoaster where you are hurled upside down in the dark, so I sat alone at the front of the train. Behind me were an upper-class British couple. The electronic American voice from the side of the train squawked something which I interpreted as 'Prepare to launch! Prepare to launch!' and the woman behind me barked, 'Lunch? Lunch? Do they really serve lunch on this thing?'

~

It's a commonplace, but true, that many Americans are not at all familiar with the rest of the world. A friend of mine from Manchester divorced her husband and married an Irish chemical engineer. He took a job with the giant Eli Lilly corporation in Indianapolis. When shopping in their local supermarket the woman at the checkout asked where they were from.

'I'm British, and my husband is from Ireland,' she said.

'Well,' said the assistant graciously, 'you speak real good English for foreigners.'

~

Americans may be the politest people on earth, and are too polite to say what they really think about the British – if they think about us at all, that is. The two main complaints they have is that we have terrible teeth – which compared to them we do – and that we are polite, courteous but distant. This can lead to social difficulty. In the 1970s I was visiting the States at the same time as British friends who had lived in New York until a short while before. They had returned to stay with American friends of theirs who lived on Long Island. I was invited to join them for a couple of days.

One morning we played badminton in the garden. It was a suffocatingly hot day, and when we came in I asked if I might have a cold beer. Our host and hostess exchanged glances. In Britain this might conceivably have implied a slight pushiness on my part; we expect to wait to be asked. But they meant the opposite. Here was some uptight Brit who thought he needed permission to get a *beer*. Probably I would be knocking on their bedroom door at four in the morning, asking to use the bathroom.

On my first night we all went out to dinner, where our hostess treated us to a detailed and grisly description of what she had suffered during the birth of her daughter. It was the kind of thing a British woman might possibly describe to her family and closest friends, but here she was telling me, a near stranger who had not at that stage even spent one night in her house. I vaguely realized that I was expected to respond in kind, with some equally emotional tale – about my brother the drug addict, or my daughter the prostitute. But since nobody in my family was a junkie, and I didn't have a daughter, I felt like the fellow in the pub who, being told it's his round, discovers that he has left his wallet at home and is uncomfortably aware that nobody quite believes him.

One day I went into New York City. I was based in Belfast at the time, and was interested to buy a newspaper published for Irish Americans. It was full of horror stories about the numerous outrages committed by British soldiers and the Royal Ulster Constabulary, without any mention of the bombings and shootings by Republican groups. Or if there were, they were depicted as heroic military actions against the enemy. You would not imagine that any civilians were involved.

I took the paper back to Long Island. Soon afterwards our hostess arrived home with another copy of the same paper which she thought might interest me. Being raised in Britain, I did not mention that I had already bought one, but thanked her warmly for being so kind.

But later, tidying my room, she found the original copy. She descended with quivering lip. There was something I had not told her. Was I so ill at ease in her home that I had not thought to mention that I already had the paper? I was thrown back twenty years to the horrible moment when it turns out that you have unwittingly broken a firm rule in a friend's house and the friend's mother is very cross indeed. As a Brit I could not have spoken the truth for fear of giving offence: 'I must say he was jolly rude, telling me he already had the paper . . .' Instead I had given as much offence by doing the opposite. As the writer Randall Jarrell said, 'To Americans, English manners are far more frightening than none at all.'

~

The incident with the paper was minuscule, but a useful reminder that social custom and practice is a field strewn with mines and mantraps, scattered randomly by a malicious goblin. We tend to assume that the social etiquette that applies in our circles is universal. No doubt there are Inuit who feel that a failure to rub noses is a sign of discourtesy. When Gorbachev came to visit Ronald Reagan for the first time, Reagan's son Ron Jr suggested that they should establish relaxed relations by tossing a football to each other. This is the most basic male-bonding process in the US; for a Soviet leader to arrive and promptly have a piece of wet leather hurled at him would have been disconcerting at best, humiliating at worst.

~

It's like language: we all know that Americans talk about an elevator rather than a lift, about a sidewalk rather than a pavement. But just as French has its faux friends ('*assister*' means not 'help' but 'attend') so does American English. 'Pavement' means roadway as opposed to sidewalk, so signs saying: 'Vehicles – keep to pavement' are baffling to a British newcomer. A 'joint' does not mean a piece of meat for roasting. 'Removal men' don't shift your furniture: they work for undertakers and carry bodies out. It's 'movers' who help you move house. 'Smart' does not imply well-dressed, but intelligent. (Seeing a friend unusually well-dressed I told him he looked 'smart'. 'Not dumb today, then?' he asked.) 'Middle-class' in British usage means 'not poor'; in America it signifies 'not rich'. Watching Barack Obama campaign with labour unions in Philadelphia, I noticed a banner declaring that one union was 'fighting for the middle classes' – not something Bob Crowe, leader of the RMT, would ever claim here.

~

Contrary to our general view of Americans as amiable blabbermouths, many of them are surprisingly taciturn. Maine, for example, is known for its laconic inhabitants. A friend was trying to moor his motorboat against a jetty north of Portland. It was low tide. 'Do I have enough water?' he shouted to a man who was sitting doing very little.

'They's plenty o' water, all right,' said the man, 'it's just spread kinda thin.' He then resumed a comfortable silence.

In Idaho I went on a guided tour with a park ranger to visit the hidden lakes in the Sawtooth Mountain Wilderness. I was the only visitor to turn up, so Ranger Lynn and I set off with just his two sons. It soon became clear why they were the hidden lakes. All his knowledge and his maps failed him. But he said almost nothing, except to point us occasionally to the next pathway. 'Just over this hill, I figure,' he said about an hour in. No lake to be seen. 'Shoot!' said the ranger. Next we crossed another ridge of which he had hopes; it also revealed nothing. 'Son of a gun!' he said, which delighted me, like when you first hear a French person say, 'oh, la la!' – it seems too perfect. Finally we climbed up a bluff behind which the ranger assured us we would see at least one of the lakes. There was a dry crater. In an unusual display of emotion, he removed his hat and banged it on his thigh. 'Well, wouldn't that smoke your hide!' he exclaimed, the longest sentence I had heard from him. We found the lakes, by accident, on the trip back down the mountain.

~

I first went to America in 1956, with my family. Dad had been chosen for a year's exchange programme with the University of Rochester in upstate New York. Thanks in part to politicking back in Hull, where he was a full-time lecturer, he was paid only his British salary, which meant that we lived the middle-class life in America, with difficulty. We travelled on the old *Queen Elizabeth*. It was the last year more people crossed the Atlantic by boat than by plane. The whole experience was so thrilling that no matter what we did in America, for me the entire year was, in part, spent looking forward to the return trip: the on-deck sports, the free films and most of all the food. Rationing took an age to finish in Britain, partly no doubt because it was not in the interests of too many bureaucrats to abolish it and their own jobs with it. Politicians constantly insist that they want to reduce bureaucracy; they then give the task of carrying this out to bureaucrats and wonder why bureaucracy rarely gets reduced.

So for a ten-year-old boy, the ship was a floating paradise. Even in third class you had almost limitless choice for breakfast, bouillon for elevenses, more unlimited choice at lunchtime, a full tea – high tea if you wanted it – then awe-inspiring choice for dinner. I gather there were late-night snacks too, but I was in bed by then, planning what I would have for breakfast the next day. One forgets how enormously food bulks in the mind of a growing boy.

We arrived in New York on a broiling hot August day. The customs shed was a heaving mass of people seemingly being checked by customs officers on a random basis. Dad said that he was pretty sure he saw folded money being exchanged. After waiting a couple of hours in heat that he must have experienced during the war in Italy but which was almost frightening to people raised in the north of England, he finally approached an officer. 'Can you help me?' he asked. 'I have three children.'

'Don't ask me, see a doctor,' said the officer.

It was the first conversation he had had with an American on American soil.

(Just thirty-nine years later I arrived with my wife and around two dozen suitcases. I was headed to work as the Washington correspondent of the *Observer.* We had piled this small mountain on to two trolleys. The customs officer, a very short but wiry young woman, took one look at it and asked, 'You got any sausages in there?' My denial satisfied her and she waved us through. The process took a few seconds. An obsession with sausages is one of the many stereotypes Americans have about the British, along with rotting teeth, aloofness, snobbery, bad food and queuing for buses, even though no bus queue has been observed, in London at least, for some decades.)

~

Americans turned out to be fabulously welcoming and generous, to an extent that embarrassed my parents then and embarrasses me now. They are in some respects the opposite of those simple native people you read about in travel books: 'Though these desert dwellers have almost nothing to their names, they will insist on sharing with you what little they have.' As in, 'Though most

Americans are, to our eyes, immensely rich with every possible material comfort, they want nothing more than for you to share their wealth with them.' Invited to spend Christmas with an executive of the company that funded the exchange scheme, we three children were given presents more expensive than anything our parents could afford. We were the simple desert dwellers transferred to the wealthy west.

~

It was a time of wonders for us children. Our car had a radio, built in! We could listen to the latest pop records as we drove along! Pat Boone, the Everly Brothers, Frankie Laine and, of course, Elvis Presley. Our mother predicted that he would be finished in no time, and in one sense she was right – she has already outlived him by thirty-three years. Dad was invited to give a talk in New York City, and whoever booked him had sprung for a flight. So the whole family trooped down to Rochester airport, to watch him take off in a Vickers turboprop – made in Britain! Imagine our pride. In those days air travel remained impossibly exotic. The airport had a dining room from which you could watch the planes taking off and landing, and if it was your birthday they provided a cake.

~

The British education system force-fed its plants, and at the age of ten I had had crammed into me as much stuff as a twelve-year-old in the US. So at school I was put into a class of children two years older than me. Most of them were immensely kind to this tiny, spindly person in round NHS glasses, seven years before John Lennon made them fashionable. It was a glimpse of the thrilling yet terrifying world of the teenager. The girls had breasts. Some of the boys smoked. Many of the older pupils were given cars the moment they were old enough to drive. They called the teachers by their first names. Ours was Cliff. He made periodic and unsuccessful attempts to persuade his class to call him by his surname. 'Sir', which is what we called male teachers in England, would have been inconceivable, not least because in the States it is now used of any male person whose name you don't know, including servers in McDonalds.

I was teased, of course. One aggressive youth informed me that his uncle could lick the whole British Army with his little finger. 'That must be some little finger,' I replied, half quoting Churchill. The remark was deemed to be incredibly witty and passed around the school and on to admiring parents. I was taught to type on a keyboard without letters by a kindly woman who went out of her way to help me. 'You know,' said some of my fellow pupils, 'the nicest thing you can say to an American woman is to call her a "bitch".' When I did so she realized what had happened and laughed.

There was a presidential election on, and all my parents' friends were desperate for Adlai Stevenson to beat Dwight Eisenhower at the second attempt. So when Miss Baldwin, the school librarian who I also adored, arrived at work with an 'I Like Ike' button on her dress, I was miserable and mortified. I played Ko-Ko in *The Mikado*, the last time I could hold a tune before my voice broke.

Probably the worst moment came when I was picked up by a schoolmate's parents who told me gravely that the British had invaded Egypt. They assumed, perhaps rightly, that this would come as a tremendous shock and produce feelings of shame, rather as if my crazed grandfather had escaped from the house and molested a young woman at a bus stop. Even then I think I was aware that some kind of corner in our national history had been turned. Back home people tended to assume that Britain and America were roughly equal in their world standing; being in the States demonstrated instantly that this was a vastly greater, vastly richer, vastly more important country. The Suez Crisis rubbed it home, even for a ten-year-old.

I went to summer day camp, and played softball. Dad's academic friends took us to sports events – baseball, basketball, ice hockey and football, none of them major league, but hotly fought and keenly supported. Here there was no division between the people who liked sports and the academically minded. It was perfectly possible to be both. Indeed, Dad's best friend among the English faculty was Jim Kaufmann, who had had a trial with the St Louis Cardinals baseball team. He implied that they would have taken him on if he hadn't preferred a university career. The man had arms as thick as most people's calves, and when you felt them they were as firm and wiry as a suspension bridge cable. The Kaufmanns introduced me to Walt Kelly's brilliant comic strip, Pogo, about a group of animals in the Okefenokee Swamp in Florida, which sounds coy and winsome, which it was, but it was also a fierce satire on the politics of the day.

~

In 1980 I went to cover the presidential election for the *Guardian*. This was before the days when computers filled every plane, and there were plenty of seats on almost every flight. I had bought, for £240, a ticket from the late, and by me lamented, airline Braniff, based in Dallas. You could buy this wonderful ticket if you crossed the Atlantic with them, and it offered absolutely unlimited first-class travel for a month. I arrived one broiling afternoon at Dallas-Fort Worth airport to find the bus driver from Hertz in a state of high excitement. 'You folks are not going to believe who I had in this bus today!' he called to us as we headed for the parking lot. 'The guy who drives the cast of *Dallas*!' As I have said, the show had monumental significance at the time, and my fellow passengers oohed and aahed appropriately.

'Maybe he shot JR!' I said to gales of laughter.

'Guess that's the famous British sense of humour!' one man kindly remarked.

That's another thing we Brits like about America: you don't have to be very funny to be thought hilarious.

~

With my cheap ticket I crossed the States from Key West off the tip of Florida in the south-east to the north-west corner plus many places in between, making sure I drank enough margaritas and ate enough fillet steak to cover almost the whole cost of the ticket, never mind the extra first-class fare. Braniff even flew Concorde between Dallas and Washington and New York, but it could only fly sub-sonically, rather spoiling the point.

Ronald Reagan was running for President and he was already a joke to the American version of the chattering classes (the 'fat-chewing classes'? Perhaps not). At one point he declared that trees caused more air pollution than cars. Opponents attending his meetings would festoon trees with signs saying, 'Cut me down before I kill again'. Far from making him look like a ninny, it did him no harm at all; a deep national distaste for Jimmy Carter had taken hold, and any of the Waltons from the eponymous TV series would have beaten him in November.

~

Reagan was often called lazy, and in one sense he was. But his career had been in motion pictures, which, like warfare, involves a small amount of action and a great deal of sitting around. For Reagan to have leapt up on set during a scene in which his character didn't appear, and insisted on taking part, would have been absurd. In the same way he saw no point at all in employing other people to work for him, then insisting on doing the job himself. He also had the example of Jimmy Carter to avoid. Carter famously checked who had booked to play on the White

House tennis court. But he had far worse habits. One Democratic senator came to see him and found him in a big chair, leafing through the USAF appropriation budget, which included everything from new bombers to the provision of Styrofoam cups. The heap of paperwork came up to his thigh, but he claimed with pride to have read every word. This is not the right way to use a leader's time.

~

By contrast Reagan often seemed at a loose end. Shortly after he was elected, the Democratic columnist Mark Shields decided he would like to interview the new President, but knowing there was no chance of a political discussion, took the always wise advice of suggesting an interview about his hobby or special interest, in this case early sporting heroes. To Shields's surprise, his request was granted, and Reagan chatted happily on the topic for two hours – until Shields had to plead that he had another appointment. There were stories of people coming for coffee, then finding themselves on a tour of the White House and invited to go bowling with the President.

In 1988 the BBC made a film about the coming tenth anniversary of Margaret Thatcher's premiership. It was made by Robert Harris, now more famous as the author of *Enigma*, *Pompeii* and *The Ghost*. It was, the team thought, a long shot but they contacted the White House and asked if Reagan would give an interview. The Americans replied that he would, but the President was a very busy man, and could spare them only five minutes and no more. If that was acceptable, they were welcome to come.

Since they probably needed only a minute or so of air time, they willingly agreed. Harris and his producer turned up with a local crew and set up in one of the many available rooms. At the appointed time Reagan appeared, along with his then press secretary Marlin Fitzwater, who reminded them that they had precisely five minutes. Reagan made a few short, laudatory but dull remarks about Thatcher. After four minutes and thirty seconds Fitzwater made the 'half a minute' sign. Then at five minutes he did the universal, throat-cut, end now signal. Reagan ambled towards the door, then stopped. 'I just thought of an anecdote about Margaret Thatcher,' he said. 'I could tell you the anecdote. Do you fellows have time?'

They assured him that their plane did not leave for ages. He told the anecdote, which was mildly amusing and forgettable. It did make the finished programme though. Then, as he was leaving, one of the American crew asked if he could give him a letter. It was from his daughter. He'd told her he was meeting the President, and she'd not understand if he didn't at least hand over the letter.

Reagan stopped and opened the letter, which was about the little girl's dog. 'My dog is a very naughty dog,' she wrote. 'Is your dog?' Reagan chuckled. 'Lucky sure is naughty. They must be twins!' By this time Fitzwater was looking ill. The President walked away, leaving the crew to assume that they had kept Gorbachev, or the Cabinet, waiting.

But twenty minutes later the young woman from the press office, who had been left behind, no doubt, to make sure they didn't steal any priceless artefacts while they were packing up, said, 'Look who's come to see us!' and Reagan stood in the doorway.

'I'm glad to find you folks still here,' he said. 'Now which of you fellows gave me the letter from the little girl about her dog? I'm sorry, but it took me this time to find a photo of myself with Lucky.'

There had been no meeting, no phone calls to world leaders, no CIA intelligence to read, just a kindly old man filling in the otherwise empty days of his retirement, rootling round in his desk, hoping to please a little girl.

~

Reagan was self-deprecating and cunning enough to turn his celebrated laziness to advantage. I attended a dinner at which he spoke before the meal, so that he could be back in the White House while we were eating the avocado and shrimp mousse. 'They say hard work never killed anyone, but I figured, "Why take that chance?" ' He had ordered – or possibly someone had ordered on his behalf – the bombing of Libya. 'So you folks can see I've really been burning the midday oil.' Not great jokes, but delivered with actorly aplomb. It never lost him. Years later I heard, from his former defense secretary Caspar Weinberger, about a speech he made at a dinner in honour of his old friend and patron, Walter Annenberg. The Alzheimer's had begun to kick in, and he said not a word, sitting still and smiling vaguely at everyone. The organizers were afraid that he simply wouldn't be able to perform. But when the time came he stood up and delivered it perfectly, getting all the right stresses, and pausing for the laughter. Then he sat down and resumed his silent smiling.

~

Reagan had become obsessed with the Strategic Defense Initiative, or Star Wars, intended to protect the country from nuclear attacks. Unlike many of the Dr Strangelove characters in the Pentagon, he thought the idea of nuclear annihilation intolerable and unbearable. He had been born in Tampico, Illinois, in 1911, when nobody woke up in the morning afraid that their life might be ended by a hydrogen bomb. It was a measure of his sincerity that he wanted to share the technology with the Soviets, a thought that caused something close to apoplexy in the Pentagon and among the right-wing Republicans who had helped get Reagan elected.

Lobbying groups for SDI showed TV commercials composed of children's drawings that depicted missiles bouncing off colourful umbrellas. Only in America could a foreign journalist, even from an allied country, ask to visit one of the country's most important defence installations and expect to be allowed in after the routine check. The Foreign Press Association in Washington vouched for me, so I found myself driving from San Francisco to the Lawrence Livermore Laboratory, where the most important work on Star Wars was being done. First we had to listen to a lecture by a man whose job was making atomic bombs. He explained that they were now working on a 'clean' bomb, which produced less nuclear fallout and so was less dangerous – to people who weren't already dead that is. He presented this as a service to mankind, rather like a man who was working on an electric car that didn't emit fumes. Then we were invited to see the kit the scientists were designing to knock missiles out of the sky. It was very impressive, like a cross between an aircraft engine and how I imagine the Giant Hadron Collider. I didn't understand any part of it or what our guides told me about it. Their secrets could not have been safer.

Later I went to visit Strategic Air Command in Omaha, Nebraska. Here they wanted something much simpler. They wanted trains. The missiles would be mounted on train trucks, and if the international situation became dangerous, they would be moved out on to the rail network and would go rattling through the night like the *20th Century Limited* or the *City of New Orleans.* This would make it impossible for the Soviets to target them. Or so they said. They took me to see the operations room, with the red telephone and its direct link to the Oval Office, and the giant screen familiar from so many Hollywood films. Instead of little dots showing incoming missiles, it had a message: 'Welcome, Simon Hoggard, London Observer.'

I told the colonel who was showing me round that I was flattered, but asked what the screen would normally show.

'Normally,' he said, 'we'd try to spell your name right.'

~

Very few people believed that SDI would make it impossible for nuclear missiles to hit big cities. But the scientists wanted it, because it meant several billion dollars in research funding. The Pentagon wanted it because it meant that a Soviet first strike would wipe out only a proportion of missile sites, so that savage retaliation was possible, indeed inevitable. Meanwhile, New York, Washington, Chicago and Los Angeles would all be smoking ruins, since there was no way they could build an SDI system that would destroy all incoming missiles. The National Security Agency wanted it because they could bargain it away against something the Soviets had. Only Ronald Reagan and a handful of other well-meaning dreamers actually thought that it, of itself, could prevent millions of people being turned into their constituent atoms.

~

Reagan, I always felt, was like the Statue of Liberty – everybody knew what she stood for and so nobody needed to ask. Of course this had its disadvantages. Since he had not uttered his views on everything that might crop up on his watch, those who worked with him spent much of their time trying to establish that their point of view would be shared by the President if only he knew that a point of view was required. As Peggy Noonan, his most successful speechwriter, put it in her memoirs: 'The battle for the mind of Ronald Reagan was like the trench warfare of World War I. Never have so many fought so hard for such barren terrain.' Yet she and Reagan were perfectly matched. On the evening after the *Challenger* disaster in 1986, when the Space Shuttle exploded on take-off, he appeared on television to speak to the nation. She had him quote the poem 'High Flight', written by a Canadian airman with the lines: ' "... slipped the surly bonds of earth", to "touch the face of God" '. Even a cynic like me could feel the goose pimples climb alarmingly neckwards.

~

In May 1980 I decided to use the wonderful Braniff ticket to visit Mount St Helens in Washington State, which was said to be about to erupt. I travelled with Simon Winchester, then with the *Daily Mail*, who is a trained geologist. We rented a vast Ford Thunderbird car at Portland airport, picked up another British journalist on the same mission, and the following morning set off north to the mountain. At the foot of the road that led to the summit was a locked gate and a sign warning that it was illegal to go beyond that point. Everyone who lived on the slopes had been evacuated, except for Harry Truman, an old settler from West Virginia who had established a fairly basic summer resort near the peak. He had become a national hero, in a minor way. Truman had declared that he had no intention of leaving; he had lived on the mountain almost all his life, and if he died there, then he died there. The authorities, realizing that clearing him out would be far more trouble than it was worth, let him stay and gave him keys to the locked gates.

There seemed little point in having flown 2,500 miles to give up, so we drove round the gate without much trouble and climbed for several miles until we came to another. We could see a logging track further on, so it seemed easy to continue. The Thunderbird eased off the road and on to the grass, then became firmly lodged on a tussock of grass that concealed a tree stump. The three of us tried to push or pull the huge vehicle off the stump, but after a few minutes we knew there was nothing we could do. Leaving the problem for later, we marched on up the mountain road. There were occasional rumbles, as if a distant giant had acid indigestion, and once or twice the ground shook gently. Winchester assured us that there was no danger. The beginning of an eruption would be marked by an outpouring of lava. Even flowing downhill, lava would move more slowly than three terrified humans pelting for their lives. He was not the last person to make that mistake.

At the top we arrived at Harry Truman's resort. It was an idyllic, jigsaw picture or chocolate-box scene. Cabins were dotted around an aquamarine lake. A few privately owned houses stood away from the water, all with picture windows through which we could see kitchens, bedrooms, televisions – a landlocked *Mary Celeste.* Garden swings creaked in the breeze. Toys strewn around the gardens showed the haste with which the occupants had left. Suddenly we were surrounded by cats, mewing, urgently rubbing against us, hoping for food. We shouted for Harry Truman, but there was no answer. 'We're not here to take you away, we're English journalists,' we yelled more in hope than expectation. But we heard no sound, apart from the creaking swings, the mewing cats and the seemingly distant rumble of the volcano on which we were standing.

We were fairly dejected when we got back to the car, though the fact that there was a police cruiser parked nearby changed things. Trooper Whitcraft told us that we'd been seen driving round the first gate. He had come up himself, spotted the stranded Thunderbird and ordered a wrecker – a tow truck – to recover it. In the meantime, he said with perfect courtesy, we were under arrest.

The wrecker arrived and took about ten seconds to get the car off the stump. Then just as we were about to be taken away, presumably to the slammer, a pick-up truck arrived, driven by

Harry Truman. 'You boys come all the way from England to interview ol' Harry?' he asked. This was a man who had lived as a hermit for most of each year, but who had suddenly discovered that he adored publicity. Most days he went down to the valley, to the nearest post office, to collect his parcel of mail. He'd had letters from around the world, and at least two proposals of marriage. 'But they don't want ol' Harry, they just want to git their hands on my spread!' he said. TV crews were waiting at the bottom of the mountain, and it was a rare day that he didn't give a few interviews. He was having the best time of his life.

'Now this here trooper is a friend o' mine,' he said. 'And I ain't gonna let him arrest you boys, not if you've come all the way from England to see me. You wanna interview me? You go right ahead.'

We asked about his early life and his life on the mountain. Did he live alone there, apart from his cats?

'Nope, got maybe a dozen coons up there too!'

Winchester, no doubt deliberately coat-trailing, asked in a shocked tone of voice, 'Coons? Do you mean black people?'

Truman stared at him for a moment, then understanding dawned. 'Oh, no,' he said, 'not niggers, *racoons*!'

One could not excuse this sort of remark, except to say that it would have seemed unexceptionable in West Virginia when Truman was born, at the end of the nineteenth century.

He gave us a cheery wave and headed back to his spread. The wrecker towed the Thunderbird down the mountain, and Trooper Whitcraft put us in his cruiser. Winchester was in front, but the other two of us were in the back behind bullet-proof glass. There were no door handles on either side. We kept up an affable conversation with the trooper. What did people do around here for fun? Hunting elk, he replied. Was there much elk around? He stopped the car and pointed into the forest. 'You see that orange flash, right there? That's an elk's asshole.'

We got to the foot of the mountain and on to the main road. We asked what he proposed to do with us. 'Well,' he said pleasantly, 'the way I figure it is, I got to write my report on this incident, then I've got to give it to my superior officer, and he's got to consider what to do about it and if he's gonna bring a charge, and by that time I figure you boys going to be back home in England. Enjoy your evening.'

With grovelling thanks we drove back to Portland for an enormous, alcoholic meal.

Two weeks later Mount St Helens erupted. There was no lava. The force of the explosion was so great that it lifted the top cubic mile off the summit of the mountain, and ash spread around the earth. I sometimes wonder how many seconds Harry Truman lived after realizing that he was certain to die. Another fifty-six lives were lost, mainly geologists who, like Winchester, assumed that they could flee whatever was exuded slowly from the top.

~

Two years after the eruption I returned, and took a plane over the summit. As you see in the pictures of meteorite damage, dead tree trunks were lined up on the ground, pointing away from the centre of the blast. But already greenery was growing back in the rich soil, and there were lakes, filled with liquids in alarming fluorescent and neon colours, as if they had been released from the centre of the earth, which was no doubt the case. In the visitor centre you could buy souvenir books that contained accounts of our visit. We had been among the last people to speak to Truman on the mountain. An assistant told me what the rescuers had found after the eruption. One man died sitting at the wheel of his car. His body had looked intact. 'But when they tried to take him out, his flesh just fell away, like a cooked chicken,' she said.

~

Later they made a not very successful Hollywood film about Harry Truman. They decided to depict him rowing out on to his lake in the perfect peace of the morning, up to the exact moment of the explosion. The line about racoons did not appear in the script.

~

Some of the very best American political journalists are women. It may be cheap psychology, but I sometimes suspect it's because they understand that politics is about the lives of ordinary people. Male columnists, especially those based in Washington, tend to write as if the only effect of political decisions was to make life easier or harder for other politicians, as if they all existed in a closed circle, a sports league in which defeat or victory pushes someone up or down the table. And American sports leagues don't have relegation; even the bottom team is around the following year. It's often the same with politicians – defeat is just an opportunity for victory next season.

Mary McGrory was a brilliant columnist for the *Washington Post.* Though already past middle age when I arrived in Washington to work, nothing would stop her from going out to discover what was really happening. She didn't peruse the morning papers, glance at the television and make a couple of phone calls to the powerful, followed by a *de haut en bas* column laying down the law on some semi-imaginary planet like so many others. Covering the Iowa caucuses in January 1988 I drove past a field full of cattle and noticed an elderly woman in the snow. It was Mary, not interviewing the cows, but plodding towards a barn to talk to a farmer and his wife.

Mind you, her determination to experience events in person could go wrong, and she taught me another vital watchword for the political writer: being there is no substitute for seeing it on television. When the Iran-Contra scandal was revealed (Reagan had agreed the sale of weapons to Iran, and the profits had been diverted illegally to support the right-wing contra guerrillas in Nicaragua) the Senate held an enquiry. One of the chief witnesses was Colonel Oliver North, who had facilitated much of the skulduggery. Mary went to the hearing, and wrote a column next day saying that North had disgraced himself and discredited the administration.

But she had been sitting in the room, behind North, and could see only the stunned, bemused and appalled faces of the senators. Those of us watching on TV saw North's face – gazing upwards, idealism etched into every wrinkle, a right-wing Che Guevara. Literally three days later there were T-shirts printed with his image: 'Oliver North – American hero'. The story was what had appeared on television. Reality was a feeble, misleading and misguided version of events.

~

Molly Ivins was from Texas. She had been to a school in the same neighbourhood as the one George W. Bush attended, and she had known him fairly well. She detested everything he believed in. She also said that he was not anything like as dumb as people thought, and had enough charm to stop a buffalo in its tracks. I got to know her at the Conference on World Affairs, a grandiose-sounding annual event held at the University of Colorado which I've attended most years since 1987. In fact CWA was, and is, a piss-up with speeches. Around a hundred or more speakers attend each year, performing several times in the course of a week, then going to parties, dinners and pub crawls. Some 60,000 members of the public attend the various sessions. Your audience might be a couple of dozen people or a thousand. Molly's were always the most crowded.

Her weekly column, like Mary McGrory's, was almost invariably about real people, living real lives. If the Republicans wanted to cut some care fund, the Washington columnists would write about its effects on Washington politics. Molly would write about its effects on the poor of Texas. She was exceedingly well read, so that when she used homely, folksy metaphors it never seemed strained or self-admiring. When her old friend Bush won his second election in 2004, she described what they did in Texas to a dog that had killed a chicken: they tied the carcase round the dog's neck and left it there until it rotted and stank. The dog would never kill a chicken again. That, she said, was what Americans would do to the Republican Party after another four years of Bush.

Molly loved a story and would embroider them, so that her party conversation was like a stand-up gig. 'The first cappuccino in West Texas' was one of her best routines, describing filling up with gas on the way to El Paso, and the shy girl at the register suggesting a cappuccino – which came from a machine and was almost undrinkable. Funny? Only the way she told it. She loved the weak but didn't hate the powerful – only those who misused their power.

She was a big woman. There was, as they say, a lot of her to love. She contracted breast cancer. At first she came to the conference in a wig. She had a double mastectomy. Then she came alternate years. Then she didn't come at all.

The last year she came we met early in the week at a bar, late at night, after the main thrashes of the evening. She was already entertaining a group of people, around a table. She greeted us late arrivals. She threw her arms around me, grasping me in a grip I thought I might never escape. 'You know,' she said, 'it's real easy to hug someone when you got no tits.' And gave an enormous smile.

~

The conference was founded and organized by Howard Higman, a man who looked like an aged bear. His parents were from England and had walked across America, which many people had to do because they couldn't afford a wagon. They would work in one spot, then if they didn't want to settle, they would walk further west. They worked in the hills above Boulder, Colorado, and built a house in the town itself. Howard was born there, and was living there when he died, eighty years later. In the meantime he had become a sociology professor, and made an enemy of J. Edgar Hoover by telling one of his classes that the FBI was a greater threat to American freedom than the Communist Party. From then on Hoover kept files on him. When the Freedom of Information Act was passed, Higman sent off for all those documents. Most of them were redacted, sheets of blackened paper, but those that were clear showed the minute depth of Hoover's snooping. 'Subject held party at home on 11th Street. License plate numbers outside included HVB 212 . . .' and so forth.

He started the conference shortly after the war. He had seen a French activist speak in New York about One World Government, which was a brief fad of the time. He asked him to speak in Boulder, at the University of Colorado. The man said he would come for $1,000. Higman knew that the university would never pay so much money for someone who most Coloradans would regard as a communist, so he invented, out of thin air, a Conference on World Affairs. He phoned friends in neighbouring states, invited them to speak, offered them no money – no fees, no transport – but said they would be hospitably entertained in the houses of the faculty. All sessions would be free and open to the public. The French activist never came.

I first met Howard at the conference in 1988. He had invited me to stay in his home, where he liked to keep a claque of various Brits. A party was in full swing. He was wearing a jacket in a multitude of colours rather like when your television goes wrong. He was roaring at a young woman, clearly a student volunteer, who had failed to keep the salad bowl full. I thought what a dreadful bully he must be. Then I saw him roaring just as angrily at a shortish man wearing a string tie. He turned out to be the governor of Colorado. I realized that Howard was an equal-opportunity curmudgeon.

He was often drunk. Of some British people it is said that they are under the impression that dry white wine is a non-alcoholic drink. Howard thought that vodka was a non-alcoholic drink. He drove a thirty-year-old Plymouth, a car built on the lines of a tank, which he said was essential for anyone driving in a university town. One year he took me for a meal in Colorado's most expensive restaurant, the Flagstaff. I had to drive the Plymouth because he had night blindness. This thing panted, clanking, up the mountainside. The valet parker looked astonished, and even more surprised when I turned off the engine but it refused to stop, shuddering and thumping for the best part of a minute.

Howard almost never slept, and every night his house resounded with CBS, NBC, ABC News, CNN and C-Span broadcasts from Congress that he had taped on his battery of video recorders. All summer he would listen to tapes of conference sessions – more than four hundred in the week – gleefully noting the famous names who had come: the designer and inventor Buckminster Fuller, the former First Lady Eleanor Roosevelt, one of the Beach Boys pop group, and Ben, or possibly Jerry, who handed out their Peace Bar ice creams. Roger Ebert, the most celebrated living American film critic, never misses a year and holds a dinner mid-way through the conference at which everyone tells filthy jokes. At one of these I sat between a porn star and Bill Nack, the celebrated reporter from *Sports Illustrated*.

In the 1990s the conference went into decline. Howard insisted that all his old friends be kept among the hundred or so speakers, even those who had nothing left to say. Audiences drifted away. The students lost interest. The university said it would not continue to fund it unless Howard resigned. He did, and died soon afterwards. It was his life, and they had taken it from him.

But now the conference is more successful than ever, and people who have been invited once are usually desperate to return.

POLITICIANS

10

Politicians

Clark, Whitelaw, Archer

It is certainly not fashionable to say this now, but I have always had an affection for most politicians. Though by no means all.

~

Few people these days remember Sir Keith Joseph, though he was John the Baptist, preparing the way for Margaret Thatcher. He had a gift for saying what he meant in a way that made it sound far worse than what he had intended. Shortly before Mrs Thatcher became leader of the Conservative Party he made a speech that might, possibly, have implied that poorer or less clever people ought not to have too many children. The whiff of eugenics, less than thirty years after Naziism had been defeated, was enough to destroy any chance of his becoming leader, which some people had thought a serious possibility.

~

For quite a while he was the industry minister, but he found it hard to cope with the demands of new technology, even the more primitive technology of the time. A chap called Brian Shallcross worked in the parliamentary press gallery for many years, mostly for TV and radio. He once interviewed Sir Keith in the Midlands. The minister had begun by talking near gobbledegook for a minute and a half. When the interview ended, he told Shallcross, 'You must take out the first ninety seconds of that.'

'But we can't, Secretary of State. It was live, and it's already been seen by millions of people.'

Sir Keith shot back: 'And I don't want any of your technical excuses.'

~

There ought to be a medical term for the condition he suffered, which was a complete inability to perceive how other people saw him, coupled with an intense and appealing desire not to hurt them. He was like a caring vivisectionist, who regarded society as a strange, half-understood organism like a frog, but who had no wish to cause harm to the frog. I followed him round one day during the 1979 election. We toured a shopping centre; he would go into the shops and accost voters, very politely, saying, 'Is there anything you would like to ask me?' Since only a tiny handful of people in the entire world woke up in the morning and thought, By Jove, if I run into Sir Keith Joseph today, I'll certainly put him on the spot! none of them ever had a question. Often they looked alarmed, and fled. But if he thought he was making it more difficult for people to do their shopping, he too would dash out of the shop, without talking to anyone.

~

He was taken to lunch in a well-regarded restaurant by a group of journalists, who, unsurprisingly, chose some of the more expensive dishes on the menu. When they asked what Sir Keith would like, he replied, 'Cake.'

Just cake? they asked.

'Yes, just cake, please,' he repeated.

Did he have any particular type of cake in mind?

'British Rail cake, please.'

It turned out that he meant the kind of slab fruit cake he had enjoyed on trains. It being the sort of restaurant that was proud to satisfy all its customers, they served him a piece of fruit cake while the hacks chewed through scallops, tournedos Rossini and other luxuries.

Because his mind was never attuned to other people, and because he had no concept of conventional wisdom, he sometimes asked the questions nobody else would think of. For instance, visiting a bird sanctuary in Scotland, he demanded: 'How do the birds know it is a sanctuary?'

~

Once while he was industry minister, he was asked in a television interview what he thought about the new Mini Metro car, the vehicle that was going to save British Leyland. It was assumed that he would launch into a gung-ho encomium about the new car, but instead he sat in silence for a while. The interviewer asked again, and again there was no reply. Finally Sir Keith gave a soft groan. 'I don't know about cars,' he said. 'You see, my car was stolen and I haven't bothered to get another one.'

~

The image of Sir Keith that lodges in my mind came on the night of the Brighton bomb, in October 1984. A young, or youngish man then, I had been drinking in the Grand Hotel until around 3 a.m. I went next door to the Metropole Hotel, where I had a room, and discovered that I was too tired and too drunk to take off my clothes and brush my teeth. So I was lying on the bed, trying to summon up the will to get ready for bed, when I heard the explosion in the Grand Hotel. The TV set in the corner of the room was an old-fashioned one, on legs, and it did a little dance, rather like the cheap East European cartoons which the

BBC used to pad out its daytime schedules. I walked over to the window and looked out. A drunk – someone far more inebriated than me – was lurching down the pavement. A policeman was calmly shifting those movable fences they use for crowd control, cutting off the area in front of the hotel. The drunk wanted to go through. The policeman told him he couldn't. The drunk objected. It was the only noise I could hear.

Finally the drunk reeled away, and then very slowly a great grey cloud of dust and smoke billowed out from the front of the hotel next door. Suddenly the area between the hotel and the sea was filled with a horde of people, yelling and screaming. I realized that there was going to be no sleep that night, so to prevent my being interrupted I called my wife, to tell her that when she got up she would hear about the bomb and that I was all right. She was very grateful to know. I then called my editor, Donald Trelford, to tell him the same thing, and to warn him that this was going to be the principal story of the year. He seemed somewhat less grateful to be woken.

By this time, someone had phoned in a bomb warning about the Metropole, and we were evacuated. It was a good night to be still fully dressed. The beach was packed with people milling about anxiously, desperate for information. Had anyone seen Chris? Yes, they had waved to him at Brighton station as he boarded the London train. But what about David, or Sandra, or Tom, or whoever – everybody seemed to have their own private list on which all their friends had to be ticked off. Roy Bradford, an Ulster MP, had been in a room at the back of the Grand with his wife. They had asked for a different room with a sea view, and finally the hotel had told them one was available. They looked at it but decided it was too small. He waved up at the building: the room had ceased to exist.

~

But the most magnificent figure was Sir Keith Joseph. He was wearing a red paisley-patterned silk dressing gown, and was carrying his red box, the reinforced wooden case that civil servants pack with important papers for the minister's attention, and plenty of dross besides, to slow the minister down. For him to have grabbed and carried his box when he could have had no idea whether there was another bomb, or a booby-trap waiting to go off, was the political equivalent of bravery under fire. People might be dying all around him, but the secrets of Her Majesty's Government must be preserved.

~

The Metropole was later deemed to be safe, and we trooped back in at around 5 a.m., two hours after the bomb. The bar was opened and there was a steady trade in large brandies.

~

For someone who was ostentatiously indifferent to other people's opinions, Alan Clark was surprisingly insecure. His diaries are full of contemptuous put-downs of colleagues, yet every compliment to himself is recorded with lavish care, as if it had been wrapped in cotton wool and placed in a wooden chest, like miser's gold, to be taken out and gloated over. There is a mention of me in the first volume of diaries to be published, the one that was such a great success and which brilliantly covered the fall of Thatcher. Apparently I told him about a poll of Young Conservatives which appeared to reveal that he was their choice for next leader of the party. I have no recollection of telling him this, or even of being aware of such a fact in the first place, but it clearly mattered to him; he took it very seriously. He was also the living representation of Gore Vidal's maxim that it is not enough to succeed: one's friends must also fail. Years before he died I wrote a rather snide piece about David Davis, who was then shadow

Europe minister, and who had made a deeply tedious speech in the Commons. I bumped into Clark the evening after the sketch appeared. 'God, David must have *hated* that!' he said, with obvious glee. It was only later I discovered that Davis was his best friend, in politics at least.

~

Once he invited me and my then girlfriend, Rosie, to Saltwood Castle for the weekend. Saltwood is alleged to be the place where the knights who murdered Thomas Becket spent the night before going on to Canterbury to carry out the assassination. I was nervous, never having been to a weekend house party before. We needn't have worried. Jane, his widow, was and is one of the kindest people I have ever met, without the faintest glint of grandeur or snobbery. We arrived, and as the peacocks squawked – only urban foxes make a noise as horrible – we rang the bell. The sound seemed to echo around the castle, from keep to kitchen to dungeon. We waited a long time. Then a footfall could be heard on stone. Finally the door creaked slowly open, as in every horror movie you have ever seen, and Clark's face appeared.

'Gosh, after all that I was expecting a hunchbacked butler,' I said.

He smiled wanly. 'You'll meet him later,' he said, and we did.

~

At dinner the hunchbacked butler appeared to serve the food and wine. Clark loved good wine – he famously said that it was impossible to entertain properly now that decent claret cost £100 a bottle – though Jane has always been a teetotaller. He himself was vegetarian, though he had provided excellent roast beef. The plates were gold – Jane remembers silver, though I do recall him apologizing for the fact that they were cold: 'You can't put gold into the oven to warm,' he explained. That, together with the speed of the hunchbacked butler, who brought the plates in one by one, meant that by the time the last guest was served all the meat was cold, a fact more than made up for by the excellence of the wine.

One of the guests was John Aspinall, the gambler, who, it is sometimes alleged, helped Lord Lucan escape after the murder of his nanny. Aspinall ran a zoo not far away in Kent, and a regrettable number of his keepers were either killed or mauled by his exotic captives. I was not predisposed to like him, and nothing he said or did changed my view. He talked loudly and at length, apparently assuming that whatever he said was necessarily of much more interest than anything anyone else might say. Rosie, who had a sharp eye for these things, noted that when he spoke his wife looked away and was clearly bored, not feeling the need to support or even listen to her husband.

At one point – we were towards the end of the 1974–79 Labour government – Aspinall launched into a long monologue about how what this country needed was a dictatorship, someone to kick the scoundrels out, do something about the bloody unions, put the place back on its feet, and so forth. Clark seized his moment and gave a passionate defence of democracy, which went against much of what he often said, but which had the happy result of silencing Aspinall.

There was, without doubt, a considerable perversity in Clark's make-up: he liked to disagree with views held by those around him, whoever they might be and whatever they might think, because it pleased him to make trouble. Sir Keith Joseph, by contrast, had little idea what the conventional view was in the first place.

In Ion Trewin's biography of Clark much of this is explained: as a boy, he was largely left alone by his parents, obliged to amuse himself night after night while they went to parties, dinners, first nights and receptions. He had a tremendous need to attract attention to himself. 'Look,' he seemed to be saying, 'I'm here, I matter too . . .'

~

He was also desperately in love with his wife. In view of his frequent and virtually public philandering, this may seem absurd, but I have often noticed the same in men who have had unsatisfactory relationships with their parents. They marry the mother they never had, the woman who gives them the unquestioning love and devoted attention their real mother never quite had time for. But then, like the most dutiful son, they feel the need to leave home. If they are attractive, rich, and bring along a whiff of louche excitement, so much the easier. Most of his girlfriends were from that class of society that gives its daughters names ending with the letters '. . . lla', usually a sign of poshness, or at least aspiration.

I had been asked to write a profile of Margaret Thatcher, to mark the first anniversary of her arrival in Downing Street. I knew Clark would be full of good stories about her, and the kind of insights nobody else would have. So I wrote to him at his Commons office and invited him to lunch (note to anyone wanting to contact a minister: always go through their Commons office, where your message will be handled by someone close to them, and often a long-standing personal friend. They will generally be happy to pass it on. A civil servant at the department will find several reasons for making sure the minister never sees it).

To my astonishment a typed reply came on Department of Employment notepaper. It explained that lunch was difficult, 'as I am usually engaged in Ugandan discussions at that time'. It was an astonishing thing to commit to any piece of paper, even more so to headed government notepaper. (The *Private*

Eye euphemism 'Ugandan discussions' had nothing to do with Princess Elizabeth of Toro being allegedly caught in flagrante at a Paris airport. It was the result of James Fenton attending a party in London where he knew almost nobody and was mooching around at a loose end. His hostess told him that another guest was a one-legged diplomat from Uganda who had recently fled from Idi Amin. 'They're upstairs, discussing Uganda,' she said. 'You should join them, it's fascinating.' When he went up to the bedroom he found the diplomat having sex with a well-known woman journalist. He told the story at the next *Private Eye* lunch and the phrase was born.)

We could meet, Clark said, for a drink before dinner. He would be entertaining a friend on the night, but we could have an hour beforehand. He chose Wiltons restaurant, and ordered a bottle of Puligny-Montrachet, the wonderful white Burgundy which there cost roughly twice what the *Guardian* would expect to pay for an entire dinner for two. Almost every word he uttered was valuable material for my Thatcher article, because he spotted things most politicians would never notice. For example, her clothing: 'When she's wearing blue, that means she is calm, in command. When she's in red, you must be careful because she's worried, *agitato*.'

At one point I asked if he liked her. He looked astonished at such a crass question. 'Like? Like? She's not there to be *liked*, you idiot! She just *is*.'

Then at 8 p.m. the door of the restaurant opened, and there was his date: a beautiful young woman with long legs and blonde hair. I can't remember her name, but I do know that it ended in '. . . lla'.

~

Once in Brussels I was chatting to Neil Kinnock, then one of our commissioners there, and he related a story Clark had told him.

Shortly after the affairs he had conducted with a judge's wife and her two daughters – 'the coven' he called them – had been exposed in the papers, the press laid siege, almost like an invading army, to the gates of the castle, undeterred by the terrible eldritch screech of the peacocks. He and Jane cooked up a plan to get him home undetected. She would leave in one of his many cars, on her own, as if to do the shopping. He would get off the train from London at the station before Hythe, just in case any hacks were waiting there. Then he would hide in the boot, and she would drive through the castle gates, lock them, and release him. The scheme worked perfectly, except that once when they had reached the sanctuary of the castle keep, she left him in the boot. In Kinnock's version, he was there for an hour, genuinely wondering whether she had left him there to die. In Clark's version, she left him for only a few minutes, but long enough to make him anxious. 'Wasn't it,' he said when he gave me his account, 'a perfectly *splendid* thing to do!' His eyes blazed with adoration.

~

A few years after he died I went back to Saltwood, to interview Jane for a BBC film about political diaries. It was December, the weather was chilly, and the castle itself was so cold you felt that it could never have been warm from the day it was built, even at the height of summer. She was camping out in the small kitchen where there was a stove, with a pot of soup on top. All sorts of things went into the soup, like a peasant stockpot, so presumably it changed day by day, and was certainly delicious when we tried it. We went outside the gates to the lawn where Clark is buried under a massive stone which was brought down from his Scottish estate, Eriboll, in Sutherland. 'I sit here and talk to him every day,' said Jane. 'I told him you were coming.'

I had asked to see the wine cellar, which I assumed would be valuable and might raise her a lot of money. It wasn't a cellar; rather it was the castle's undercroft, and it was filled with the detritus of years: broken lawnmowers, old toys, gardening equipment, swathes of tarpaulin and rubble. Scattered around were cases of wine, most very good indeed: famous Bordeaux châteaux, the greatest names in Burgundy, others generic wine for everyday drinking. I was startled, even shocked, since anyone who knew about this collection could have come in the night, or when Jane was away, spent perhaps ten seconds breaking down the ancient door, and whisked the whole lot away in a van. Later on Jane did get a valuer down, and the collection sold for an extraordinary £52,767, a sum undoubtedly inflated by the provenance of the bottles.

~

In 1993 the first volume of Clark's diaries was published, and he was asked to speak about them at the Cheltenham Literary Festival. A week or so before the event I got a call from the festival organizers to say that Clark had decided that he couldn't be bothered to write a speech. 'Why don't you get a hack to interview me?' he asked. 'Get Hoggart, or somebody.' So I turned up an hour beforehand in the writers' room. Clark was looking at a bottle with obvious distaste. 'The wine here is *filthy*,' he said. 'Let's go out and find some *ale*!' (He generally talked in italics.)

Outside it was a cold October night and slightly foggy. Cheltenham has many pubs, but few seemed to be near the Town Hall and every bright light we saw turned out to be an upmarket clothes shop or an estate agent. Finally, through the murk I saw a familiar face hurrying in our direction. 'Ah, Melvyn!' I said. 'Do you know if there's a pub near here?'

He was very helpful, saying that we should go down that alleyway where we couldn't miss it – the place was very noisy. I thanked him, adding, 'You two know each other, I assume,' and there was that British grunt that doesn't indicate assent; more a desire not to dissent or get into hand-shaking, because time presses and which of us needs any more acquaintances? I don't know if Melvyn was out of earshot, but as we went our opposite ways Clark turned to me and said, 'Who the hell was *that*?' and I realized there were limits to the fame of even Melvyn Bragg.

~

(A complete indifference to popular culture has always been a characteristic, if in some cases an affectation, of the upper classes. Julian Fellowes tells a story about the filming of *Gosford Park*, for which he wrote the screenplay. The film contains an exceedingly grand dinner party at which one guest is a Hollywood producer, in Britain to make a film called *Charlie Chan in London*. Another guest asks him what happens in the picture; he replies he can't say – he doesn't want to spoil it for them. At which Maggie Smith says, 'Oh, none of us will *see* it,' in the same tone of voice she might use for saying that none of us will be dressing up as babies for rag week.

Robert Altman, the director, wanted to cut the line because, according to Fellowes, no Hollywood director could conceive of the idea that anyone might not want to see a Hollywood film. But Maggie Smith had said, 'I think I can make it work, Bob,' and it usually got one of the biggest laughs.)

~

The former Tory Chancellor Nigel Lawson has always had a streak of vanity, which perhaps makes him unexceptional among politicians, though of course it is more noticeable in someone who has a fair bit to be vain about. I often wonder how he reacted to the enormous fame of his daughter Nigella (how astounding to call your baby girl by a name, which while describing a genuine if unusual herb, is almost unknown to anyone else. A John might call his daughter Joanna, and I suppose I could have called mine Simone, but Nigella is the equivalent of Barrietta, or Terencelle).

When he was a junior minister, a newspaper ran an article about up-and-coming politicians, to be illustrated with pictures taken by a famous photographer. All those selected arrived at the site, the House of Commons terrace, in good order and on time. Only Lawson gave them any trouble. He demanded to see the pictures before they appeared in the paper.

'Do you know,' said the famous photographer, 'in all my professional career, only one other person has made that request?'

'And who was that?' asked Lawson.

'Zsa Zsa Gabor,' said the photographer, smiling sweetly.

~

A colleague and I had lunch with Lawson while he was still a junior minister. We understood him to say that when the Tories returned to power they would have to consider taxing some of the extras that went with jobs, chiefly company cars, health insurance and so forth. Soon afterwards I was asked to write a piece for the *Guardian* about up-and-coming politicians, and mentioned this, including the line: 'The Tory party divides into two groups about Nigel Lawson: there are those who hate him, and those who loathe him.'

The day the piece appeared he tackled my boss, the paper's political editor, Ian Aitken. 'What your assistant wrote about me was outrageous!' he said.

Ian was inclined to agree. 'Yes, I thought the line about hating and loathing was a little bit strong.'

'Oh no,' said Lawson, brushing it aside. 'That's perfectly true. But the suggestion that I would support a tax on company perks is outrageous!'

~

Lawson's refusal to work with Sir Alan Walters, Thatcher's personal economic policy adviser, in 1989 caused him to resign from his job as Chancellor, and prepared the way for the fall of Thatcher the following year. Walters, an academic economist, had views that accorded with Thatcher's instincts but had never worked in the world of political economics where you have to raise and spend real money, rather than manipulate theories. It is a little like – and I exaggerate here – the difference between being a property developer and enjoying a game of Monopoly. Walters had a job in Washington, where I met him at a British embassy bash. I asked where he was living, and he said, 'Georgetown. I cannot bear to live near poor people. So I took out a map of Washington, worked out where the poor people were, and found the neighbourhood that was furthest away from them.' In Washington the word 'poor' is more or less synonymous with 'black'.

I assume that, since I worked for the *Observer* at the time, he was taking pleasure in winding me up. And in any case, like most British reporters in Washington who didn't live in the suburbs, we had a house in Georgetown too. Even so, a slight chill ran down my spine.

~

Lord Carrington resigned as foreign secretary over the Argentine invasion of the Falklands, and this is now regarded as the last great noble resignation in politics. In the face of failure, everyone else clings on desperately by their fingertips, like Cary Grant on Mount Rushmore in Hitchcock's *North by Northwest*, or else crashes down the rock face after the prime ministerial boot has crushed their knuckles. Before the invasion, however, I was sent to cover Carrington's tour of Central and South America. We flew out on an RAF VC-10. The cabin crew were WRAFs and were delightful. I asked in my immature way for Drambuie to wash down dinner. The stewardess left the whole bottle on the seat next to me. 'It'll save me scurrying up and down every time you want some more,' she said. This kind of thing lodges in a young man's memory.

We landed in Recife, Brazil. Carrington was to visit an area where there had been a drought for several years. As our bus bumped down the dirt road to a village we passed the corpses of livestock that had died from lack of water. In the village itself people were hollow-eyed and emaciated, the children with those unspeakable pot bellies sticking out from below ribcages that protruded from their skin, like bone-handled knives in a box. An old blind man was singing to his own accompaniment on an accordion. The music was not entirely to my taste, but then it came from a quite different culture. Carrington evidently didn't enjoy it either, and asked, rather grumpily, what the song was about.

'He is singing a song for rain,' said our interpreter.

Carrington was not mollified. 'Tell him he can have some rain from my farm,' he said. 'It's almost underwater.'

This absurd suggestion was passed on to the blind man, who looked pleased, as if it were a genuine offer. As we disappeared in, literally, a cloud of dust I wondered whether for weeks the stricken people of the village would look yearningly every day to see if suddenly a tanker might bump along the road, labelled 'Rain from Lord Carrington's farm'.

I recorded all this, together with the banalities of conversation between world leaders. This never fails to disappoint, but in a way I find ironically pleasing. (I especially enjoyed a conversation I overheard in the late 1970s, in the eastern part of West Germany, when Jim Callaghan had gone to visit British troops there. Helmut Schmidt, then the German Chancellor, arrived by helicopter for a meeting. Schmidt had faultless English, and the conversation began thus:

'Helmut, you're looking very well.'

'You too, Jim, you're looking very well.'

'I saw Henry yesterday.'

'Henry who?'

'Henry Kissinger.'

'How is he?'

'He's looking very well.'

No doubt the level of discourse was raised when there were no journalists listening.)

When Carrington met the mayor of Mexico City one of them, I forget which, remarked that his city and London had much in common, including an underground railway system. This astounding coincidence clearly affected both of them, and Carrington eagerly suggested a return visit, no doubt so that the mayor could experience the Northern Line in the rush hour – fractionally less crowded, I suppose, though probably also less efficient.

The breach came in Venezuela. By this time I had realized that absolutely nothing of importance was being transacted beyond a vague attempt to remind the South Americans that Britain still existed. We had some businessmen in tow, and I think they were supposed to make valuable contacts. However, I devoted myself, as so often, to cheap and meaningless jokes. I wrote that when Carrington had arrived in Caracas, his car had pulled to a halt, and was immediately surrounded by heavy-jowled men in need of a shave. 'And that was just the embassy staff.'

The Foreign Office cabled the press coverage of the visit overnight, every night, and since apart from the man from the BBC World Service I was the only reporter on the trip, this can't have taken long. Carrington's man of affairs approached me at one of the many cocktail parties. 'The foreign secretary has asked me to ask you which members of the embassy staff were in need of a shave.'

I said that it had been a not very good joke, and that as it happened, I had not criticized the foreign secretary himself.

'Precisely,' he said. 'The foreign secretary does not mind criticism. He does, however, expect to be taken seriously.'

This adage strikes me as being true of nearly all politicians, at least those who reach a certain level, and I have not forgotten it.

~

Actually there are many sayings and jokes that sum up those aspects of politics that are not always visible to the public. When I first started working at the Commons I was asked to keep an eye on the Liberal Party, which then had six MPs and was led by the flamboyant, louche figure of Jeremy Thorpe. In the summer of 1973 there was much talk of a hung parliament, and indeed a few months later a hung parliament was what we got. Thorpe had spent a day on a hovercraft tour of the north-west, arriving at coastal towns and emerging from the waves in his homburg-hatted, Edwardian dandy outfit. At one point I asked him what he would do if neither main party had a majority and he replied gravely, indeed pompously, 'The Queen's government must go on.' I took this to mean that he would give his party's support to whichever main party he thought fitting, and wrote as much in the paper.

The Liberal conference loomed, and on the constant principle that news rushes in to fill a vacuum, Thorpe's opinion on coalition assumed great importance. There was nothing else to write about. Many Liberals had been angered by his remarks, and had attacked him. He deflected the hostility by blaming me, 'this ignorant, junior reporter'. I heard myself denounced at least a dozen times on radio and television. This was slightly frightening – I already knew enough about him to be aware that Thorpe could be a determined enemy – and professionally worrying too, since, I assumed, none of his MPs would want to speak to me. This would make the job of Liberal correspondent far more difficult. In fact, the other five MPs could not have been more helpful. I told my boss, Ian Aitken, that I was puzzled by this. 'You have to remember,' he said, 'that when you make one enemy in this place, you automatically make 639 friends . . .'

~

There's a similar joke that's told to new MPs. A first-timer takes his place in the chamber, and, looking across to the other benches, says to the older MP next to him, 'It's good to get a sight of the enemy.'

'No, dear boy, that is the opposition,' his colleague says. 'You will find the enemy on this side.'

~

Another has a newcomer making his maiden speech. After it's over he runs into an old hand. 'My dear fellow,' says the veteran, 'that was a Rolls-Royce of a speech!'

The younger man is delighted until he's taken on one side by another: 'What he meant was, it was almost inaudible and it went on for ever.'

~

The following story is one I often tell when I give talks about politics. It includes a very bad word, and I always warn audiences beforehand, saying they should leave if the word might offend them. Nobody ever does walk out, and didn't even in Frinton-on-Sea, which I regard as a small triumph.

Bill Stones was a former miner and union official who became MP for Consett, one of those Labour seats where they weigh the votes rather than bother to count them. Miners were sometimes awarded a safe seat by the local party as a thank-you for long service down the pit and with the union. Stones also suffered from pneumoconiosis, or miner's lung. He was not one of those MPs who believed in actually doing very much, or imposing his opinions on others, and he spent much of his days in the corner of the Strangers' Bar, drowning the pain in his lungs, and occasionally going to vote the way the whips told him. But he was well liked.

One time he was eavesdropping on a conversation taking place around the bar itself. The group was talking about the membership of the Commons. 'The trouble with this place,' said somebody, 'is that it's full of cunts!'

Bill put down his drink, wiped his mouth, and said in his broad northern accent, 'They's plenty of cunts in country.' He paused. 'And they deserve some representation.'

I know of no better definition of parliamentary democracy.

~

Willie Whitelaw was a dedicated centrist among Tories, what Margaret Thatcher used to call a wet. But after he had been swept aside by her in the 1975 leadership election he demonstrated complete loyalty to her, in her company at least, and in the broadcasting studios, though he could be astringent about her when among friends or like-minded colleagues. 'That woman,' he once expostulated to the late Julian Critchley, 'thinks that *Question Time* is her hotline to the British people! She is wrong!' But his presence at her side was a guarantee to the party's left, or 'wet' wing, that they had not been entirely forgotten. Whenever she came up with some particularly mad scheme, he would be there to gaze at her with those eyes, like an oyster with a hangover, and tell her, with great regret, he was sorry to have to be so blunt, he apologized for being so candid, but duty called and the fact was, that the scheme was entirely unworkable. It is not a coincidence that Willie's influence was in decline when she decided to press on with the poll tax.

But he was most famous for his 'Willieisms', remarks that were simultaneously nonsense and yet perfectly easy to understand. I first came across these when he was appointed Secretary of State for

Northern Ireland in 1971. He arrived at Aldergrove airport outside Belfast and gave a press conference. One of the matters of most concern to reporters – especially those from nationalist newspapers or from the South – was a series of paramilitary parades being held by a former home affairs minister, William Craig. As a mini-Oswald Mosley, Bill Craig was slightly less threatening than P.G. Wodehouse's Black Shorts leader Roderick Spode, but some of his supporters were less comical, and the parades were thought alarming and a further threat to the peace of the province, such as it was.

The reporters pressed Willie several times, but he had clearly not been briefed on the topic, and had no intention of pronouncing on it. In the end he said firmly, 'I have always said it is a great mistake ever to pre-judge the past!' I thought at the time that would make an excellent watchword for almost any politician.

~

Willie was a big man and liked a big drink. Now and again he would come into Annie's Bar in the House of Commons, which no longer exists but in those days was the exchange and mart for MPs, ministers and journalists to swap information. Willie, who was Deputy Prime Minister at the time, would appear only when he had something he wanted to see in print, or when he wished to hear the gossip among the hacks. We would welcome him warmly, and offer him a drink.

'I would like a little whisky,' he said.

'When you say you would like a little whisky, do you mean you would like a small whisky?' I asked.

'No, when I say I would like a little whisky, I mean I would like a large whisky, thank you very much.' He would drink that quickly, then buy a drink for everyone in the bar. It was as if a Pall Mall club were sharing premises with a Wild West saloon.

~

In Northern Ireland Willie drank copiously. After he had left I reported that he worked his way through a bottle of Scotch every night. His former press officer, Keith McDowell, upbraided me. 'You got it completely wrong,' he said.

I replied that I had the information on good authority.

'Maybe,' said Keith, 'but you didn't have a clue about the bottle of gin he drank every lunchtime.'

Twice I covered him campaigning in his constituency of Penrith, in the far north-west by the Scottish border. He was delighted to see me, or at least managed to give that appearance. 'I expect you have come to hear some of my favourite *remarks*!' he said. He then descended upon the electorate roughly in the way that a combine harvester meets a field of wheat. 'Delighted to meet you! Vair pleased to meet you! So glad to meet you!' he would say, two dozen times in a minute, processing pedestrians, shoppers, drinkers so fast that he would encounter the same people two or even three times, bestowing the same blessing upon them. (A colleague told me about seeing him in action at a local Conservative Association. As he shook each hand, he said, 'Marvellous, marvellous!' He asked one woman how she was, and she replied that her husband had just died. 'Marvellous, marvellous!' he replied.)

On one occasion he invited me back to his home for lunch, revealing on the way that he was on the wagon. This turned out to mean that he drank only wine, and we shared a bottle of hock before the meal.

He had a tremendous gift for recovery. At a by-election he had gone to a constituency in support of the Conservative candidate, who was of a right-wing disposition. Willie appeared at the regular morning press conference, and was asked about a report on the probation service that had just been published. He said it was an important report, and should be considered very carefully.

'But your candidate said it should be screwed up and thrown into the waste-paper basket,' said one reporter.

Willie didn't miss a beat. 'Quite right. It should be screwed up, thrown into the waste-paper basket, then taken out, smoothed down, and considered very carefully.'

~

He had an extraordinary ability to shut people up without actually producing any kind of argument. I once saw him being questioned, rather persistently, by the *Observer*'s political correspondent, Nora Beloff, a woman never lightly rebuffed. As she returned to the attack, he finally announced, 'So there it is, there you are, and there you have it!' She could not find a reply. Another time a different reporter was trying to persuade him to apportion blame for some disaster or other. Willie was far too careful to do any such thing. 'I do not blame anyone,' he said, 'except perhaps all of us!'

~

Willie's most celebrated remark came in the second 1974 election campaign, when he wanted to accuse the Labour Party of misleading people into thinking that the economy was in better shape than it actually was. 'They are going about the country stirring up complacency!' he said. This is usually quoted as 'stirring up apathy', which would be entirely meaningless instead of being just somewhat meaningless. At another press conference during the same campaign, he was asked about morale among Tory workers. He insisted that it was good. (You could always tell he was lying, because he looked so miserable.) He was challenged. How could he know? He replied, 'I have the thermometer in my mouth, and I am listening to it all the time.'

~

Denis Healey was a man who never underestimated his own abilities. Once when Milton Friedman, the Chicago economist (how distant monetary theory seems now, like flared trousers and the Bay City Rollers!), was in Britain making a series of TV programmes, he interviewed Healey. 'You know,' he said afterwards, 'you're the cleverest man I've met in Britain.'

'You're right!' Healey shot back.

He loved playing with ideas, some complicated, some very simple. While he was Chancellor, a group of us took him to lunch and he mused that the one thing that would make his life easier was a tax on sex. He could manipulate figures like a master baker kneading a lump of dough. When inflation was roaring away in the mid-1970s, he managed to produce a figure indicating that it had fallen to 8.4 per cent – a figure that it didn't quite reach until four years later.

~

Tory MP Norman Tebbit, the 'semi-house-trained polecat', as Michael Foot called him (the prefix 'semi' pointlessly spoiling the rhythm, I thought, just as Denis Healey's description of shadow Chancellor Sir Geoffrey Howe's speeches, 'like being savaged by a dead sheep', would have worked better without the 'dead') was another man delighted by his own image. Tebbit was in fact a very courteous and even rather shy man, and I often suspected that the aggressive persona he had crafted for himself was designed to cover up for that. He was like an actor playing the demon king, happy to be booed by the children since he knows it's his part they are jeering, not him.

He certainly specialized in a particular lip-curling aggression. During the 1980 American election, I asked if he supported Ronald Reagan. 'I'm more of a Bush man myself,' he said. 'I would vote the double ticket – Reagan and a heart attack.'

As the votes were being counted in the 2001 British election, it was clear that William Hague was going to lose badly, and would have to resign. I was chatting to Norman when another reporter arrived to say that Michael Portillo appeared to be saying that he wouldn't run for leader. Did Tebbit think he'd got cold feet?

'I wouldn't know,' he said. 'I have never slept with him.'

~

Tony Benn's reincarnation as one of the best-loved figures in British public life, almost a national treasure, has been startling. Shortly before he left parliament he appeared on stage at the Festival Hall in a debate with David Davis, the Tory front-bencher. The great auditorium was largely, though not completely, full. Benn was at his most cosy and reassuring even when he talked about the misery and gloom ahead. One imagined an old grandfather, chuckling gently, smoking his pipe and patting the children on the head while warning them that they'd never find jobs when they grew up . . . They were talking about globalization. He reflected amiably on Dyson vacuum cleaners – 'marvellous machines, we have one at home' – which had recently moved manufacturing from Malmesbury in Wiltshire to the Far East. 'And do you know why they moved?' he asked, his voice thick with suspense, like a grandpa getting to the end of a ghost story. 'For profit!' Some of the audience gasped at this terrible allegation, rather as if he had accused the firm of moving so that its executives could enjoy sex tourism.

I remember thinking at the time that they had actually moved for survival. Since Hoover, Electrolux, Miele and all the rest made their cleaners abroad they were able to charge, say, £50 less for them. If everyone who wanted to buy one was happy to make a £50 contribution to the Distressed British Vacuum Cleaner Workers' fund, that would solve the problem, but it didn't seem very likely. If Benn had said, 'Look, we can keep jobs at home by running a siege economy, or we can have cheaper goods, make your choice,' that would have been honest, but not at all in keeping with his image.

I was covering the event for Radio 4. In the interval we went to talk to members of the audience in the bar. We moved in on the most middle-class, middle-aged couple we could find. They came from Guildford, Surrey. Had they come to hear David Davis? No, said the wife, we really like Tony Benn. I asked if they had always been revolutionary socialists. They both looked baffled, and the wife said, 'No, we always vote Conservative, don't we, darling?'

~

It was a long time since Benn had been regarded as a swivel-eyed extremist, more commonly known as Anthony Wedgwood Benn. The journalist Bernard Levin felt able to say, 'The head is the thick end of the Wedge.' Benn always struck me as being a blend of cold, clear-eyed opportunism and an extraordinary naïveté. He lived in Holland Park, in a fine house where, in the front garden, he kept the park bench on which he had proposed to his wife.

One morning a friend and I were driving to work at the House of Commons. This was sure to be difficult since there was a train strike which affected all lines in and around London; the traffic would be terrible and the buses full. Thatcher had not been long in power and this was an early skirmish in her protracted fight with the unions. We saw Benn walking just beyond his house and offered him a lift. He was full of enthusiasm for the strike. 'I think they should have collecting boxes at the main London stations,' he said, 'so that commuters can show their support for the strikers.'

Like many fundamentalists, Benn lived in a community of like-minded people, those who agreed with him on all political matters and saw the world in the way he did. To those folk it was a given that the railway workers were right to be on strike, but they also assumed that other workers would be eager to offer them support, even if their own lives were being hugely inconvenienced. This, I have noticed, affects people who have strong belief systems of any kind – political or religious, even ecological – because they rarely if ever have a serious discussion with anyone who doesn't agree with them, and hence find it hard to realize that their own views appear extreme or sometimes crazed to the majority. To these people, Benn's intimates, it was perfectly obvious that desperate commuters, faced with a bank of train indicators showing 'cancelled', would race to press fivers into the hands of those who had caused them to be cancelled.

~

This inability to comprehend how the rest of the world thought and lived extended into many areas of life. Once he summoned me to his office to acquaint me with some speech, or initiative, or project he wished to see recorded in the *Guardian*. He asked if I would like a drink. He himself did not drink alcohol, but he kept a bottle of whisky in his filing cabinet. I nodded gratefully, and he gave me the Scotch – a whole tumbler, full to the brim, without water or space for any water. I thought it strange that he had got through four or five decades without realizing that this was around three times the size of the most generous Scotch you would offer the greediest drunk.

~

Like many upper-class friends of the proletariat, he tended to assume that all its members were much the same. It went without saying that they were decent, hard-working, proud, loyal to their own, and oppressed. When he was the industry minister he made it his business to meet as many trade union representatives as possible. They were welcome to see him in his office, more or less at all times. Eric Heffer, one of his junior ministers, the son of a carpenter and a genuine member of the working classes, found this incredibly annoying. 'Anyone with a trade union badge can turn up at the department and see Tony,' he said, no doubt exaggerating a bit. 'You can't get anything done; you plan a meeting and Tony's off seeing some member of the boilermakers or whatever and telling them what a great job they're doing.'

Benn had seen working people drinking beer and eating sandwiches, and assumed this was their staple diet – like cats, or gerbils, they would be happy to eat the same stuff every day. So when union officials were invited for talks, that's what they were served. Heffer remonstrated. 'When these people come all the way to London to see the Secretary of State, they expect proper hot food,' he said. So Benn switched the order to macaroni cheese.

~

Benn had a penchant for runic remarks, which probably made perfect sense to him. I met him in Bristol during the 1979 election, when he lost his seat – in spite of his tenacious support for Concorde, which, though a remarkably expensive aircraft designed to provide transport for very rich people, happened to be partly built in his constituency. A colleague and I asked how he felt about the opinion polls which seemed to indicate a victory for Mrs Thatcher. He was scornful. 'Opinion polls,' he said, 'are the enemy's intelligence reports.' I have often wondered what he meant by this. A polling organization that produced figures skewed in order to create a particular result would quickly be out of business. Perhaps he meant that the polls revealed to the other side what the electorate would let them get away with. I suspect that since the polls suggested that the working people of Britain were not flocking to the banner of socialism, then he thought there must necessarily be something crooked about them. I don't know.

~

The 1983 election was a terrible defeat for Labour, partly because Thatcher had shed much of her early unpopularity following the 1982 victory in the Falklands, partly because Michael Foot was the Labour leader, and partly because the campaign was organized with catastrophic incompetence (and some pointless cunning too: Foot, already frail, was sent on a tour of seats that would have been unwinnable in any year, but had very left-wing Labour parties – often the case in safe Tory seats where the Labour power brokers saw no point in operating. These isolated left-wing groups were to be rewarded for the extremity of their views by a visit from the leader). Labour also had a hard-left manifesto, a document that Gerald Kaufman memorably described as 'the longest suicide note in history'.

When the result came in – it would have seemed humiliating in any election year – Benn declared it a triumph. More people had voted for an explicitly socialist programme than ever before, he said. He was always a proponent of the 'socialism has not failed; it has never been tried' line of argument. You hear the same from the right wing: free markets haven't failed, it's just that no government has had the guts to try them. Such opinions are like that stuff you used to pour into car radiators: whenever the radiator springs a leak, the gunk mixes with the incoming air and seals it off. So many followers of Tony Benn took the view that the electorate chose Margaret Thatcher because Labour was not left-wing enough. The argument was leak-proof.

~

Benn's diaries are also slightly less frank than you might imagine. Bernard Donoughue, who worked with Jim Callaghan in

Downing Street, records a time when Benn planned to go to Bristol to address a mass rally – 'Usually four shop stewards in a room,' Donoughue said sourly. Number 10 got wind that this was going to be one of Benn's speeches in which he attacked the Labour government for being insufficiently Bennite. The switchboard tracked him down and the Prime Minister spoke to him. 'The moment you open your mouth to give this speech, you cease to be a member of this government,' he said. Benn cancelled the speech. You'd think he might have found space for this interesting story in his diaries, but apparently more pressing events intervened.

Benn also used to tape virtually every word he uttered in public. But he often switched off the machine when other people were talking. The record of his own words was all that was required. Partly because he was convinced, with considerable justice, that the press would twist everything he said, so he needed an unchallengeable record. But another of the many bees that buzzed around in that bonnet was a conviction that readers hungered to read the words of politicians in their pure, unvarnished entirety. Papers should print screeds of speeches, so that the public could make up its own mind. The notion that the public might be more interested in David Beckham, or *Big Brother*, or indeed anything beyond the thoughts of Mr Benn and his colleagues, apparently never struck him.

~

(It is a common complaint among politicians that their speeches are always filtered through the press, and I do have some sympathy. Words get dragged out of context, sentences twisted to fit some kind of narrative that exists principally in the mind of the reporter. And times have changed. When I first went to work at Westminster, *The Times* had a team of sixteen parliamentary reporters who recorded something from more or less every speech made in the chamber. Now there is none, and a speech only makes its way into the paper if it advances a news story or appears, mocked, in a parliamentary sketch. There is a Sherlock Holmes story, 'The Cardboard Box', in which Dr Watson describes a dreary August: 'Parliament was not sitting, so there was little of interest in the newspapers' – a thought that would be inconceivable today.)

~

Benn aroused as much dislike among his immediate colleagues as he received adoration from the public, at least in his later years. They had had to live with all the disappointing compromises and shabby second-bests that are the fate of anyone trying to run a government. After Thatcher's 1979 win, he embarked on a long campaign against the failures of the Wilson and Callaghan administrations that had preceded Thatcher. For ministers who had been in Cabinet and who had seen him accept everything, often without demur and without a hint that he might resign, this became a source of rage. A speech he gave at the 1980 Labour conference in particular made many of them feel physically ill.

I remember asking Gerald Kaufman about one of Benn's coat-trailing speeches. He said, 'I once got a letter from a constituent saying that whenever he saw my face on television, he could reach the set and switch me off within two seconds. Well, whenever I see Benn's face, I can switch it off in half a second. Because I have a remote control.'

~

Another left-winger is Dennis Skinner, with whom it was sometimes difficult to rub along. Dennis was a sea-green incorruptible, and like so many of that type, greatly admired his own incorruptibility. He would not eat sandwiches at the Labour Party's National Executive Committee meetings, on the grounds that he had not paid for them. He had been abroad but didn't like it – even Soviet Russia, where he had paid a parliamentary visit. The group had been down a mine, and had had hot baths afterwards. Dennis was so appalled at seeing a vast woman approach his tub with a scrubbing brush that he had, according to colleagues present, climbed out and fled. He didn't have a passport. He wasn't opposed to all things foreign, however, and had been an Elvis impersonator briefly in his youth. Like old soldiers who have never quite coped with the end of their military career, with its camaraderie and sense of shared danger, Dennis mourned the end of the class war, which had given such meaning to his own life. He would talk about strikes, and picket lines, and police baton charges in the same way that a retired major might describe an attack on a German machine-gun nest.

~

He never trusted me, partly – I like to think – because as a northerner myself I didn't entirely buy his blunt-spoken, no-nonsense, we-call-a-spade-a-spade northerner image. I used to treasure his occasional insults. I was once on the Commons terrace with Joe Ashton, another northern Labour MP, and his wife, and my then girlfriend. Dennis approached us, and put his hands on the back of my girlfriend's chair. ''Oo's this, then?' he asked, as if she did not exist (a soft, fancy-pants southerner might have said, 'Good afternoon, I don't think we've been introduced.').

'That's Rosie, Simon's girlfriend,' said Joe.

'We all have our cross to bear,' said Dennis, ambling off.

~

In 1982 I was standing in the Members' Lobby with a colleague. The Falklands War was near the end of its phoney stage and the fighting about to begin. Skinner came out of the chamber in conversation with Ian Gow, who was then Margaret Thatcher's parliamentary private secretary. 'It must be serious,' I said *sotto voce* to my colleague, 'she's offering Skinner a job in a government of national unity.'

At that instant, he left Gow's side and raced over angrily. 'I heard that,' he said. 'Up north where I come from, we say what we have to say to each other's faces.'

Something in me snapped. 'Don't be daft,' I said, 'I come from the north and northern people are just as snide and gossipy and backbiting as anyone in the south.'

'But *you're* middle class,' he said, again rolling off with a slight swagger, as one who has made his point with lethal effect.

~

(Joe Ashton I liked a lot. He wrote a partly autobiographical novel about being a working-class lad who goes into politics. He made the point that for the poor, all round the world, there were only four ways out of poverty: sport, show business, politics and crime. We toured Sheffield with its working-class terraces – then – steel mills, and finally the vast and celebrated Fiesta Club, the ultimate in a luxury night out for the working man and his wife. Everyone was seated at little tables, where they would be served food, such as chicken or scampi in the basket. These vast clubs had recognized three things: that working-class people had more money to spend, that the men did not only want to spend their evenings drinking with each other in the pub, and that they were happy to have their wives with them.

All day Joe had been telling me how much local people admired Arthur Scargill, whose fierce negotiating skills had won the miners an extra 50p an hour, a reasonable sum in those days. The act at the Fiesta that night was Bernard Manning – scarcely a national treasure, but not yet the source of hatred he was to become. Manning's act went down extremely well. At the end, he said, 'Arthur Scargill? Arthur Scargill? Yer know what I'd like to do wi' Arthur Scargill?'

At this point Joe nudged me. 'They're not going to like this,' he said. 'They worship Arthur Scargill round here.'

'I'd like to tekk 'im out, buy 'im the 'ottest curry in Sheffield . . .'

Joe tensed beside me.

'And sew his arsehole up!'

The place collapsed in laughter and cheers. Joe ushered me out quickly.

I had seen Manning perform once before, at his club in Manchester. He was more famous then for being filthy rather than racist. As ever, the relief for his audience came from being able to laugh at things they could never say at home or in polite society.

'This RAF plane was shot down. Nine men on it and a WRAF managed to swim to this desert island.

'After a week, the WRAF was so ashamed of what she was doing, she killed herself.

'After another week, the men were so ashamed of what they were doing, they buried her.

'After another week, they were so ashamed of what they were doing, they dug her up again.'

Funny? Up to a point. But such jokes are the equivalent of the *Playboy* nude behind the locker door – the point is not that it's erotic but that it's forbidden.)

~

Skinner had a certain innocence which you find in all people whose lives are built round a particular view of how the world works. Like Benn and like Thatcher – a comparison that would enrage him – he often found it difficult to understand how other, non-ideological, people might view things. For example, Jane Fonda had agreed to come to the House of Commons and address the left-wing Tribune Group about her opposition to the war in Vietnam. She had been asked to come to St Stephen's Entrance, the main door for visitors to the Commons, where Skinner was to meet her. It was St Patrick's Day and he was wearing a spray of shamrock in his lapel.

There was no sign of her there, and someone suggested that she might have gone by mistake to St Stephen's Tavern, a pub across the road. Skinner popped over to the pub but she wasn't there either. He shuttled back and forth for a while, then asked the barmaid if she had seen Jane Fonda.

'No, she usually sits over there with a bottle of Guinness, but she hasn't been in today. Now get out of here, you drunken Irish git, before I call the police.'

~

The next Skinner story is, I am sure, apocryphal, yet like many apocryphal stories contains an inner truth. In the tale he is approached by Nicholas Soames, the grandson of Sir Winston Churchill, and an Old Etonian. 'You know, Skinner,' he said, 'you miners and us public schoolboys have more in common than you might think.'

'Aye, and what might that mean?' asked Skinner.

'Well, for one thing, we all take our showers together.'

Skinner allegedly growled, 'But we can risk bending down to pick up soap.'

It is certainly true that Soames enjoyed winding Skinner up. Once he told him that he was going to be in Derbyshire, visiting friends – the Duke and Duchess of Devonshire, as it happened. But he would like to pay a call on the Skinners too. 'So tell that wife of yours to get her hair out of curlers, and get some food in. Just a snack, some quails' eggs will do . . .'

~

Another person who sees the world in a quite different way from the rest of us is Jeffrey Archer. It is a commonplace that he is a liar. Actually he is more of a fantasist, someone who has the ability to invent a world preferable to the one he is living in. This can be a huge help to a novelist, who has a far more difficult task than any writer of non-fiction. We have only to note what we observe or hear, or learn in some indirect way; novelists must create a world out of nothing. Very few people can do this, which is one reason why Archer is so successful and so rich. For a long time the *on dit* among the chattering classes in London was that Archer's books were really written by Richard Cohen, a publisher who edited all his early novels. As it happened I was at university with Richard, and over lunch one day I gingerly raised the suggestion.

He sighed as one who has heard the same story far too many times before. 'Look,' he said, 'if I had written Jeffrey's books, they would be much better written, because I know how to write. I know the difference between "their" and "there", and I know that you need more than two punctuation marks per page. Jeffrey doesn't know any of that. But if I did write them nobody would read them, because I can't tell a story, and Jeffrey can.' In fact Richard spent a year of his own time on each of the early Archer books, taking the rattling, page-turning yarn and turning it into English.

~

You always felt with Archer that his life was a series of dramas – some tremendous, like his trial for perjury, others minuscule, scarcely worth even his own attention. Once I arrived at Waterloo station and noticed that my tie had an egg stain on it. I had a lunch that day, so went to buy the cheapest new one I could find at Tie Rack. It was a jazzy, multicoloured tie, long since given to charity, and it was only after I'd bought it that I noticed it had the Olympic rings worked into the pattern. I passed Jeffrey in a House of Lords corridor that day.

'Ha!' he said. 'I see you are wearing my tie!'

I made a feeble joke about it not being his tie; I had bought it that morning.

'No, no, no,' he clucked impatiently, 'the tie I designed for the British Olympic Federation.'

This seemed improbable, and when I got it home I discovered it was an Italian tie, designed for the Italian Olympic Federation.

People rarely remonstrated with him; for one thing, he was impervious to criticism, and for another, it was better to have the original story to relate rather than whatever limp explanation he would provide.

Take the time at a Tory conference in Blackpool when he hosted a lunch for various political journalists in his suite at the Imperial Hotel. The conference resumed at two thirty, but they were all enjoying stickies such as port and brandy when the phone rang in the bedroom. He took it, then hurried back. 'I'm sorry, I'm going to have to ask you to stand outside in the corridor for a while. It's the Prime Minister on the line.'

They were waiting outside when Nicholas Soames walked past. He asked what they were doing, standing around like a bunch of whores touting for business. They explained that Archer was speaking to John Major.

Soames harrumphed off to his room, then a moment later stuck his head round the door and said, 'If he is talking to the Prime Minister, he's doing it by telepathy, because the Prime Minister is on live television, on the platform, and he's not speaking to anyone!'

A colleague of mine who was present did make the mistake of challenging Archer, but got an evasive reply about how Major had called him from underneath the stage, just before stepping up to the platform seats . . .

~

A couple I know, both of them political writers, found themselves at the same reception as Archer one evening. As the bash wound down, he said cheerily, 'I know, why don't we all eat at the Ivy? On me!'

The husband joshed him; even he could not get a table at the Ivy at 9 p.m. on a week night.

'Oh, I think I can,' Archer said, before disappearing to make the call.

'That's fine,' he said, returning, 'we'll get a cab there now.'

He was, as always, as good as his word and paid the bill before disappearing to the Gents. My friend teased the maître d'. 'It's all right if Lord Archer phones asking for a table,' he said, 'but it would be a different story if a pleb like me tried to book at the last minute.'

'No,' the maître d' said, 'I don't understand. Lord Archer booked this table three weeks ago.'

As I said, not a lie, or, if it were, an entirely pointless one. Instead it was a small drama, a moment of mild but satisfying excitement.

Raymond Chandler used to cut sheets of typing paper into four, horizontally. He would put each slice of paper in the machine and write – with double spacing – around twenty-five words. If nothing exciting happened, or there wasn't a particularly vivid phrase, or the introduction of a new character, he would rip out the paper and start again. I felt that Jeffrey Archer lived his life on the same pattern: there had to be something going on at every instant. Hence the celebrated moment when someone at one of the parties he held in his riverside penthouse asked the way to the toilet, and was told, 'Down the corridor, and turn left at the Picasso.'

I sometimes attended his Tory conference bashes, the ones where he served Krug and shepherd's pie. (It is vulgar, I gather, to refer to champagne by its brand name, or in some circles even as champagne. Instead it is 'wine'.) Unusually for a private party, the guest list was chosen by rank. You had to be a newspaper editor, a political editor, a political columnist, or a Cabinet minister. Mere junior ministers and similar riff-raff were not welcome. On one occasion I turned up with my colleague Paul Routledge who was technically, nominally, my junior on the *Observer*, a fact that troubled me greatly since he was far more experienced and competent than me, but which didn't seem to trouble Paul at all.

Jeffrey came over, looking cross. 'You,' he said, 'are a political editor, and so are invited to my party. He' – he pointed at Paul, who was admittedly trying to open a bottle of Archer's champagne – 'is a mere reporter. Tell him to leave!'

Being fairly drunk myself, I replied, 'It's your party. Tell him yourself.'

Jeffrey marched towards the recalcitrant gatecrasher who gave him a look that would have sent a basilisk running for its mummy. It was a blend of venom, class hatred, and sheer 'you-looking-at-me?' loathing I have rarely observed in a human face, and I can still see the swerve Jeffrey executed to avoid it. Again, a mini-drama had been played out.

~

One evening my wife and I were guests at a dinner party given by a mutual friend. Jeffrey was there, and Mary Archer was down from Grantchester, where they live in the house made famous by Rupert Brooke. The house is celebrated for many reasons, principally Brooke's lines, 'Stands the Church clock at ten to three? / And is there honey still for tea?' – puzzling since who is finishing tea at 2.50 p.m.? Surely it would have been better to write something more convincing, such as 'Stands the Church clock at five forty-two? And is it yet time to open the 'poo?' The house is also behind what many crossword fans regard as the greatest clue ever produced by the greatest of contemporary crossword compilers, John Graham, whose pen name is Araucaria: 'Chaste Lord Archer vegetating at poetic site', which is an anagram of the first four words, leading to THE OLD VICARAGE GRANTCHESTER. John works out his anagrams with the letters from a Scrabble set; even so, this is a near miracle of apposite clueing.

Jeffrey did most of the talking at the dinner, and Mary said very little. (Later he wrote to our hostess saying, 'I loved the food, the wine, and the company. Mary loved the food and the wine.') He told stories, some true, some I suspect not true, others retold and embellished for effect. Mary had been in charge of fundraising for the Fitzwilliam Museum in Cambridge and had wanted £500,000 to create a Japanese room there. They had, he said, been offered £100,000 by a Japanese businessman, but this was not enough. He had told Margaret Thatcher, who immediately offered to entertain the man to tea. He was shown into Number 10, where, in Mary and Jeffrey's presence, they talked about Anglo-Japanese relations, world trade, prospects for peace and so forth. It was only at the very end of the allotted hour that she said, 'As you know, Mary needs £500,000 to endow her Japanese room. You have already made a most generous offer. But if you were to give her the full amount, I would make this promise: the room would be named after you, and I would personally make the journey to Cambridge to open it, in your presence!' According to Jeffrey, the man had the cheque written before he left the sitting room.

On their way out, he added, Mary turned to him and said, 'I always knew that you were the most vulgar man in England, but I had not realized that she was the most vulgar woman.'

This story appears to be very largely true though the businessman's company, the Shiba corporation, was upset by his generosity – which involved a somewhat smaller sum. Mrs

Thatcher did open the room, but it has been named after Shiba and the businessman was not present.

~

A much more dramatic event came with his trial for perjury in 2001. I was sent to cover the verdict, which was a long time in coming. I suspect, without any first-hand knowledge, that the jury spent five days or so debating the man being tried with him, Ted Francis, who had backed up Archer's evidence in his original libel trial, but who years later revealed that he had been lying at Archer's behest. He too might have been guilty as charged, but at least he had recanted; indeed without his change of heart, neither man would have been on trial.

It was a pleasant week, for us reporters at least. Daytimes we spent chatting to each other, with lunchtimes in the pub. I caught up on some Jeffrey Archer novels which, as Richard Cohen had said, turned out to be ripping yarns. The clerk of the court was an astonishingly beautiful black woman called Deidre, who I later learned had paid for her training by working in a gentleman's club. She had caught the eye of the late David Fingleton, who wrote about food for the *Spectator*, and he would take her on his arm to the opera. There was never any suggestion of impropriety in her professional or social life, though since she was so gorgeous I assumed she was much in demand. I thought at the time that her career would make a good short story plot for Jeffrey Archer, or even Somerset Maugham. Perhaps she would reach the pinnacle of her career, as chief clerk at the Old Bailey, when someone would reveal that she had once worked in a gentleman's club. These days, when Page 3 girls and porn film makers can stand for parliament with only mild tutting in the press, it might not seem like much.

Deidre made it her business to look after the press, letting us know when the judge had friends in and so when we had longer for lunch. It was during one of these midday sessions that Valerie Grove of *The Times* suggested that we kept a bottle of champagne ready for the verdict. I, the fusspot, said that we had nowhere to keep it cold and that nobody liked warm champagne. 'Oh, I don't know,' said A.N. Wilson, then writing for the *Telegraph* in the days before they sacked nearly all their good writers, 'we could always leave it between Mary Archer's thighs for ten minutes.'

And Mary Archer did look ice cold when the verdict came down. It must take quite a lot of stern effort to be so apparently unmoved by anything, including the incarceration of your husband. The foreman of the jury was a young Rastafarian – which was unusual, since in my limited experience juries almost always choose the most middle-aged, middle-class person among them. Deidre asked if they had reached a verdict, and the Rasta replied that they had. I thought it made a fascinating vignette of modern British society: two young people, both of immigrant stock, producing the formulae that would send a peer of the realm to prison. For the first time in the trial, as he found himself living inside the plot of what might have been one of his own short stories, a nerve in Archer's cheek began to twitch.

The judge, Humphrey Potts, began by saying, 'Sentencing you, Lord Archer, gives me no pleasure at all . . .' As Andy Hamilton said on *The News Quiz* a day or so later, 'Why did they give that job to the one person in Britain who could make that remark?'

~

As sketchwriters we are, I suppose, verbal caricaturists. Nicholas Garland, the brilliant cartoonist for the *Telegraph*, once described to me how his profession worked. A new person swims into the public gaze. They may have an apparently quite ordinary face, like John Major or Tony Blair. The cartoonist then finds something, anything, about their appearance that is even slightly off-normal. The example he gave was Neil Kinnock's freckles, a minor facial detail that even people who knew him quite well would scarcely notice. So you draw the freckles prominently. You add the slight bifurcation or dimple at the end of his nose. Make the sandy hair a little stragglier than it is, and by the end you have a sort of basic, ur-Kinnock, which can be used as a convenient basis for a host of adaptations. Meanwhile, the readers begin to notice the freckles, nose and hair, so that after a while the victim comes to resemble their caricature. This was especially noticeable in TV's *Spitting Image*. By the end of the first series, the puppet had become the reality and the flesh-and-blood human a lacklustre copy. The effect was heightened by the fact that as we grow older, our skins begin to wrinkle and look more like latex.

Various cartoonists fastened on to John Major's upper lip, on which a sort of phantom moustache seemed to hover. Tony Blair's protruding ears were a convenient shorthand for him. My colleague Steve Bell spotted that Blair had, like Margaret Thatcher, one mad staring eye. (I claim credit for noticing that this was sometimes the right, sometimes the left, as if the daemon within took its pick each morning.) By the end of Blair's period in office, Bell was able to draw the eye inside an electricity pylon, as the viewing hole in a prison door, or as an untethered balloon floating away into the sky and achieve instant recognition.

~

In the same way, we sketchwriters develop our own shorthand for the people we write about, exaggerating language, absorbing verbal tics, fastening on to some minor eccentricity and pumping it as hard as we can. One of my favourite characters has always been Michael Fabricant, the Tory MP for Lichfield. When I returned to sketchwriting in 1993, I noticed how he was always ready with a grovel for the then Prime Minister, John

Major. 'Is my Right Honourable friend aware that the people of South Staffordshire are united in their delight at the success of the economy . . .' and so forth. I also noticed, and no one could fail to notice, his extraordinary hair, silky, shiny, lustrous and blond, very much like the tail of a My Little Pony toy. It also changed length at alarming speed. Seeing it long one day and short the next was not perhaps surprising, but the opposite seemed impossible. The only conclusion was that he was wearing a wig, something he always denied. When his local paper asked him about it, he offered to jump out of a plane, with a parachute but without a crash helmet, just to prove his point. The paper decided not to take up the offer because of the cost of insurance. Then a House of Commons official found himself following Fabricant down the colonnade that connects the Members' Entrance with Westminster tube station. This is open on one side to New Palace Yard, and a gale was blowing. Fabricant's hairstyle substance lifted up and revealed a system of netting, presumably designed to keep the hair in place.

~

It would be hard to imagine a more trivial subject, but I learned two things. Fabricant hated it but the readers loved it. They mailed in clippings about him. One sent a photograph of a waiter in Lyon who looked alarmingly liked him. They sent snaps of French shops with the word 'Fabricant' on the front. Some had reminiscences of his early days in Brighton, where his father was a rabbi, and I even got a CD of Fabricant the disc jockey doing a stint on the local radio station. (He had spent a brief time in pirate radio.)

Meanwhile he grew more and more angry. He would beard Labour MPs in the Tea Room and beg them to tell him how to make me stop, as if they had any idea, or would have told him if they knew. Suddenly his annoyance came to an end. After the

1997 election, when he was lucky to hold on to his seat, I pointed out that his majority was roughly the same as the *Guardian*'s readership in his constituency – so, I claimed mendaciously, he had me to thank for his continued success. Now we are on friendly terms, and there are even embarrassing photos of him and me sharing a manly hug at a Tory conference. I am not proud of this; it is yet another example of the continued impotence of all satirists of whatever stripe.

~

I am also on Christmas-card terms with Sir Peter Tapsell, the last of the knights of the shires, the grandest of all grandees. Sir Peter has the right attributes for a commanding orator: he has a slight speech impediment, and does not speak so much as boom. He utters each word with thunderous precision, as if he were a goose and it was a golden egg that he was laying with the utmost care. The running joke is that Hansard writers fling aside their pens and notepads, and record Sir Peter's words on illuminated manuscripts, or arrange for them to be cast in bronze at tiny foundries in Birmingham, saved from bankruptcy by the work.

Sir Peter's interventions are greatly prized in the Commons, and whenever his name is called, the place goes quiet – though, it must be said, this is sometimes only a prelude to mocking laughter. No matter. He showed me how he had incorporated a sketch of mine into his election material: 'When Sir Peter Tapsell speaks, the whole House falls silent,' I had written. This is the exact equivalent of a theatre taking a bad review: 'The fabulous scenery cannot make up for the appalling acting and the dreadful script,' and quoting the one word 'Fabulous!' over the posters.

He does take his utterances with great seriousness and is one of the few MPs who mounts to the Hansard office in the Commons to make sure they have recorded every speech, question or intervention correctly. Once a Hansard reporter, trying to get his work finished in time for a deadline, suggested that he could check what had been recorded on the internet. 'I am afraid,' said Sir Peter glumly, in the manner of one who has not yet caught up with the twentieth century, never mind the twenty-first, 'that I don't have an internet.'

~

(The same morose desire not to accommodate modern technology afflicted the late Auberon Waugh. He phoned me once to commission a book review for the magazine he edited, the *Literary Review*. I said I expected he would like me to send it by email.

'I suppose so,' he said unhappily.

I said I would need an email address.

He brightened up when someone evidently came over to put it in front of him. 'It starts "litrev",' he said. 'I expect that is short for "literary review".' Then he groaned. 'There's a little curly thing, I suppose you'll know what that is . . .')

~

The person who caused the Hansard writers most trouble over the years was, unsurprisingly, John Prescott, former Labour Deputy Prime Minister, a man who on any day could go three rounds with the English language and, like Tigger, emerge asking, 'Have I won?' Hansard even used tape recordings of his speeches to train newcomers on the grounds that they could face no sterner test. It is a myth that Hansard provides an accurate transcript of what MPs say: in fact, it provides an account of what they were trying to say. They won't alter a sentence merely because the MP has changed his mind, or been told to get back on message by the whips, but if someone has simply jumbled up his words, as Prescott generally did, they will untangle them. On some occasions the version that communicated what he really meant was around half the length of what he had actually said. Once or twice they simply left whole chunks out.

~

Prescott was extremely chippy about his coverage in the press, which he attributed to his working-class origins, even though his father had been a manager on the railways and so was, by any standards, middle class. But he himself had been a steward on passenger liners, and MPs – like school bullies, ever willing to find weakness and exploit it – would play on that. 'Another gin and tonic, Giovanni!' Nicholas Soames would shout at him, secure in the knowledge that it would wound. He attributed the sketchwriters' tormenting to our public school background, though the two he hated most, me and Matthew Parris, hardly fit that bill. Matthew had gone to boarding school, but had been raised in Africa, so his parents had had a limited choice. My parents, I used to stress, had not paid one penny for my schooling. Prescott somehow discovered that for two years I had gone to Hymers College, Hull, in the city he represented. This is now a fee-paying independent school, though in my day it was direct grant. I had a scholarship and so all my costs were paid by the (Labour) council. These matters seem unimportant, but to Prescott they meant a lot. He regarded it as the smoking gun, the proof that I really was yet another toff out to humiliate him for being a son of the workers.

~

One characteristic of many MPs is not that they are venal, arrogant, corrupt or crazed by power. Many – no, most – are none of these things. But they can be dreadfully boring. There was one Labour backbencher who held a Midlands seat through much of the seventies and eighties who was notorious for his nit-picking interpretations of official documents. You'd be having a quiet drink in Annie's Bar, hoping that something interesting would happen or someone interesting arrive, and this fellow would appear bearing an obscure ministerial document as if it were the German plans for the invasion of Britain in 1940. 'May I call your attention,' he would say, 'to page 57, paragraph 9, subsection (iii)?' You would, out of weary politeness, read the thing. He would snatch the paper back, flip to page 102, paragraph 17, point at it triumphantly and say, 'Compare it with this! You do take my point!' Usually it was impossible to see what his point was, or if there was one it was generally too trivial and obscure to be worth reading, never mind writing an article about.

We soon decided that he was the second most boring man in Britain, on the grounds that to be the most boring man in Britain would be, in its way, quite interesting. We developed a system of avoidance, called International Rescue, as in the *Thunderbirds* puppet series. If you needed help getting rid of him, or any other bore, you put your hand on top of your head and rubbed it, as if relieving an itch, until a colleague noticed it. They could then go to one of the many internal phones around the Commons, call the appropriate bar or café, and ask for you. A short message – 'The news desk needs you to ring them' or, 'Your grandmother is dangerously ill' – was enough to provide an excuse to flee.

~

Booze played an enormous part in the life of parliament. Since the House rarely rose before 11 p.m., and often went on into the small hours, there was little for many MPs to do apart from vote when they were told, and drink when they wished. Alcohol was, and is, substantially cheaper than it is in the outside world, since the bars have no rates or rents to pay. Journalists in particular were anxious to use their expense accounts to prise information out of those who might have it. My boss Ian Aitken was the master of this. He knew the favourite drink of almost every minister or senior opposition MP.

During Harold Wilson's government there was another of the routine emergency Cabinet meetings at which massive cuts in public spending were demanded. Knowing what problems this would cause, ministers did everything they could to keep the decisions secret until they could be leaked out, or at least presented with gloss to make them almost acceptable. All the papers were naturally desperate to find out what had happened. Ian relaxed. He waited in Annie's Bar, his Scotch and water being topped up at fairly frequent intervals, until in walked a Cabinet minister he knew well. Ian also knew that he drank pints of Federation Ale, so he had one poured, handed it to the minister, placed his hands on the wall on either side of the man's shoulders rather like an American cop, and demanded information. The minister gave him half of what had happened, which was half more than anyone else obtained, and it led the paper the next day.

~

Ian's ability to get the story out fast and readably – in those days of copytakers he would write his first paragraph on the back of an envelope, then ad lib the rest – was highly valued. Ted Heath was to make a speech to mark the UK's entry into the Common Market. Copies of the speech would be delivered to the political correspondents in advance, so it was agreed that Ian would write for the first two editions of the paper, and Hella Pick – the thunderously grand diplomatic editor, a rare example of a female panjandrum – would attend the dinner and write up the speech for the last two editions, which, in the minds of all metropolitan media folk, were the only ones that mattered.

Next day Ian was puzzled but pleasantly surprised to see that his account had survived all four editions, possibly because it was better written than Hella's. So it was with a light heart that he walked into the Gay Hussar restaurant for lunch. Sitting at the very end of the room, which is long and shaped rather like a bus with the maître d' hovering around the driver's end, was Hella, who rose to her considerable height, pointed at Ian, and declared: 'What you did to me last night was outrageous!' Several of the diners broke into applause.

~

(The Gay Hussar was the office canteen for many politicians, chiefly though not exclusively of the left. It provided reliable and tasty food in immense portions. It also provided Victor Sassie, who owned and ran the place as if it were a reform school for youths who might, given his full attention, be redeemable. He came from Barrow-in-Furness but had trained in eastern Europe, giving him a whiff of the exotic. Victor liked to boss the diners around. He once threw out George Brown, then the foreign secretary, for groping a woman at the next table. On one occasion I watched him trying to change the order placed by a customer.

Victor: What have you ordered?

Customer: Roast pork.

Victor: Nah, you don't want that. You want the goose.

Customer: But I don't like goose.

Victor: Nah, there's too much garlic in the pork. The girls in the office won't want to kiss you.

Customer: But I don't want the girls in the office to kiss me.

Victor, to the waiter: Bring this customer the goose.)

Ian could put away an enormous amount of Scotch without any apparent effect, and I only saw him drunk once. He had been summoned by phone from a party in Downing Street where he happened to be talking to the Prime Minister, Jim Callaghan. He blamed me and the news editor, Peter Cole, and upbraided us in strong language. Next day he was full of remorse, and insisted on buying us dinner and champagne at his club, the Garrick. Here his self-reproach led him to offer me his place at the Guadeloupe summit of world leaders. In Britain we had the winter of discontent, the weather was foul, and so I said in awed gratitude, 'Ian, you don't mean that!'

'No,' he said after brief thought, 'as a matter of fact I don't.'

Ian had lost the sight in one eye from a disease he picked up reporting the Algerian war for the *Daily Express*. The eye is on permanent display in Moorfields Eye Hospital. It was replaced by a glass eye that was cunningly linked to the appropriate muscles, so that it looked and moved just like a real one. Unfortunately it would occasionally pop out, once when he was near the top of the escalator in Highgate tube station, one of the deepest in London. It also popped out while he was swimming in Guadeloupe, and he and a friend had to walk down the beach asking the sunbathers, '*Pardonnez nous, mon ami a perdu son oeuil de verre . . .*'

A day or so later they were in the press room, and an American tourist put his head round the door. 'Has one of you fellows lost a glass eye? We were swimming and we saw this thing – we heard one of you was missing it . . .'

~

It was the booze in the Commons, and especially the Tory whips' office, that got me off smoking, something I had always planned to do. Indeed the fact that I was always about to give up made me feel it was quite safe to smoke even more. I reached sixty cigarettes on some working days. Disaster loomed on terrible nights when the Commons rose at 11 p.m., which meant that the pubs outside were closing at exactly the same moment as the Commons bars. However, Ian could sniff out strong drink with the skill of a truffle hound, and on this occasion we quickly found our way to the Conservative whips' office. Whipping is a difficult and demanding job, and greatly resented by many backbenchers who are not whips, and who dislike being told where to be and when, and how to vote. For this reason they tend to relax strenuously. As the late political columnist Alan Watkins once put it, 'Every night is Burns night in the SNP whips' office,' and the same was true of the larger parties.

We began drinking Scotch from the hospitality cupboard. Other whips and other journalists, hearing the noise, came in. By the end there were, I think, fourteen of us, and at 4.30 a.m. it was clear that there was no more Scotch to be found. I have a vague memory of handing round a bottle of Blue Curaçao, and somehow finding my way out to Whitehall where I managed to hail a taxi. Next day I woke at around 1 p.m., feeling as ill as I have ever felt. It seemed a good time to stop smoking, so I did. It was fantastically difficult, a matter of small, incremental achievements: the first article written without a fag, the first pint, the first party negotiated without nicotine. But I still have a recurring dream in which I smoke one cigarette, then the rest of the packet, and am hooked again. Like alcoholics, smokers never actually lose their addiction; they just try to ignore it.

~

The whips were frantically busy during the end of the 1974–79 Labour administration, when the government was in a minority and every single vote counted. One of the many stupid rules parliament clings to is that an MP can vote only if they are on the premises. They don't have to pass through the division lobbies, and they don't even need to be conscious for their vote to be counted. During this hectic period relations between the two whips' offices broke down. Labour had clearly and deliberately cheated, obliging one of their men who was 'paired' to vote anyway. So the Tories sent one of their men to look round the ambulances parked in New Palace Yard. In one they saw the MP for St Helens, Leslie Spriggs, lying unconscious. 'How do we know he's not dead?' asked the Tory whip.

The Labour whip looked desperately around till he saw a tempting button, which he biffed. A loud 'ping!' rang out. 'Three hundred and seventeen!' he said triumphantly, as the government secured another hair's-breadth win.

Peter Snape was one of the most resourceful Labour whips, but he was defeated when Michael Cocks, the tough Labour chief whip, sent him round to see Maurice Edelman, an MP and novelist who was not the most assiduous attender at the Commons. He was to be told to turn up at 10 p.m. for a crucial vote. No excuse whatever would be tolerated. Snape drove round to his expensive Belgravia flat. He was, Edelman said, tremendously sorry, but he had a dinner party that night, and it was quite impossible for him to abandon his guests. The government would have to struggle by without him. Snape begged and bullied, plucked and pleaded, but nothing worked.

The government won by a couple of votes anyway, and Snape drove home to West Bromwich. On the last part of the trip, he heard a late-night news bulletin: Maurice Edelman had died. He walked into his house to hear the telephone ringing. He picked it up to hear Cocks say, 'Snape! Overkill.'

~

At present I work as a parliamentary sketchwriter for the *Guardian*. This is a job that is almost, but not quite, unique to Westminster – there are sketchwriters in Dublin and Edinburgh too, and their work, like ours, is fairly incomprehensible if you don't recognize the names or know the references. In America, the notion of impairing the purity of the news with humour would be thought outrageous. Jokes are permitted, of course, but corralled into their own pens, such as late-night TV or humour columns. It is, however, a long tradition here. Currently there are five of us, the others working for *The Times*, the *Independent*, the *Daily Telegraph* and the *Daily Mail*. We like to think of Charles

Dickens as our greatest predecessor, and some of his *Sketches by Boz* convey the same backbiting, paranoia and conspiracy that political journalists report today, if in less exciting and enticing prose. For a long time, however, sketchwriting was largely reverential. Before television, and while radio was kept firmly in its box by the authorities, it was the nation's great conversation with itself and was treated with all the respect due. Harry Boardman, who wrote the *Guardian* sketch during and after the war, published his selected columns as *The Glory of Parliament* – a title that would be inconceivable today.

The first modern sketchwriter was Bernard Levin, who wrote a weekly sketch in the *Spectator* under the soubriquet Taper. Levin could make words spin dazzlingly, and he was ferocious about anyone he disliked or mistrusted. (Sir Hartley Shawcross, a Labour lawyer of uncertain political views, became Sir Shortly Floorcross, an almost Trollopian name. Sir Reginald Manningham-Buller, a Tory lawyer, was Sir Reginald Bullying Manner. Levin had a particular antipathy for Selwyn Lloyd, Macmillan's foreign secretary, whom he called Hoylake UDC, after the Lancashire seaside town where he had once led the council.)

He was even rude about Hugh Gaitskell, the almost universally admired – at least by the chattering classes – leader of the Labour Party, but then Levin was a contrarian who instinctively reacted against anything that had become received wisdom. He memorably described trying to stay awake during one of Gaitskell's speeches: 'No soldier facing a court-martial and firing squad could have fought sleep as tenaciously and ingeniously as I did. I propped my chin on the point of my pencil (very painful) . . . in vain; if martial law prevailed in the press gallery I would be saying "To hell with the handkerchief!" at this very moment.'

~

Norman Shrapnel wrote sketches for the *Guardian* for seventeen years. He wrote long, elegant, extended metaphors: parliament as a ship, or an unruly school, or an amateur drama company riddled with rivalries. His prose was chamfered, tongued and grooved, put together with as much care as a Chippendale cabinet. MPs loved him, and would occasionally penetrate to the press bar at the top of the building. They would spot him, and sometimes ask to be introduced. I would agree, though I knew exactly what would happen. He would greet the member with courtesy, but exceedingly brief courtesy. Once he had shaken hands, he would return to the bar and to his drink. Once I asked him why he was so terse with these people who were among his greatest fans. 'Because,' he said in a voice that always reminded me of Eeyore on his birthday, 'I am afraid that if I got to know them, it would spoil the purity of my hatred.'

People occasionally ask how we find something to write about every day, though as another of my predecessors said, 'It's easy when you have 649 helpers working to help you.' Often the sketch writes itself: Geoffrey Howe, Norman Lamont and Robin Cook all made thunderous resignation speeches, for example. You could provide a verbatim account, tack on a couple of adjectives and go off for a drink. Or there's a particularly rancorous Prime Minister's Questions.

At other times, it's more difficult, though even so there seems to be some unknown, minor god looking after us. Once I was covering defence questions, which ought to be exciting, but rarely is. I was desperate for something – anything – to happen. Then John Spellar, a junior defence minister, got on to the subject of funds for forces' healthcare. 'The honourable gentleman is right,' he said to a Tory, 'these cuts in defence medical services have gone too far.' Except he inserted an extraneous letter 'n' in the word 'cuts', and there was a two-second pause while people gazed at each other, asking by eyebrow, 'Did he say what I thought he said?' before they all collapsed in laughter. That was an easy one to write.

Do MPs hate us? Not often. Now and again, an MP will send a message, usually through another MP, to say that their feelings were hurt, or – more shamefully – that their mother's feelings were hurt. Politicians should not hide behind their mothers. But for the most part, unlike academics, they take the knocks with resignation and even a degree of pride. In the days of *Spitting Image* the main complaints came from politicians who didn't have puppets. Their children felt let down.

Index